1: The Arduous Business of Getting Rescued

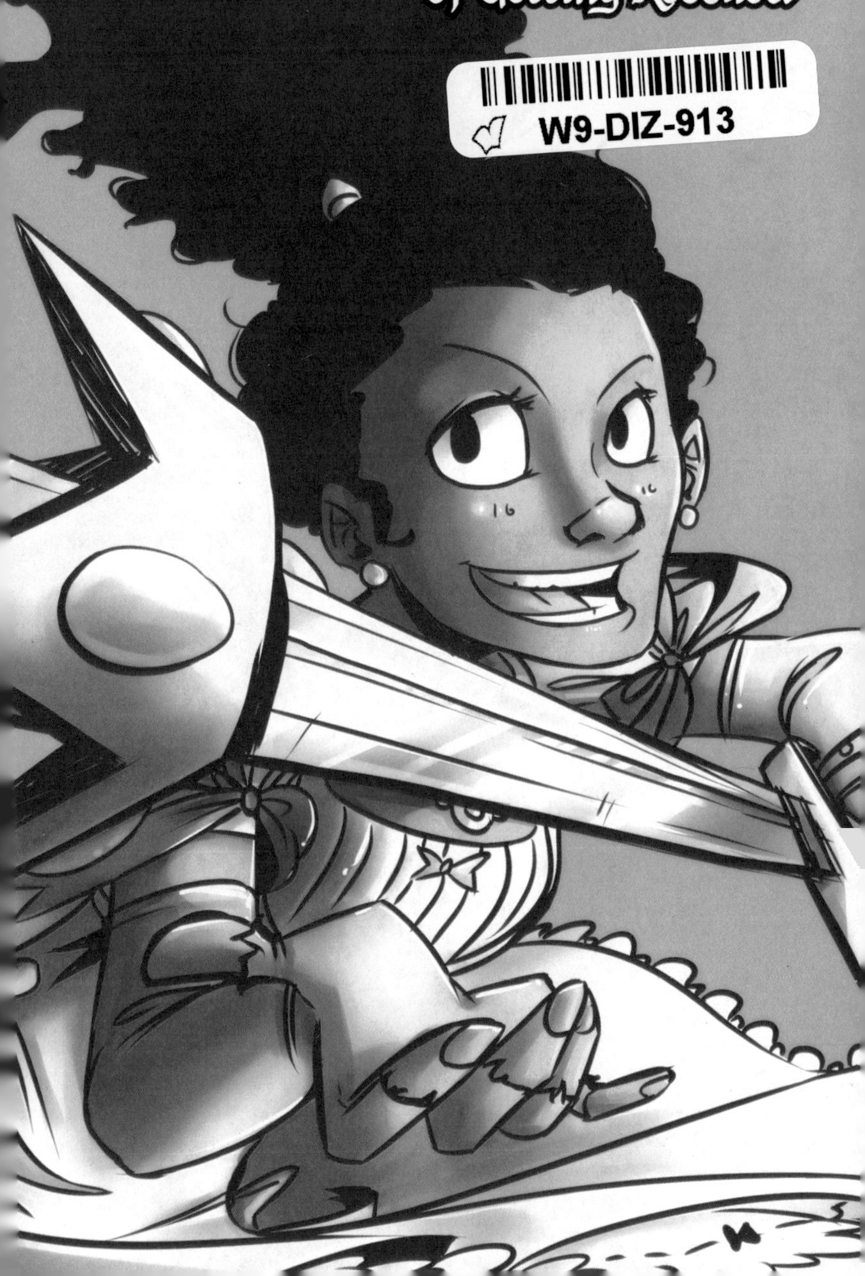

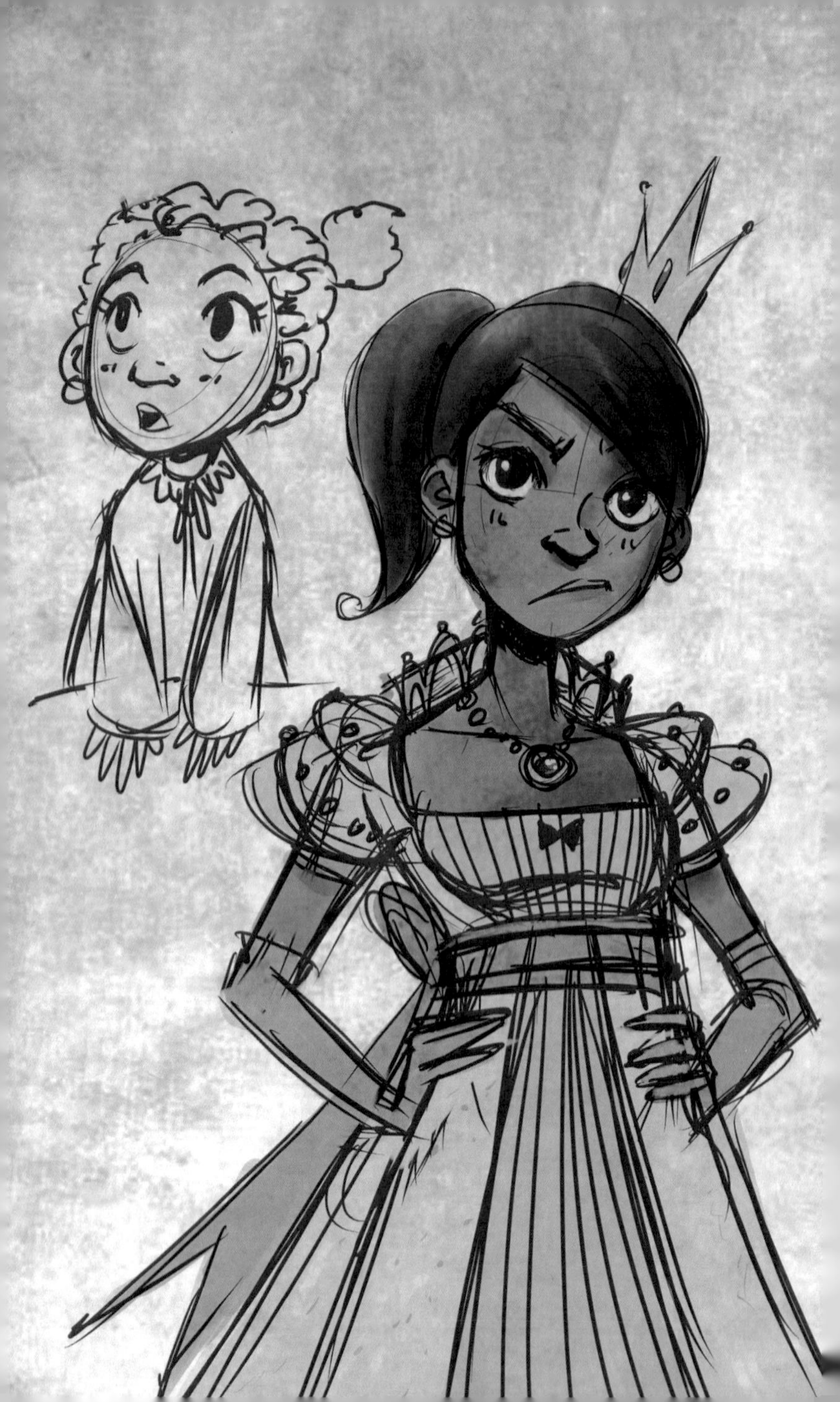

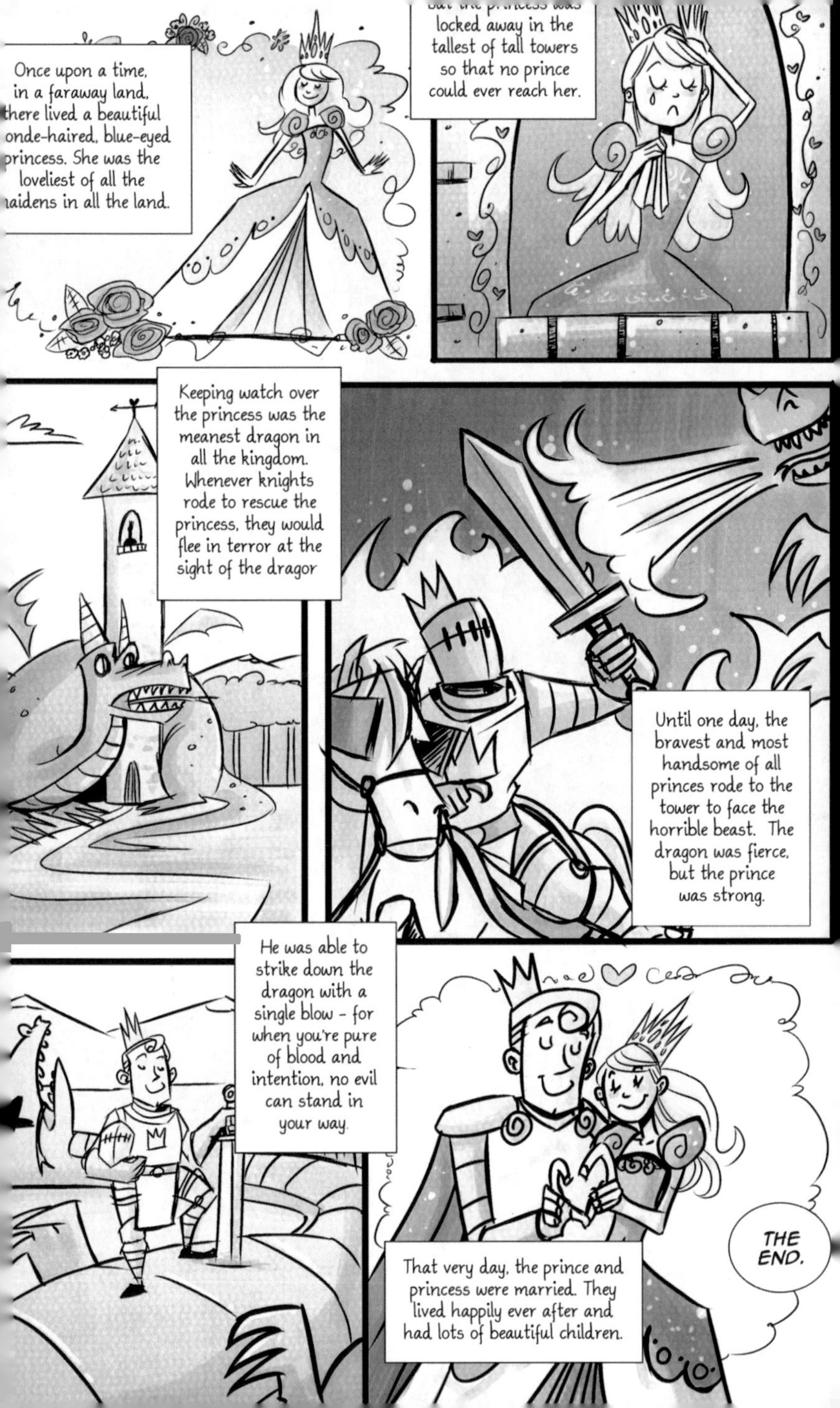
Once upon a time, in a faraway land, there lived a beautiful onde-haired, blue-eyed princess. She was the loveliest of all the aidens in all the land.
locked away in the tallest of tall towers so that no prince could ever reach her.
Keeping watch over the princess was the meanest dragon in all the kingdom. Whenever knights rode to rescue the princess, they would flee in terror at the sight of the dragor
Until one day, the bravest and most handsome of all princes rode to the tower to face the horrible beast. The dragon was fierce, but the prince was strong.
He was able to strike down the dragon with a single blow - for when you're pure of blood and intention, no evil can stand in your way.
That very day, the prince and princess were married. They lived happily ever after and had lots of beautiful children.
THE END.

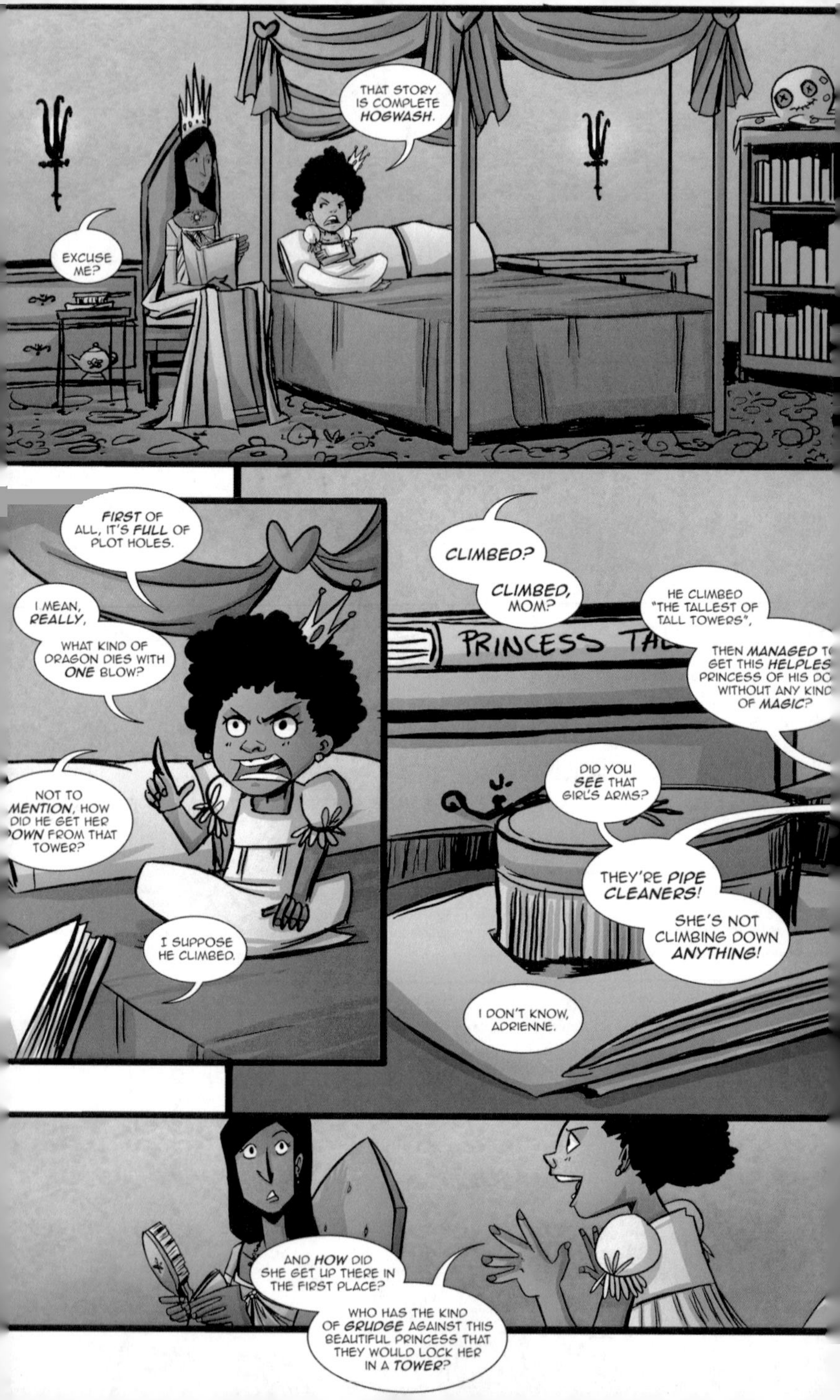
THAT STORY IS COMPLETE HOGWASH.
EXCUSE ME?
FIRST OF ALL, IT'S FULL OF PLOT HOLES.
I MEAN, REALLY,
WHAT KIND OF DRAGON DIES WITH ONE BLOW?
NOT TO MENTION, HOW DID HE GET HER OWN FROM THAT TOWER?
I SUPPOSE HE CLIMBED.
CLIMBED?
CLIMBED, MOM?
PRINCESS
HE CLIMBED "THE TALLEST OF TALL TOWERS",
THEN MANAGED T GET THIS HELPLES PRINCESS OF HIS DO WITHOUT ANY KIN OF MAGIC?
DID YOU SEE THAT GIRL'S ARMS?
THEY'RE PIPE CLEANERS!
SHE'S NOT CLIMBING DOWN ANYTHING!
I DON'T KNOW, ADRIENNE.
AND HOW DID SHE GET UP THERE IN THE FIRST PLACE?
WHO HAS THE KIND OF GRUDGE AGAINST THIS BEAUTIFUL PRINCESS THAT THEY WOULD LOCK HER IN A TOWER?

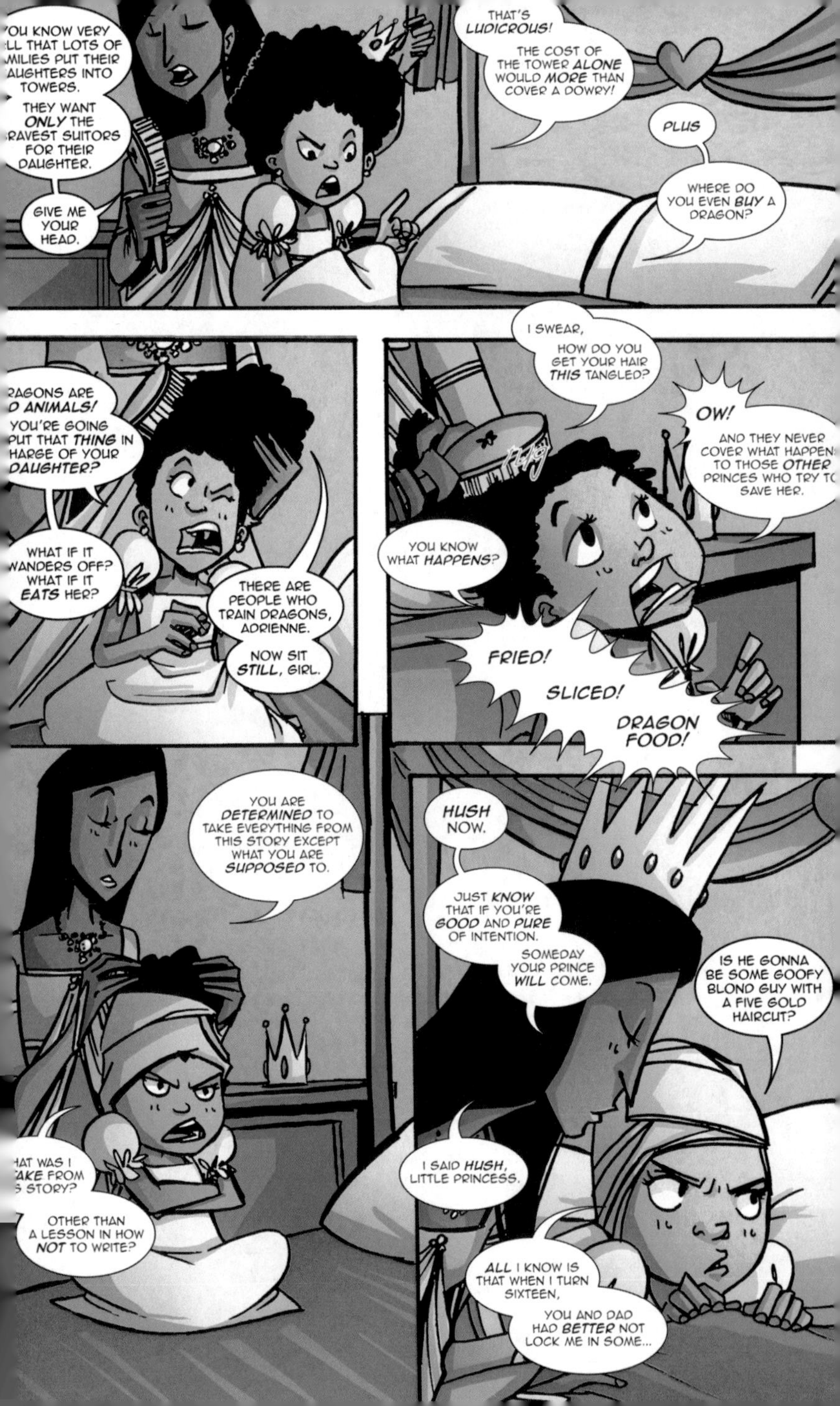

OU KNOW VERY
LL THAT LOTS OF
MILIES PUT THEIR
AUGHTERS INTO
TOWERS.
THEY WANT
ONLY THE
RAVEST SUITORS
FOR THEIR
DAUGHTER.
GIVE ME
YOUR
HEAD.
THAT'S
LUDICROUS!
THE COST OF
THE TOWER ALONE
WOULD MORE THAN
COVER A DOWRY!
PLUS
WHERE DO
YOU EVEN BUY A
DRAGON?
RAGONS ARE
D ANIMALS!
YOU'RE GOING
PUT THAT THING IN
HARGE OF YOUR
DAUGHTER?
WHAT IF IT
WANDERS OFF?
WHAT IF IT
EATS HER?
THERE ARE
PEOPLE WHO
TRAIN DRAGONS,
ADRIENNE.
NOW SIT
STILL, GIRL.
I SWEAR,
HOW DO YOU
GET YOUR HAIR
THIS TANGLED?
OW!
AND THEY NEVER
COVER WHAT HAPPEN
TO THOSE OTHER
PRINCES WHO TRY TO
SAVE HER.
YOU KNOW
WHAT HAPPENS?
FRIED!
SLICED!
DRAGON
FOOD!
YOU ARE
DETERMINED TO
TAKE EVERYTHING FROM
THIS STORY EXCEPT
WHAT YOU ARE
SUPPOSED TO.
HAT WAS I
AKE FROM
S STORY?
OTHER THAN
A LESSON IN HOW
NOT TO WRITE?
HUSH
NOW.
JUST KNOW
THAT IF YOU'RE
GOOD AND PURE
OF INTENTION.
SOMEDAY
YOUR PRINCE
WILL COME.
IS HE GONNA
BE SOME GOOFY
BLOND GUY WITH
A FIVE GOLD
HAIRCUT?
I SAID HUSH,
LITTLE PRINCESS.
ALL I KNOW IS
THAT WHEN I TURN
SIXTEEN,
YOU AND DAD
HAD BETTER NOT
LOCK ME IN SOME...

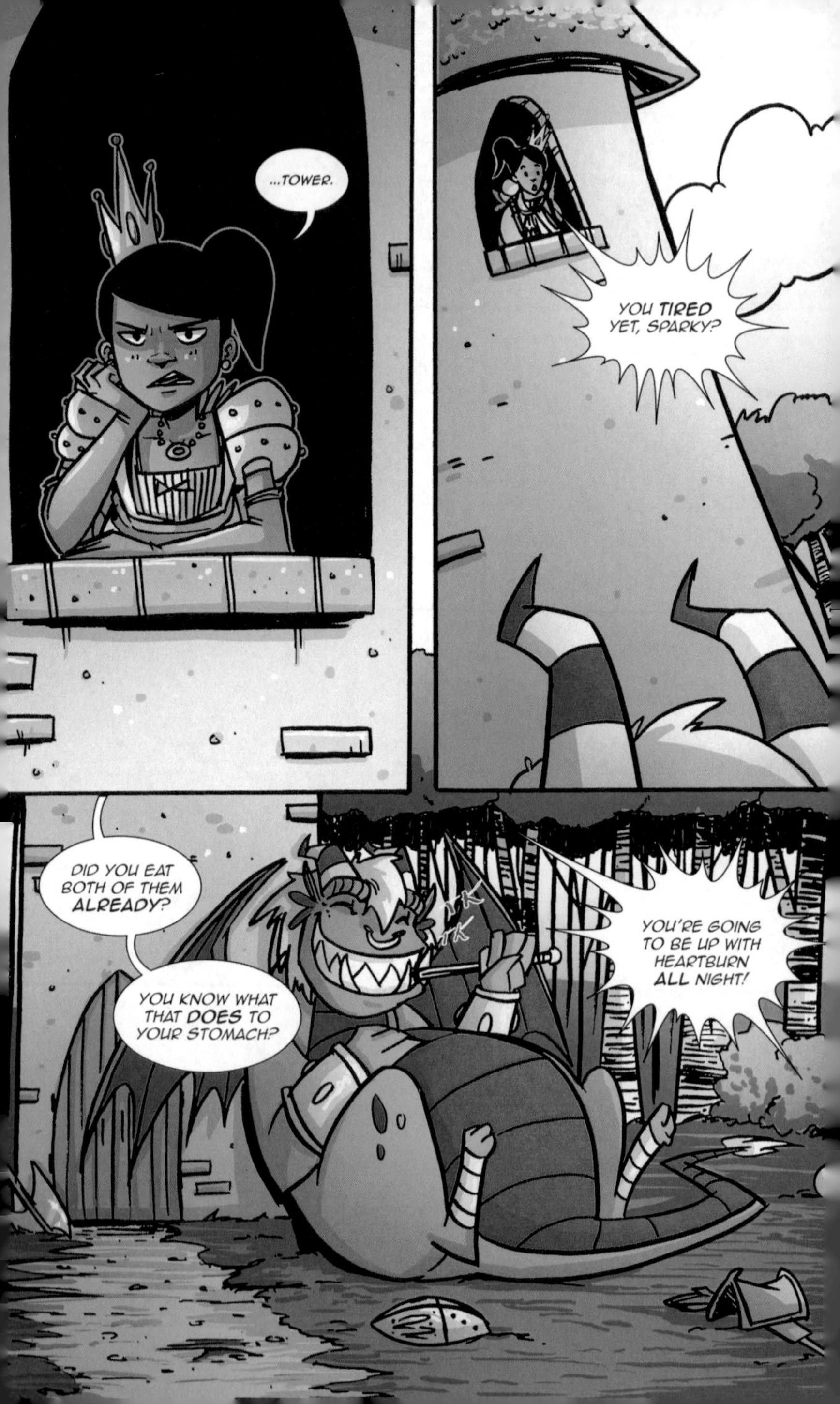
...TOWER.
YOU TIRED YET, SPARKY?
DID YOU EAT BOTH OF THEM ALREADY?
YOU KNOW WHAT THAT DOES TO YOUR STOMACH?
TK
TK
YOU'RE GOING TO BE UP WITH HEARTBURN ALL NIGHT!

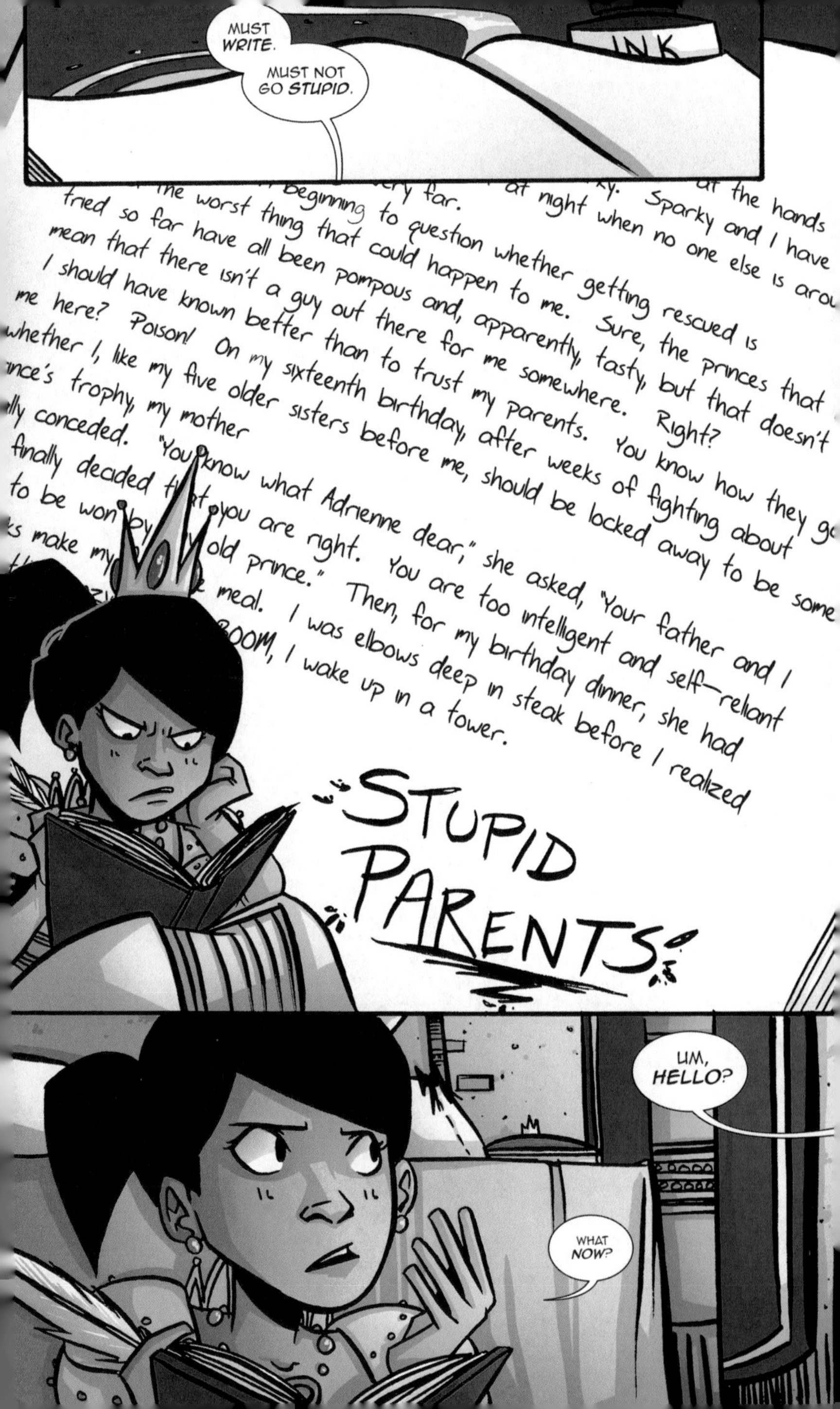

MUST WRITE.
MUST NOT GO STUPID.
INK
...at the hands
...ky. Sparky and I have
...ery far. ...at night when no one else is arou
...beginning to question whether getting rescued is
...the worst thing that could happen to me. Sure, the princes that
tried so far have all been pompous and, apparently, tasty, but that doesn't
mean that there isn't a guy out there for me somewhere. Right?
I should have known better than to trust my parents. You know how they go
me here? Poison! On my sixteenth birthday, after weeks of fighting about
whether I, like my five older sisters before me, should be locked away to be some
...nce's trophy, my mother
...lly conceded. "You know what Adrienne dear," she asked, "Your father and I
finally decided that you are right. You are too intelligent and self-reliant
to be won by ... old prince." Then, for my birthday dinner, she had
...ks make my ... meal. I was elbows deep in steak before I realized
...OOM, I wake up in a tower.
STUPID PARENTS!
UM, HELLO?
WHAT NOW?

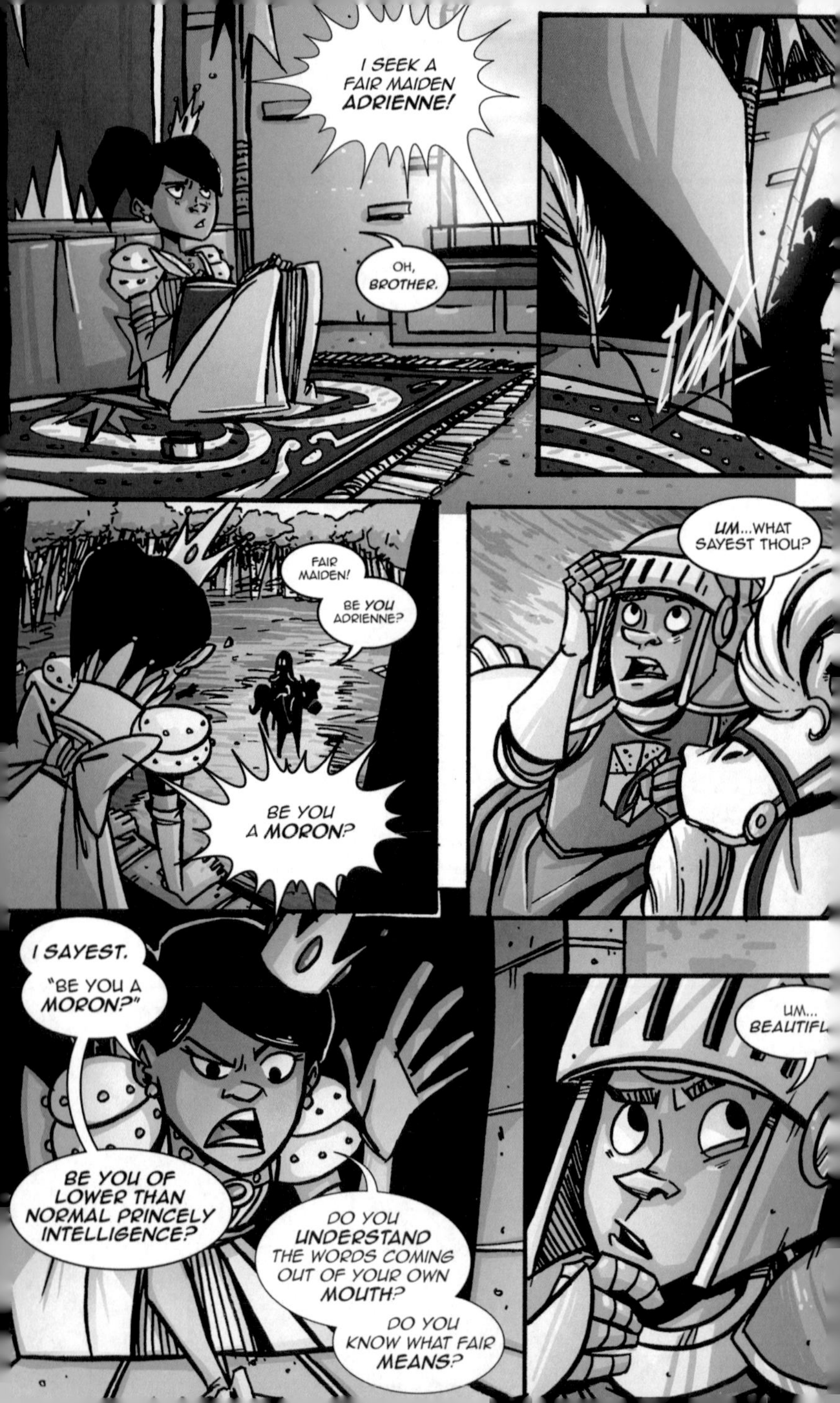
I SEEK A FAIR MAIDEN ADRIENNE!
OH, BROTHER.
FAIR MAIDEN!
BE YOU ADRIENNE?
BE YOU A MORON?
UM...WHAT SAYEST THOU?
I SAYEST.
"BE YOU A MORON?"
BE YOU OF LOWER THAN NORMAL PRINCELY INTELLIGENCE?
DO YOU UNDERSTAND THE WORDS COMING OUT OF YOUR OWN MOUTH?
DO YOU KNOW WHAT FAIR MEANS?
UM... BEAUTIFU

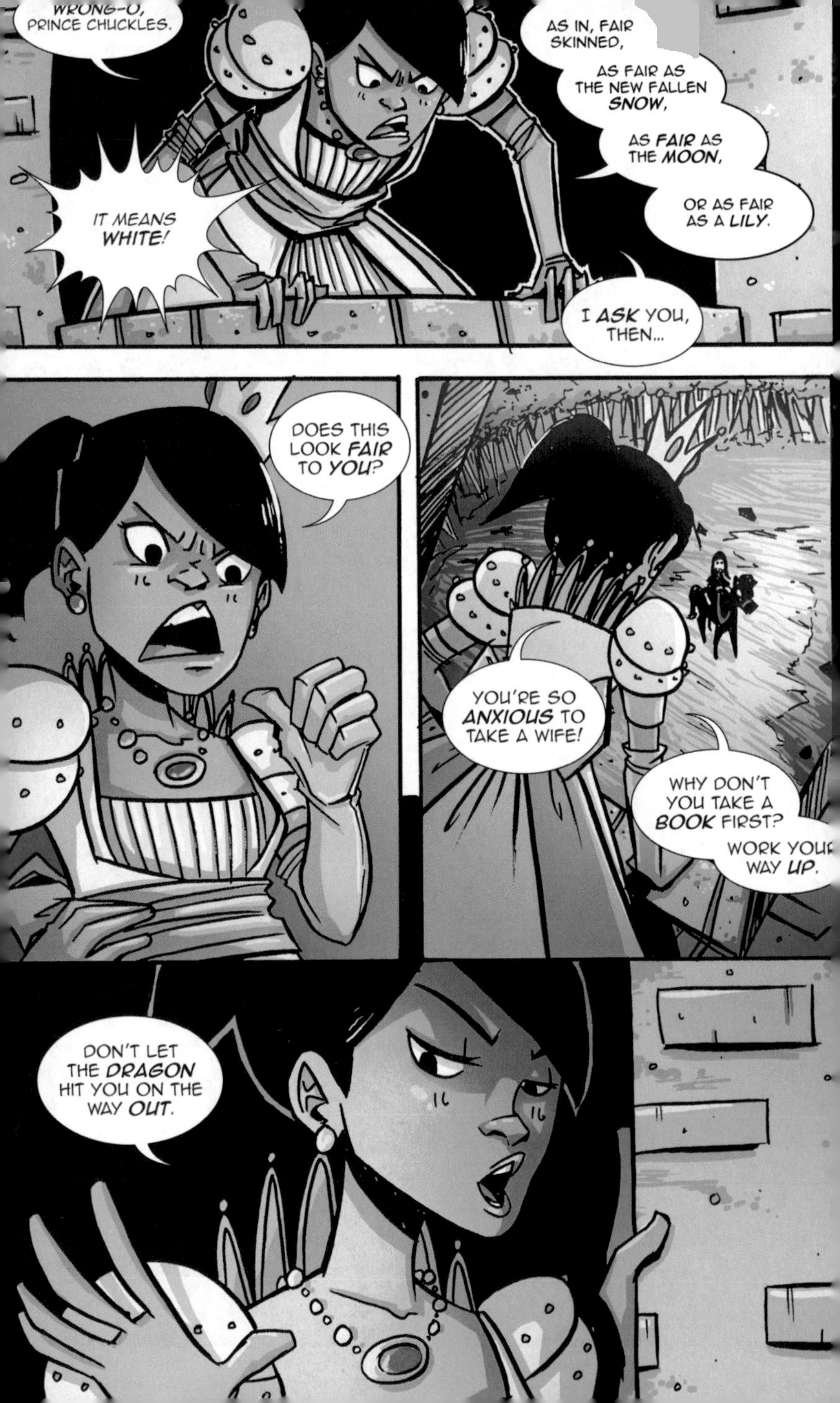
WRONG-O, PRINCE CHUCKLES.
IT MEANS WHITE!
AS IN, FAIR SKINNED,
AS FAIR AS THE NEW FALLEN SNOW,
AS FAIR AS THE MOON,
OR AS FAIR AS A LILY.
I ASK YOU, THEN...
DOES THIS LOOK FAIR TO YOU?
YOU'RE SO ANXIOUS TO TAKE A WIFE!
WHY DON'T YOU TAKE A BOOK FIRST?
WORK YOUR WAY UP.
DON'T LET THE DRAGON HIT YOU ON THE WAY OUT.

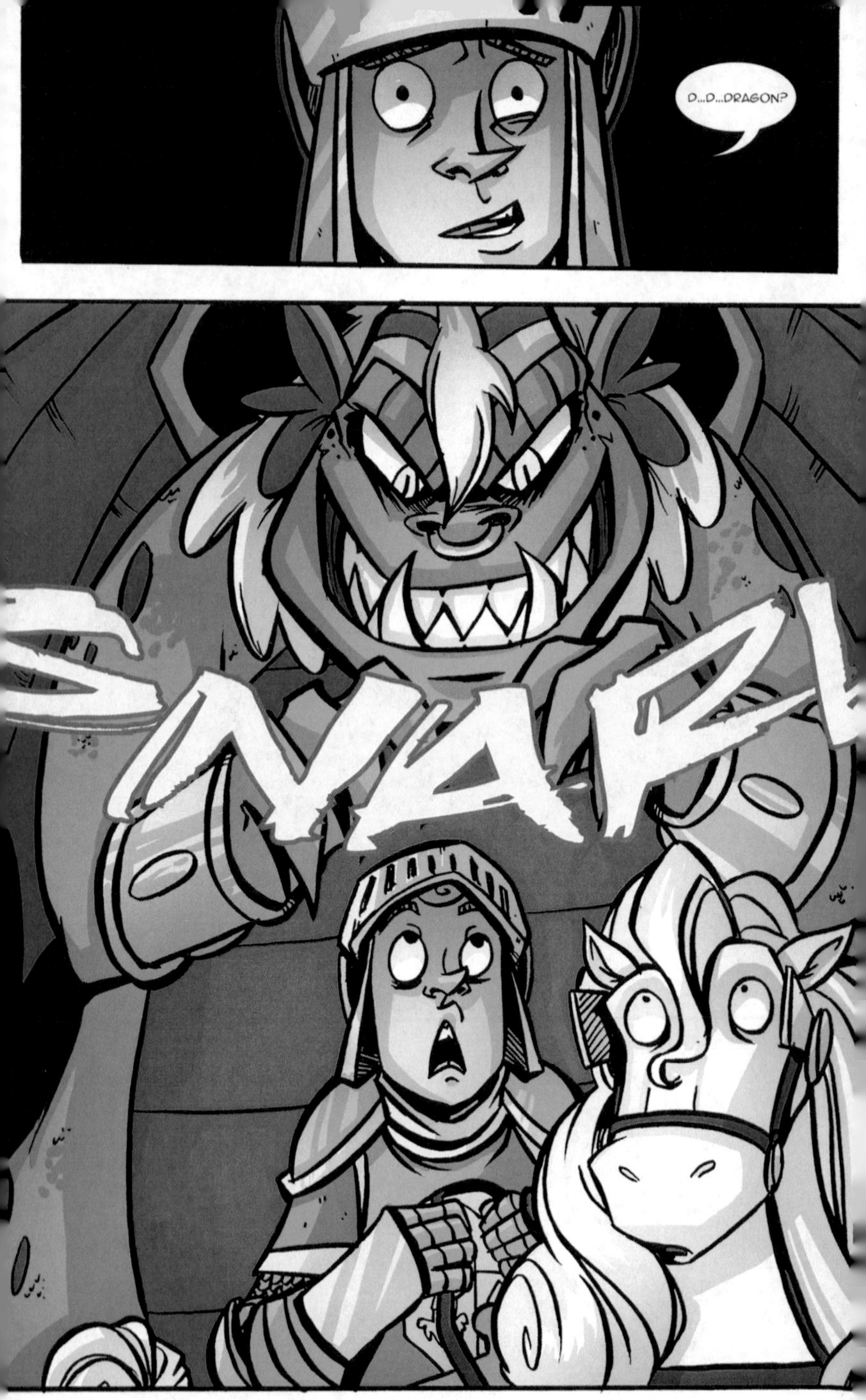
D...D...DRAGON?

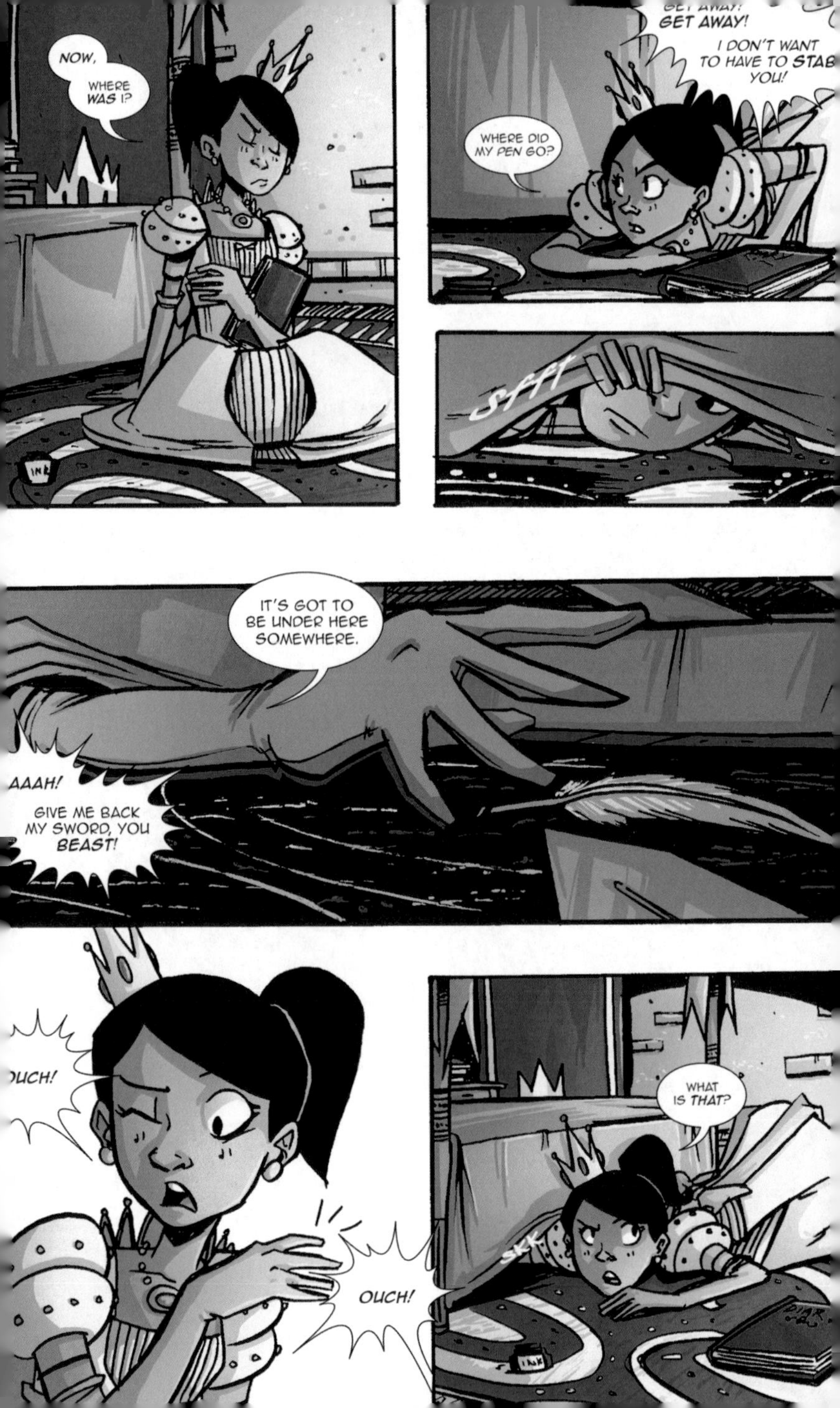
NOW, WHERE WAS I?
INK
GET AWAY!
I DON'T WANT TO HAVE TO STAB YOU!
WHERE DID MY PEN GO?
SFFT
IT'S GOT TO BE UNDER HERE SOMEWHERE.
AAAH! GIVE ME BACK MY SWORD, YOU BEAST!
OUCH!
WHAT IS THAT?
SKK
INK

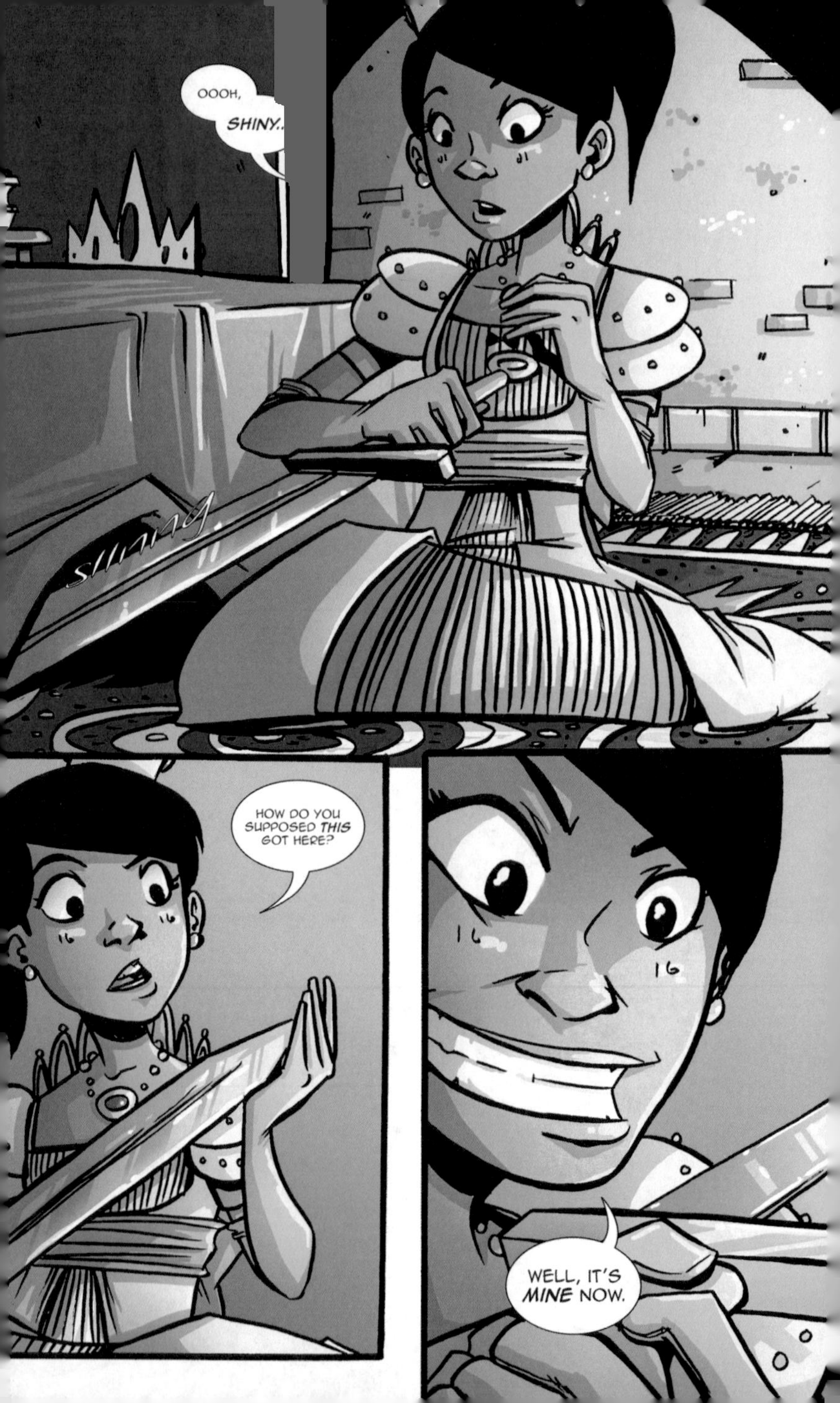
OOOH,
SHINY...
SHING
HOW DO YOU SUPPOSED THIS GOT HERE?
WELL, IT'S MINE NOW.

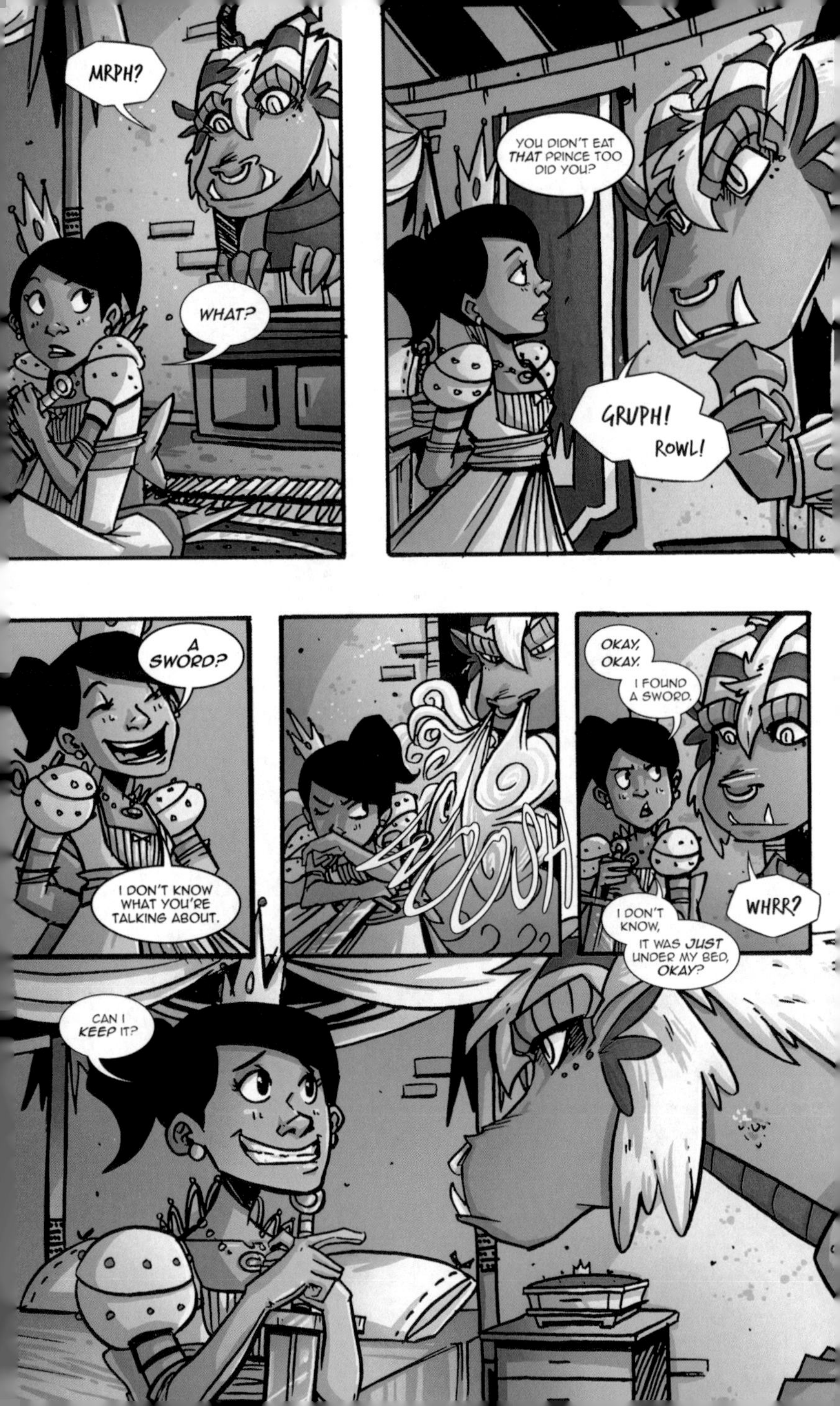
MRPH?
WHAT?
YOU DIDN'T EAT *THAT* PRINCE TOO DID YOU?
GRUPH!
ROWL!
A SWORD?
I DON'T KNOW WHAT YOU'RE TALKING ABOUT.
WOOOSH
OKAY, OKAY.
I FOUND A SWORD.
WHRR?
I DON'T KNOW,
IT WAS *JUST* UNDER MY BED, *OKAY*?
CAN I *KEEP* IT?

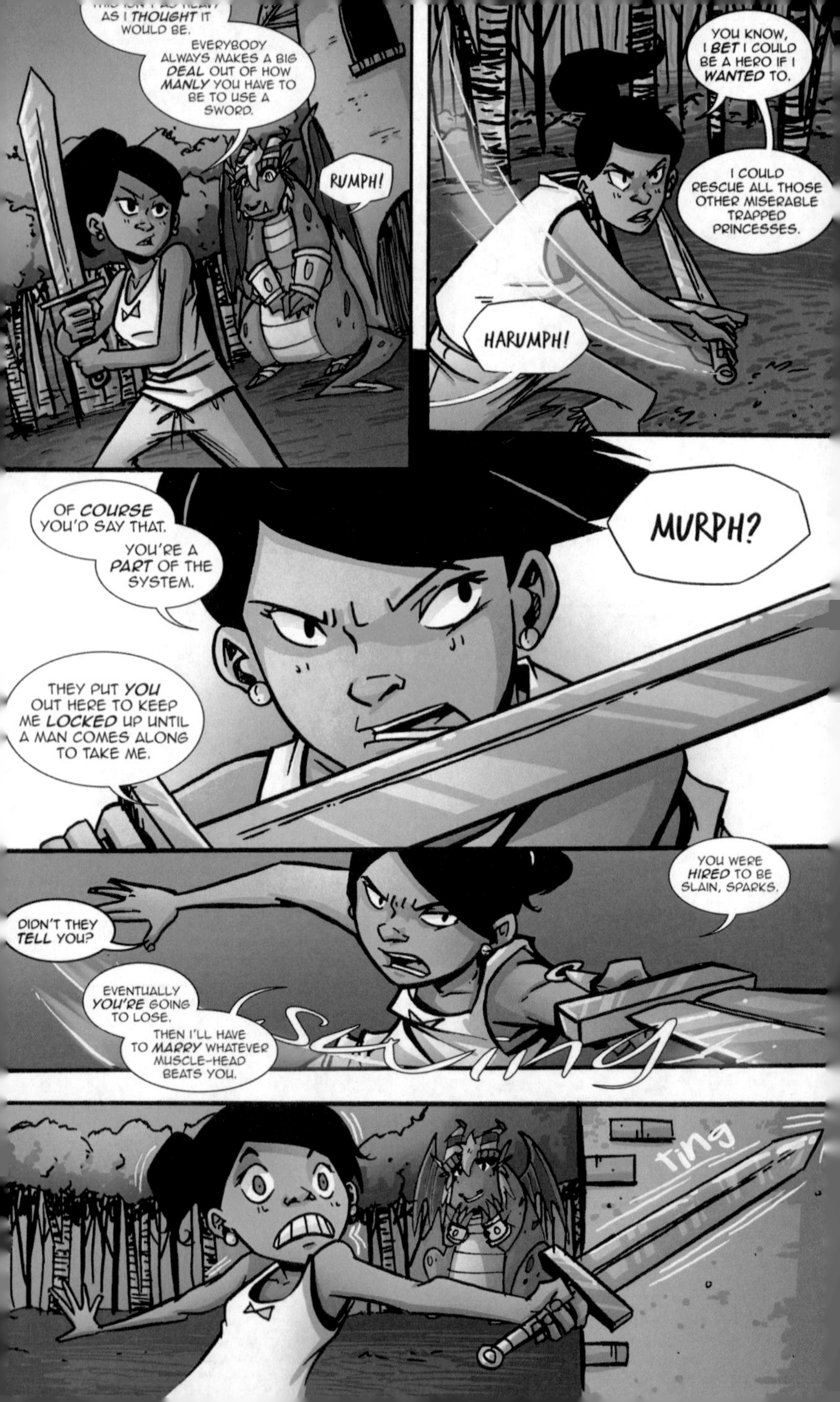
AS I THOUGHT IT WOULD BE.
EVERYBODY ALWAYS MAKES A BIG DEAL OUT OF HOW MANLY YOU HAVE TO BE TO USE A SWORD.
RUMPH!
YOU KNOW, I BET I COULD BE A HERO IF I WANTED TO.
I COULD RESCUE ALL THOSE OTHER MISERABLE TRAPPED PRINCESSES.
HARUMPH!
OF COURSE YOU'D SAY THAT.
YOU'RE A PART OF THE SYSTEM.
MURPH?
THEY PUT YOU OUT HERE TO KEEP ME LOCKED UP UNTIL A MAN COMES ALONG TO TAKE ME.
YOU WERE HIRED TO BE SLAIN, SPARKS.
DIDN'T THEY TELL YOU?
EVENTUALLY YOU'RE GOING TO LOSE.
THEN I'LL HAVE TO MARRY WHATEVER MUSCLE-HEAD BEATS YOU.
swing
ting

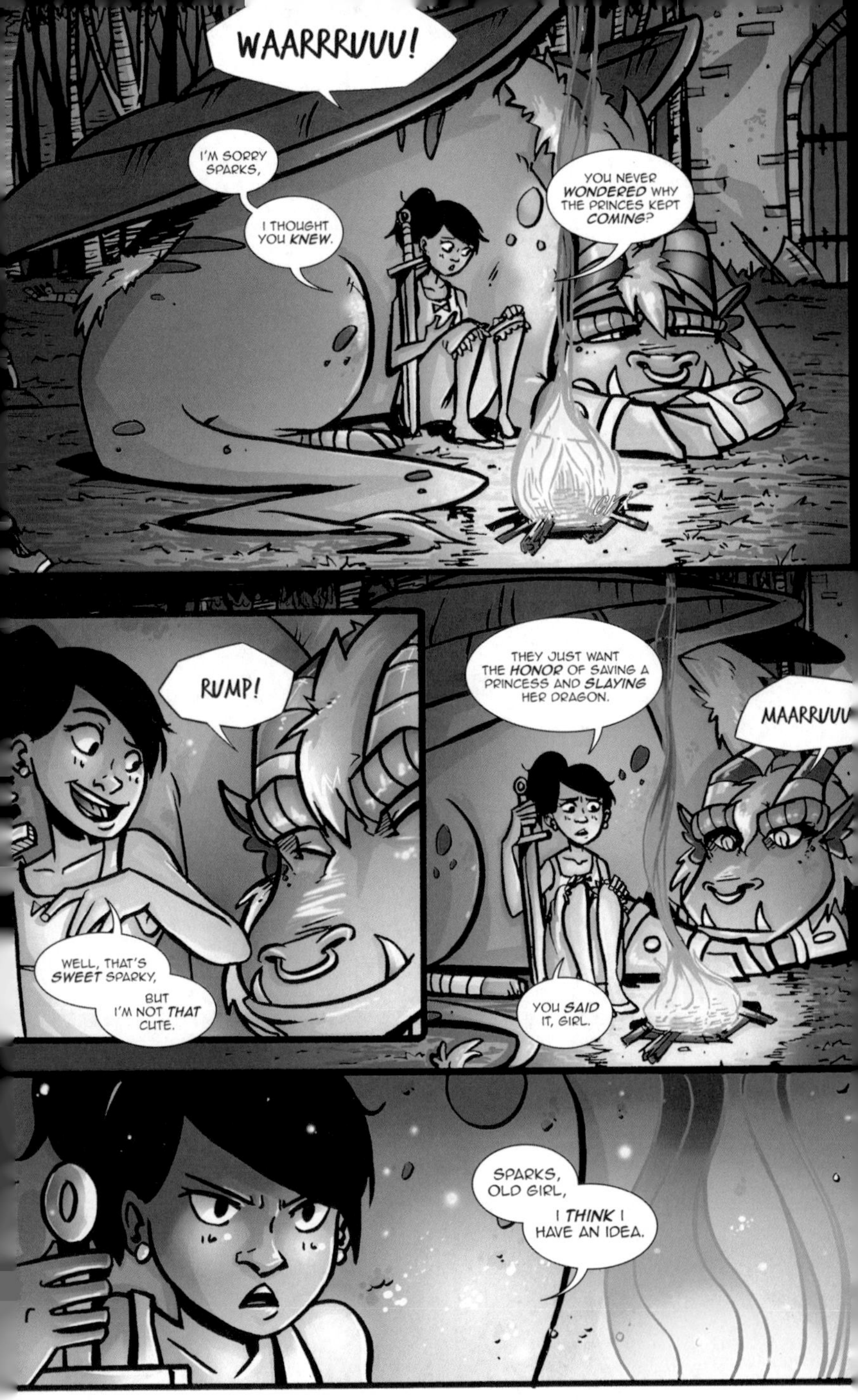

WAARRRUUU!
I'M SORRY SPARKS,
I THOUGHT YOU **KNEW**.
YOU NEVER **WONDERED** WHY THE PRINCES KEPT **COMING**?
RUMP!
WELL, THAT'S **SWEET** SPARKY,
BUT I'M NOT **THAT** CUTE.
THEY JUST WANT THE **HONOR** OF SAVING A PRINCESS AND **SLAYING** HER DRAGON.
MAARRUUU
YOU **SAID** IT, GIRL.
SPARKS, OLD GIRL,
I **THINK** I HAVE AN IDEA.

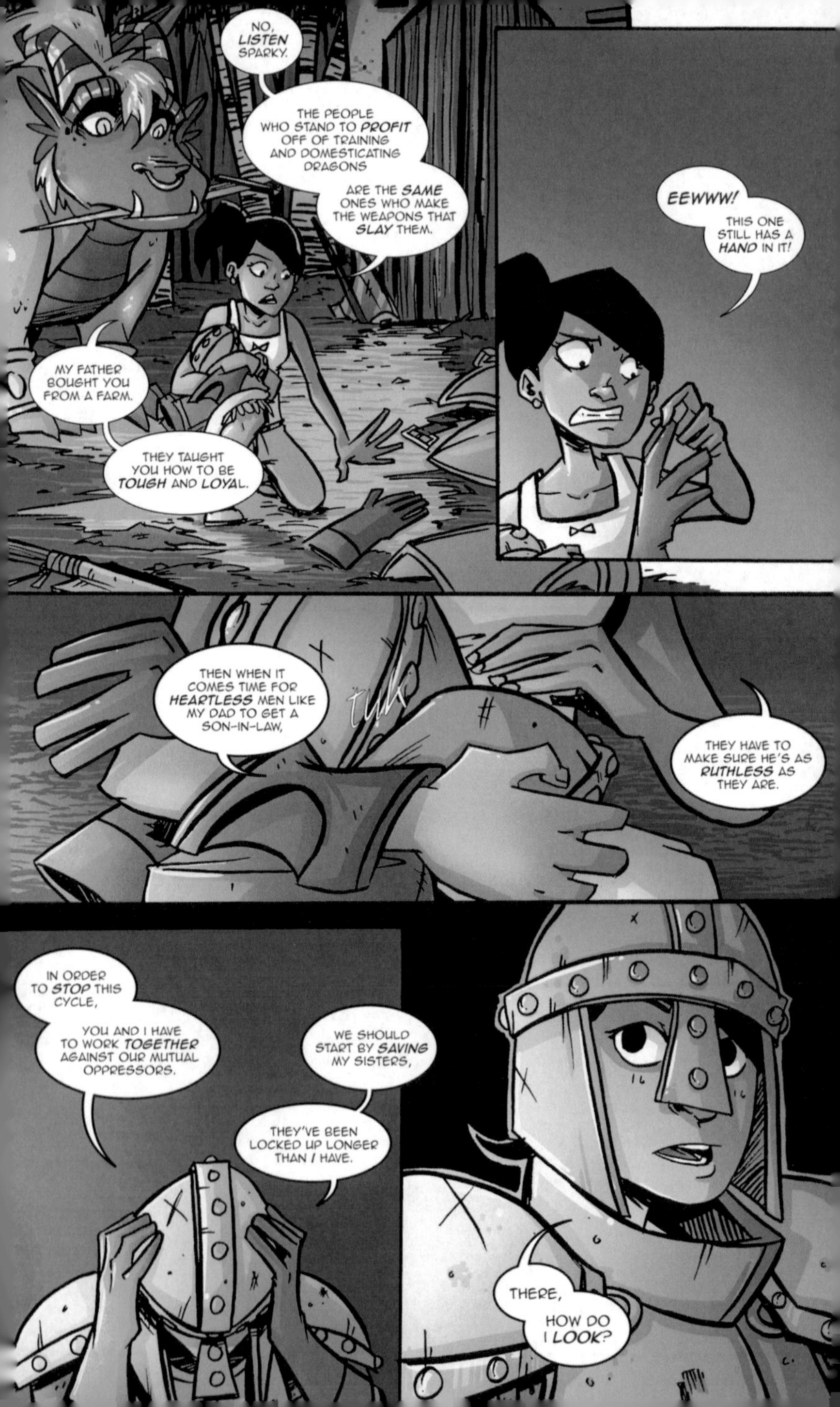

NO, *LISTEN* SPARKY.
THE PEOPLE WHO STAND TO *PROFIT* OFF OF TRAINING AND DOMESTICATING DRAGONS
ARE THE *SAME* ONES WHO MAKE THE WEAPONS THAT *SLAY* THEM.
MY FATHER BOUGHT YOU FROM A FARM.
THEY TAUGHT YOU HOW TO BE *TOUGH* AND *LOYA*L.
EEWWW!
THIS ONE STILL HAS A *HAND* IN IT!
THEN WHEN IT COMES TIME FOR *HEARTLESS* MEN LIKE MY DAD TO GET A SON-IN-LAW,
tuk
THEY HAVE TO MAKE SURE HE'S AS *RUTHLESS* AS THEY ARE.
IN ORDER TO *STOP* THIS CYCLE,
YOU AND I HAVE TO WORK *TOGETHER* AGAINST OUR MUTUAL OPPRESSORS.
WE SHOULD START BY *SAVING* MY SISTERS,
THEY'VE BEEN LOCKED UP LONGER THAN *I* HAVE.
THERE,
HOW DO I *LOOK*?

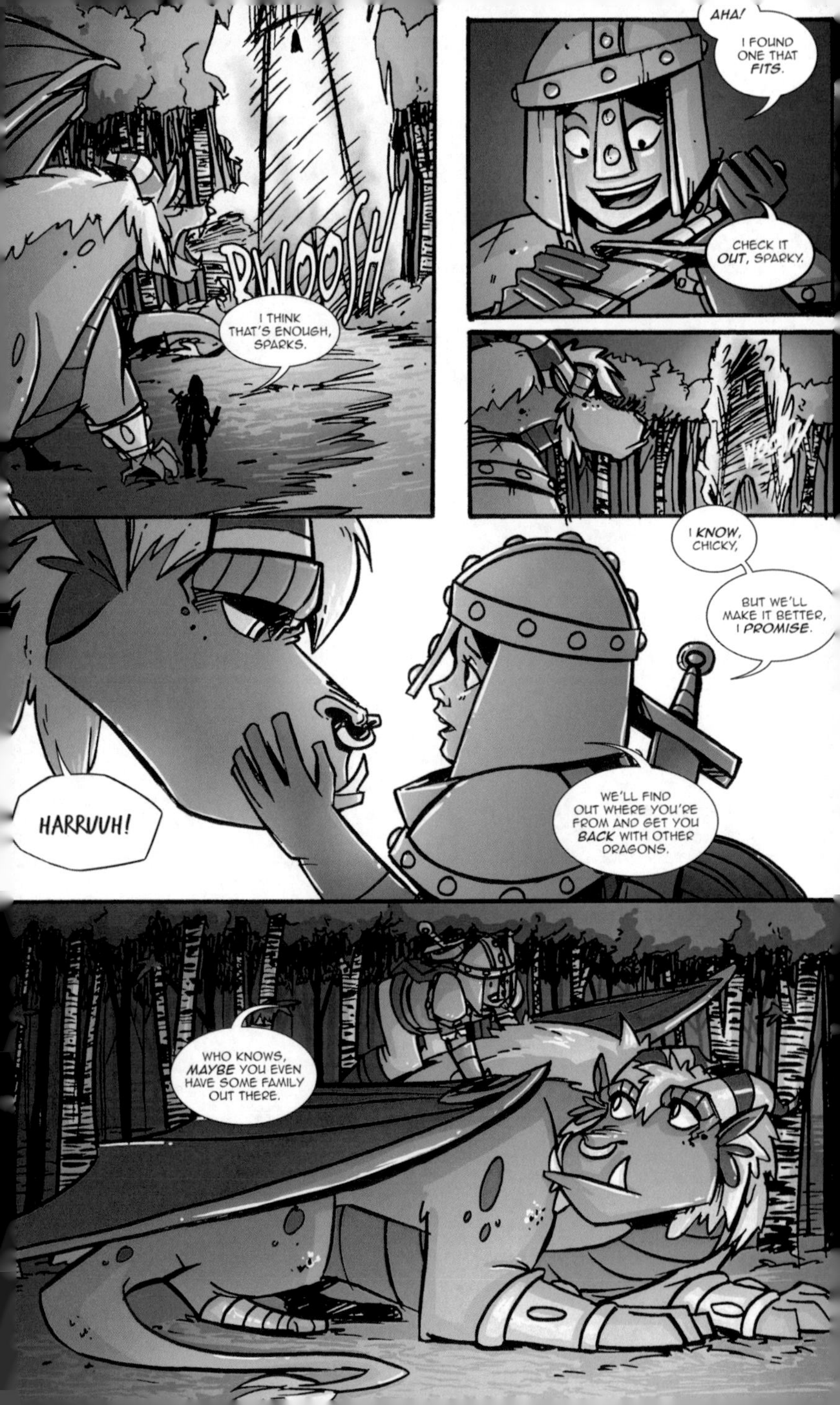

FWOOSH
I THINK THAT'S ENOUGH, SPARKS.
AHA!
I FOUND ONE THAT FITS.
CHECK IT OUT, SPARKY.
I KNOW, CHICKY,
BUT WE'LL MAKE IT BETTER, I PROMISE.
HARRUUH!
WE'LL FIND OUT WHERE YOU'RE FROM AND GET YOU BACK WITH OTHER DRAGONS.
WHO KNOWS, MAYBE YOU EVEN HAVE SOME FAMILY OUT THERE.

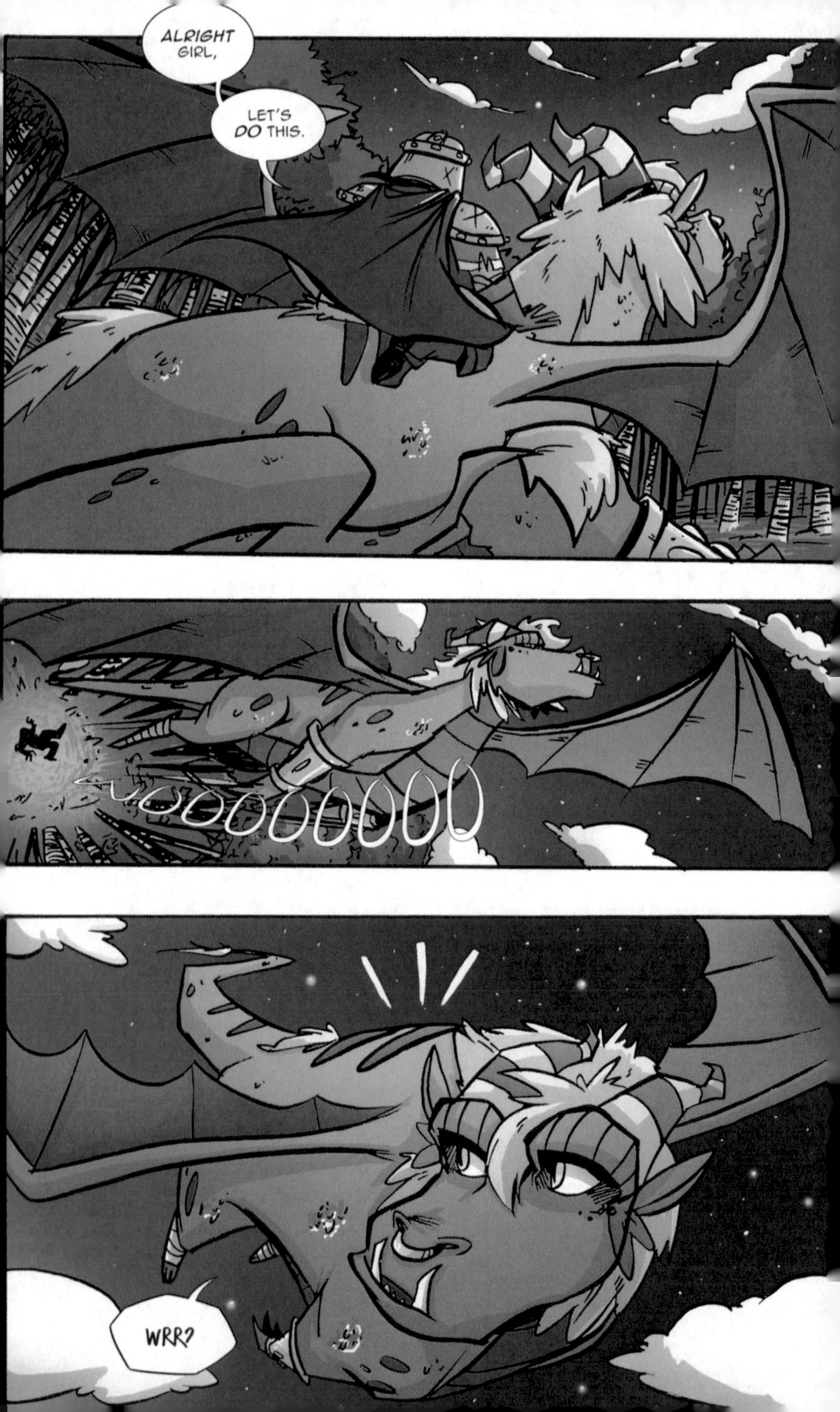
ALRIGHT GIRL,
LET'S DO THIS.
WOOOOOOOOOO
WRR?

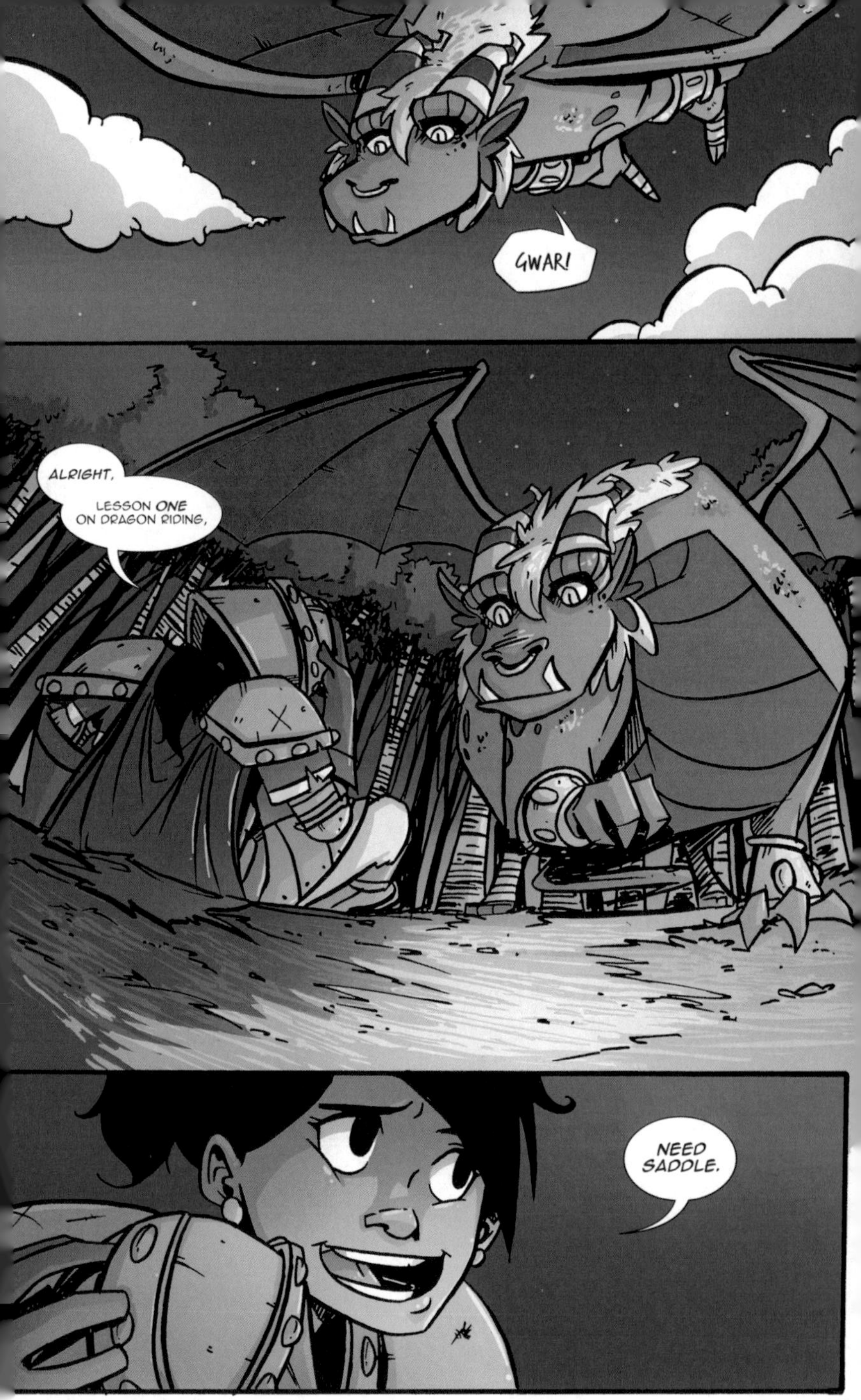
GWAR!
ALRIGHT,
LESSON ONE ON DRAGON RIDING,
NEED SADDLE.

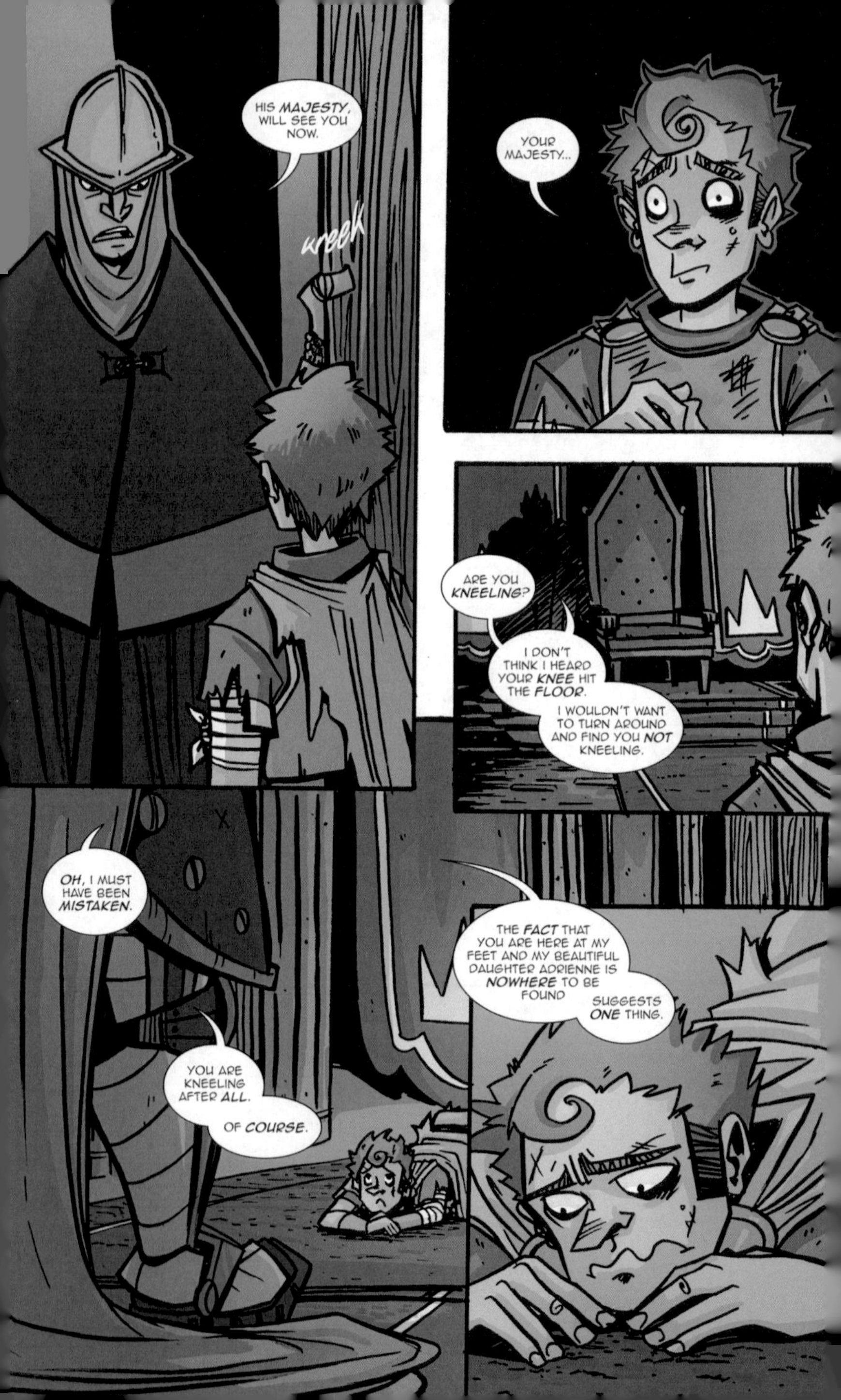
HIS MAJESTY, WILL SEE YOU NOW.
kreek
YOUR MAJESTY...
ARE YOU KNEELING?
I DON'T THINK I HEARD YOUR KNEE HIT THE FLOOR.
I WOULDN'T WANT TO TURN AROUND AND FIND YOU NOT KNEELING.
OH, I MUST HAVE BEEN MISTAKEN.
YOU ARE KNEELING AFTER ALL.
OF COURSE.
THE FACT THAT YOU ARE HERE AT MY FEET AND MY BEAUTIFUL DAUGHTER ADRIENNE IS NOWHERE TO BE FOUND
SUGGESTS ONE THING.

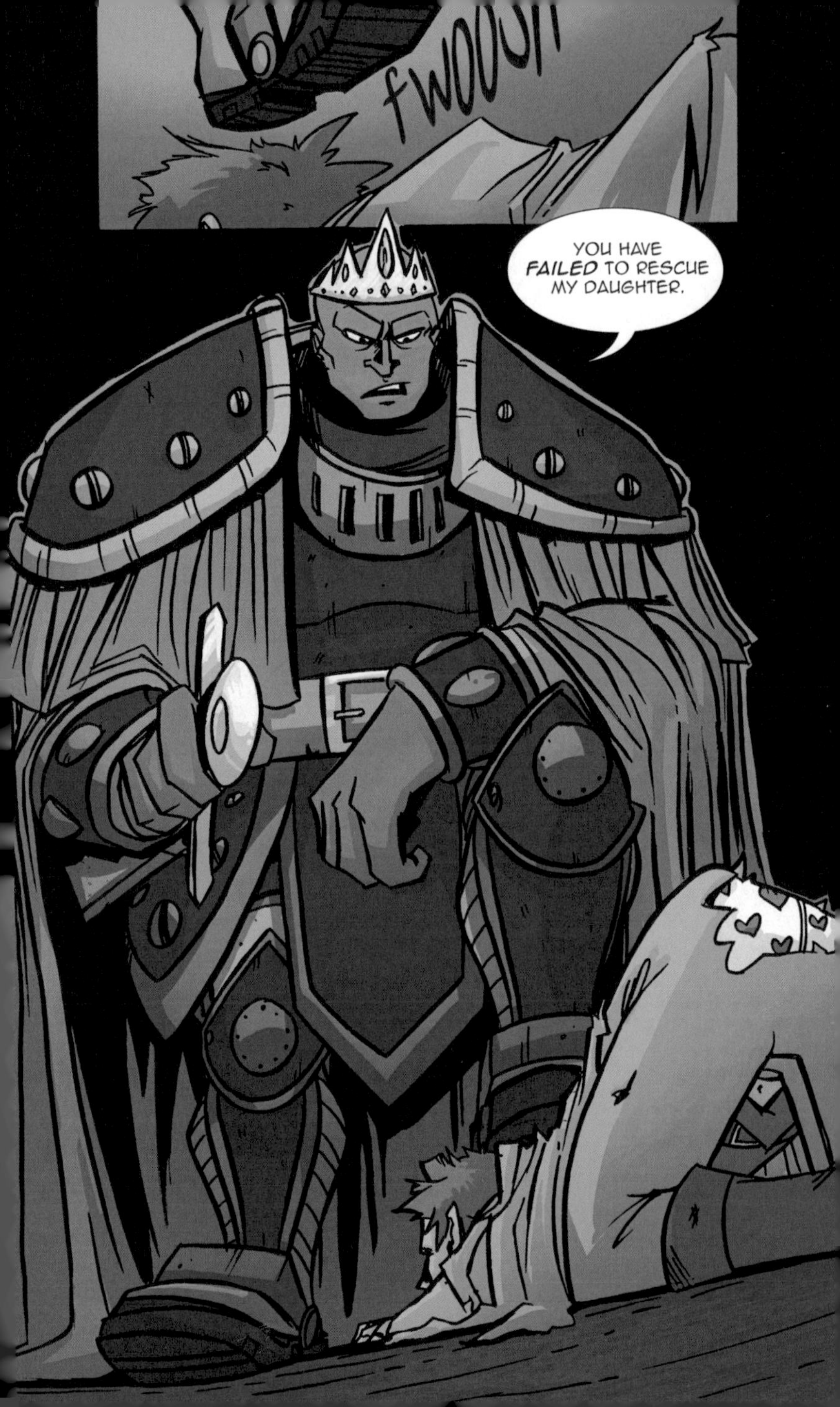
FWOOSH
YOU HAVE *FAILED* TO RESCUE MY DAUGHTER.

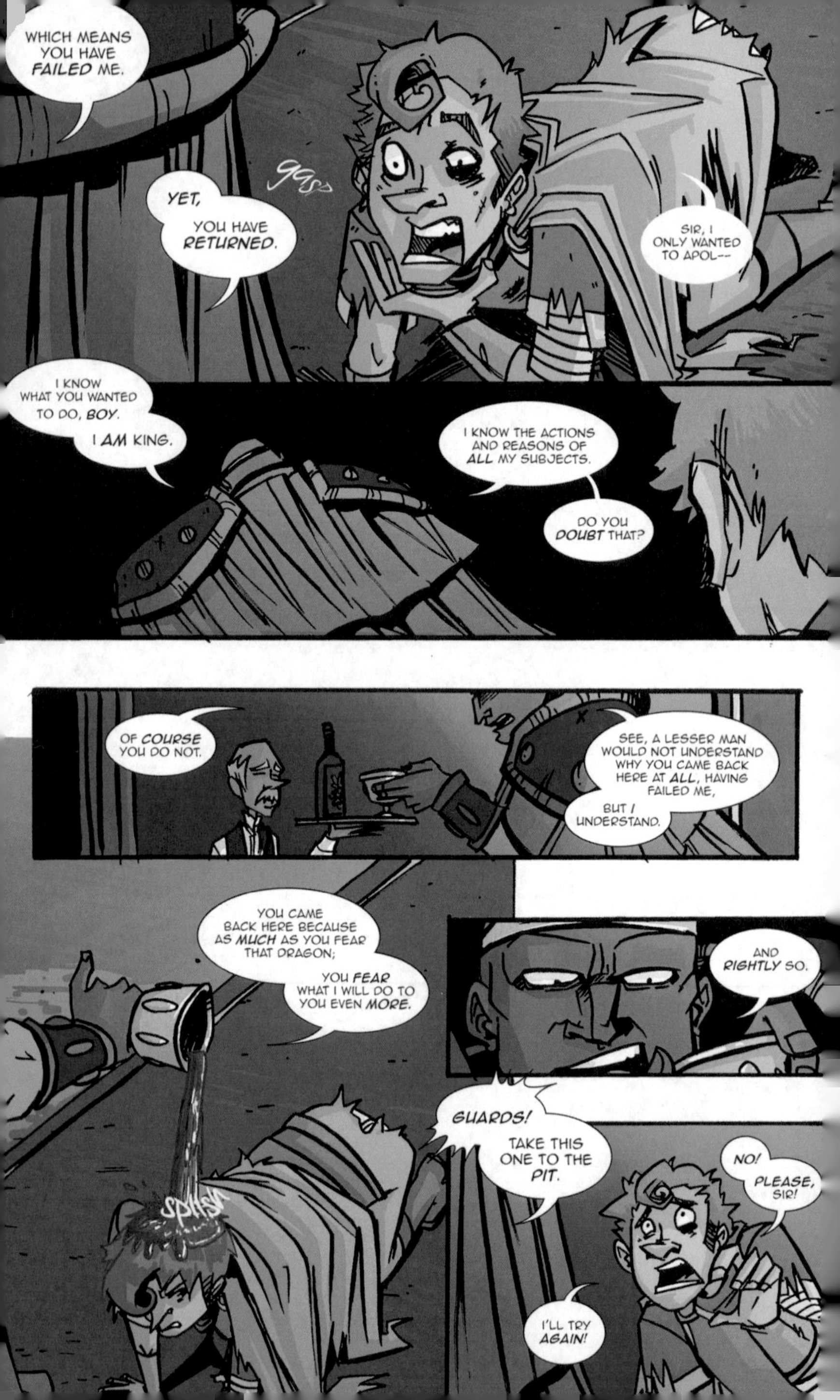
WHICH MEANS YOU HAVE *FAILED* ME.
YET, YOU HAVE *RETURNED*.
SIR, I ONLY WANTED TO APOL--
I KNOW WHAT YOU WANTED TO DO, *BOY*.
I *AM* KING.
I KNOW THE ACTIONS AND REASONS OF *ALL* MY SUBJECTS.
DO YOU *DOUBT* THAT?
OF *COURSE* YOU DO NOT.
SEE, A LESSER MAN WOULD NOT UNDERSTAND WHY YOU CAME BACK HERE AT *ALL*, HAVING FAILED ME,
BUT *I* UNDERSTAND.
YOU CAME BACK HERE BECAUSE AS *MUCH* AS YOU FEAR THAT DRAGON;
YOU *FEAR* WHAT I WILL DO TO YOU EVEN *MORE*.
AND *RIGHTLY* SO.
SPLISH
GUARDS!
TAKE THIS ONE TO THE *PIT*.
NO!
PLEASE, SIR!
I'LL TRY *AGAIN!*

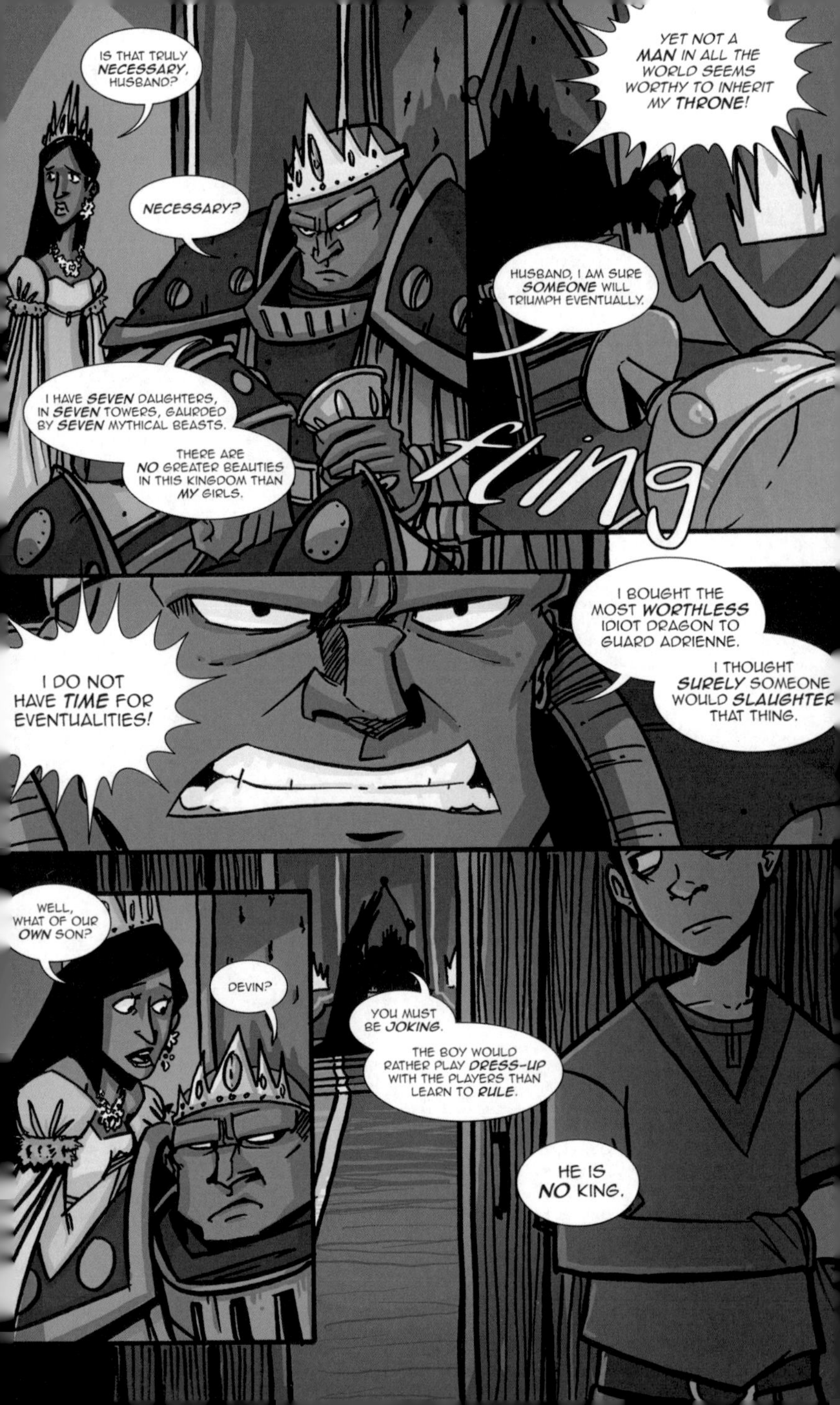

IS THAT TRULY NECESSARY, HUSBAND?
NECESSARY?
I HAVE SEVEN DAUGHTERS, IN SEVEN TOWERS, GAURDED BY SEVEN MYTHICAL BEASTS.
THERE ARE NO GREATER BEAUTIES IN THIS KINGDOM THAN MY GIRLS.
YET NOT A MAN IN ALL THE WORLD SEEMS WORTHY TO INHERIT MY THRONE!
HUSBAND, I AM SURE SOMEONE WILL TRIUMPH EVENTUALLY.
fling
I DO NOT HAVE TIME FOR EVENTUALITIES!
I BOUGHT THE MOST WORTHLESS IDIOT DRAGON TO GUARD ADRIENNE.
I THOUGHT SURELY SOMEONE WOULD SLAUGHTER THAT THING.
WELL, WHAT OF OUR OWN SON?
DEVIN?
YOU MUST BE JOKING.
THE BOY WOULD RATHER PLAY DRESS-UP WITH THE PLAYERS THAN LEARN TO RULE.
HE IS NO KING.

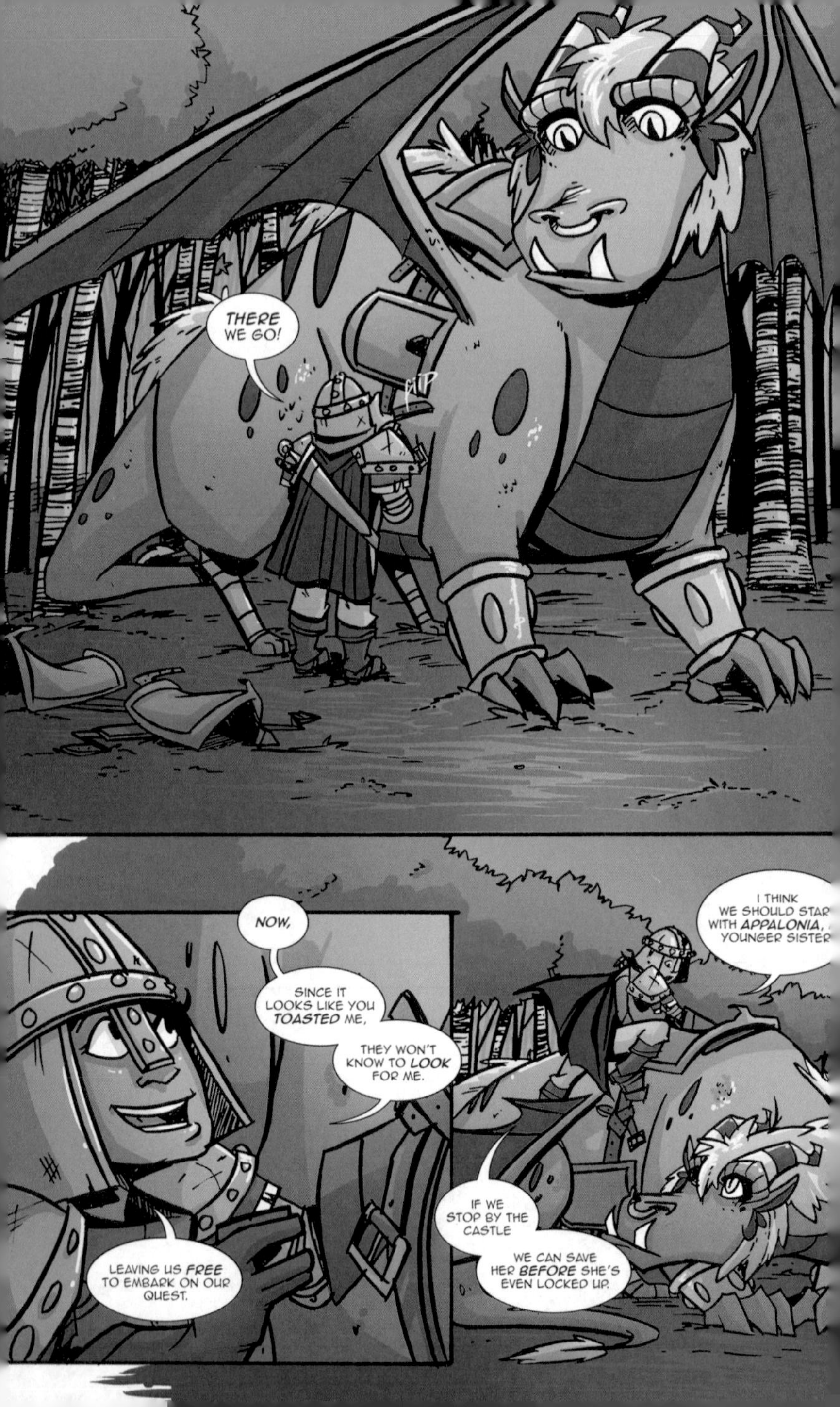
THERE WE GO!
NOW,
SINCE IT LOOKS LIKE YOU TOASTED ME,
THEY WON'T KNOW TO LOOK FOR ME.
LEAVING US FREE TO EMBARK ON OUR QUEST.
I THINK WE SHOULD STAR WITH APPALONIA, YOUNGER SISTER
IF WE STOP BY THE CASTLE
WE CAN SAVE HER BEFORE SHE'S EVEN LOCKED UP.

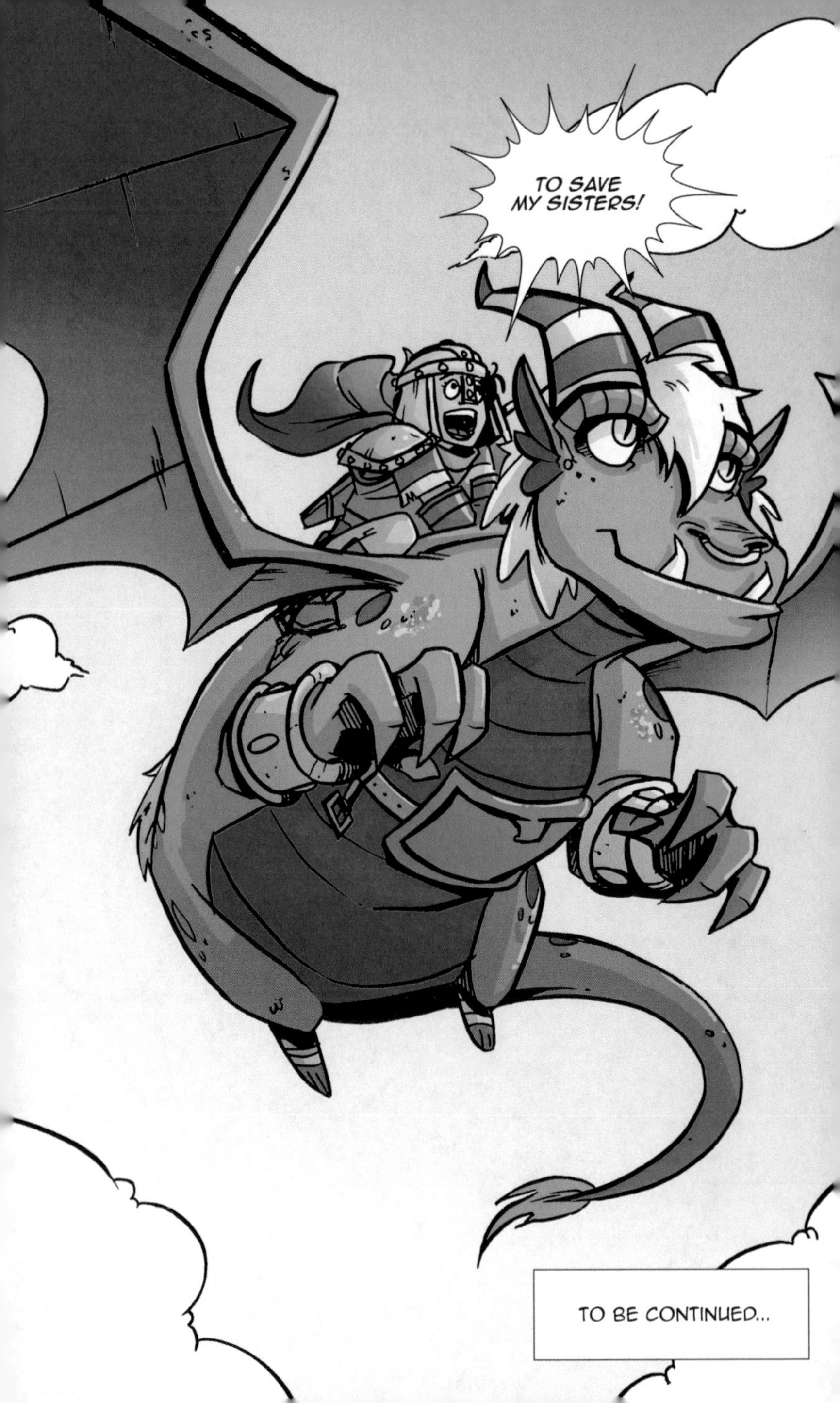
TO SAVE MY SISTERS!
TO BE CONTINUED...

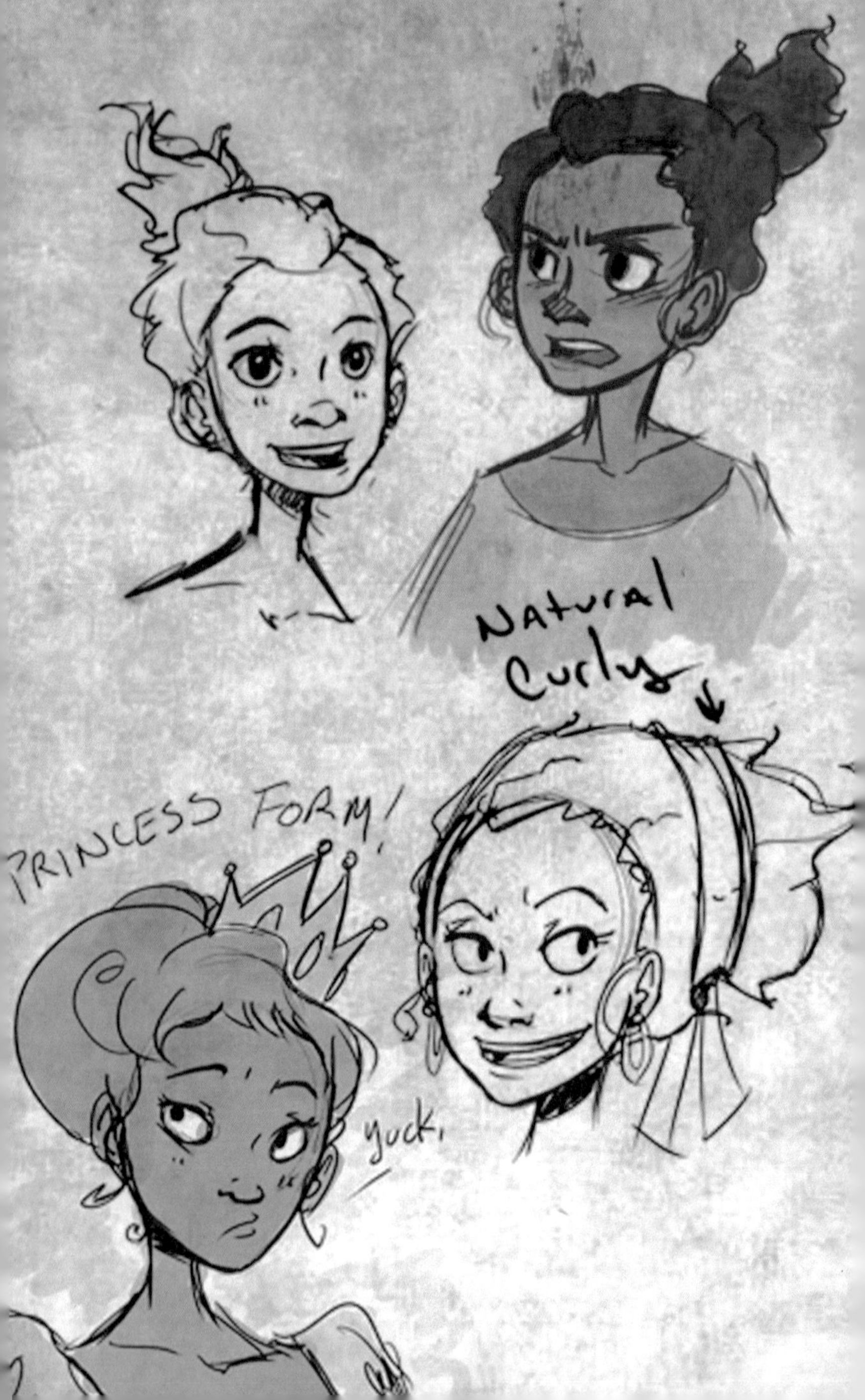
Natural Curly
PRINCESS FORM!
yuck.

2: All for the Want of a Proper Belt

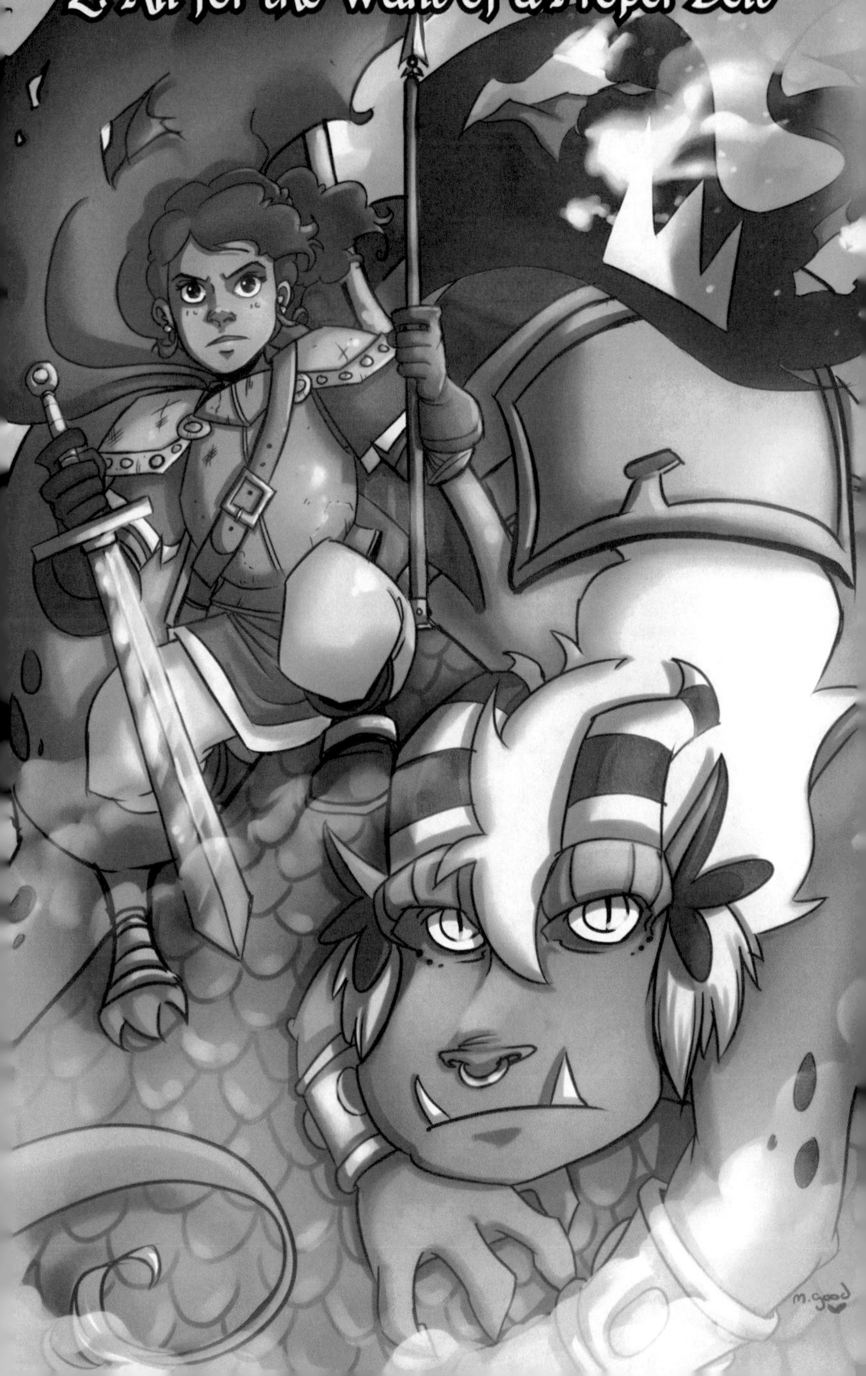

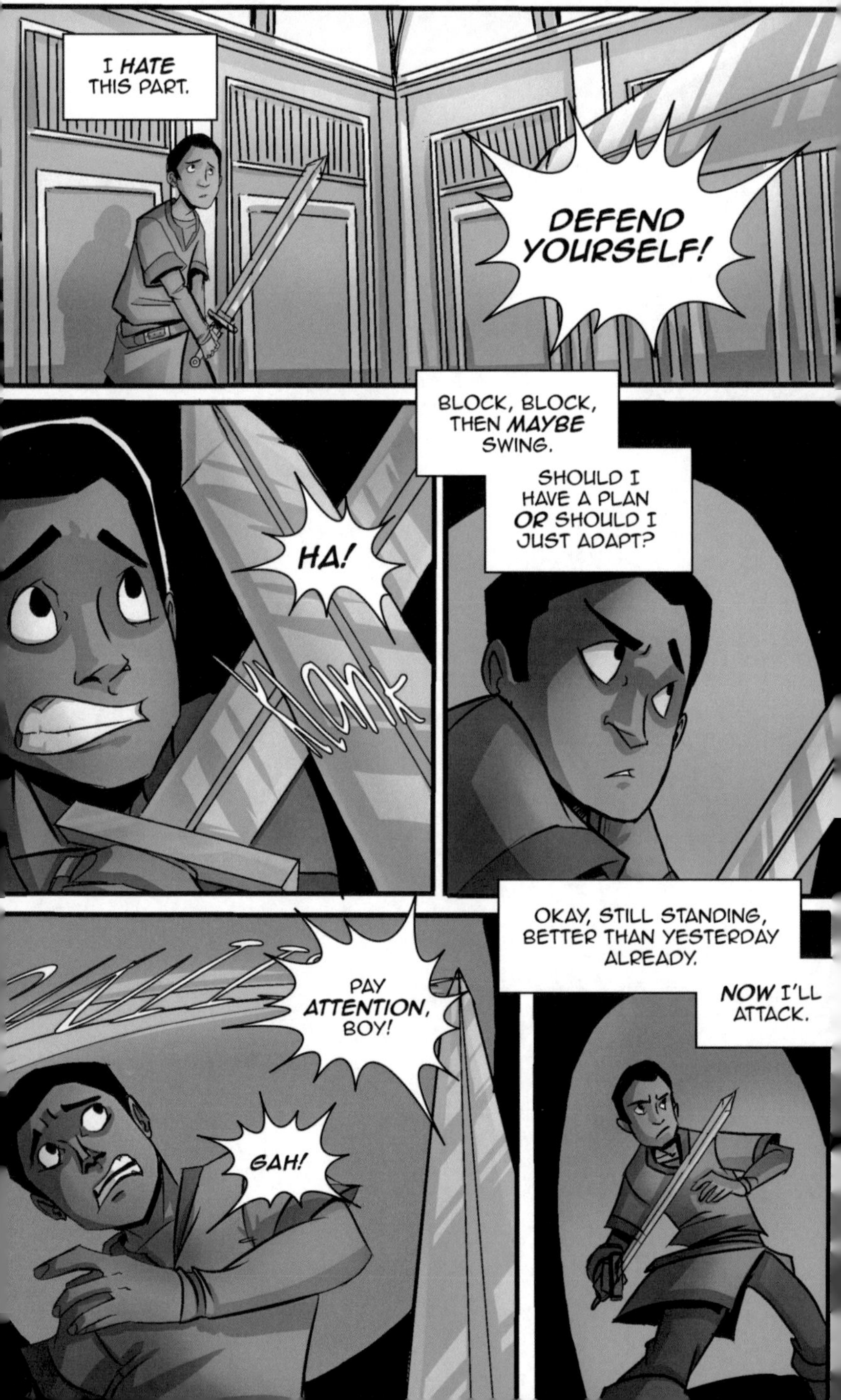

I HATE THIS PART.
DEFEND YOURSELF!
BLOCK, BLOCK, THEN MAYBE SWING.
HA!
SHOULD I HAVE A PLAN OR SHOULD I JUST ADAPT?
PAY ATTENTION, BOY!
GAH!
OKAY, STILL STANDING, BETTER THAN YESTERDAY ALREADY.
NOW I'LL ATTACK.

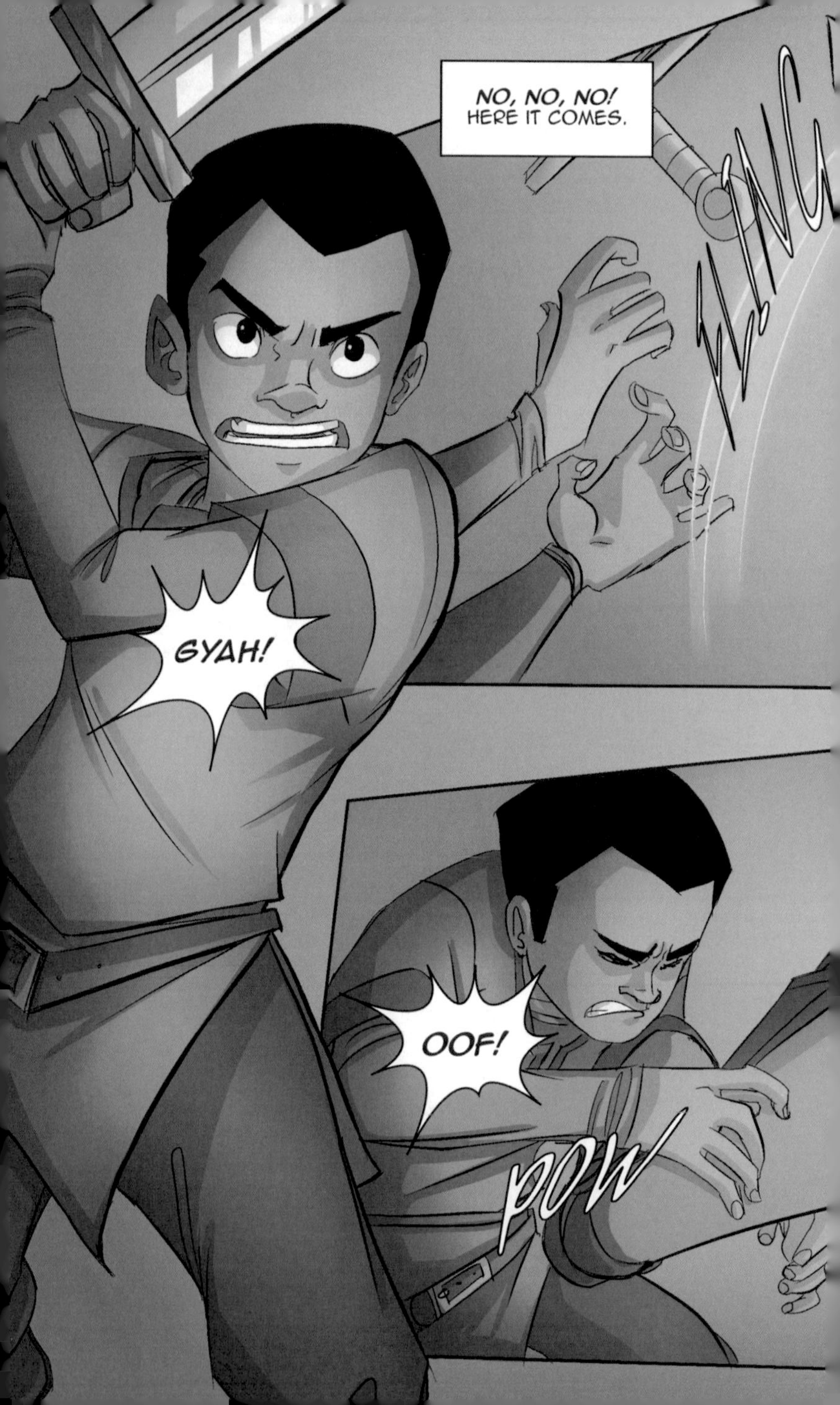
NO, NO, NO!
HERE IT COMES.
FLING
GYAH!
OOF!
POW

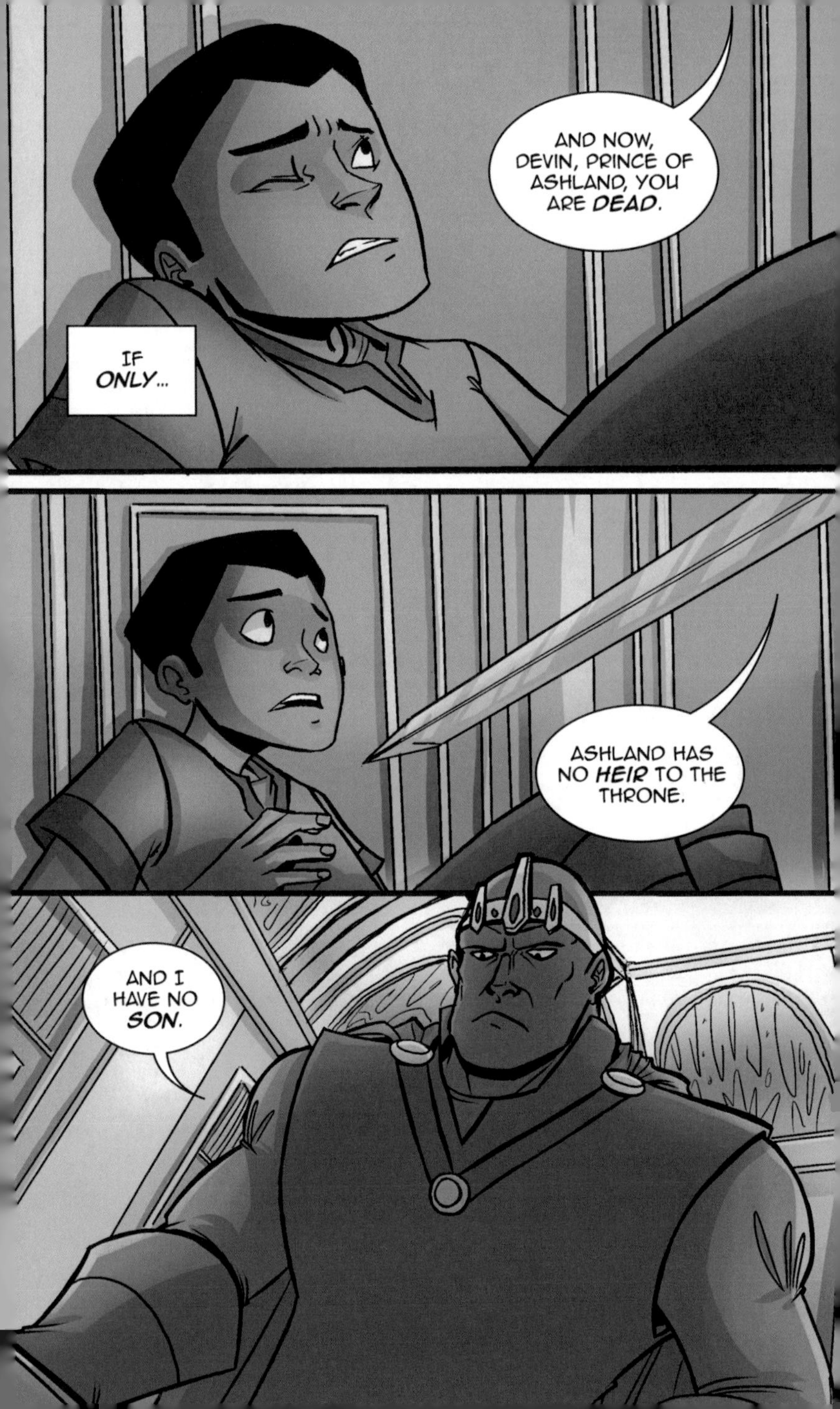
AND NOW, DEVIN, PRINCE OF ASHLAND, YOU ARE DEAD.
IF ONLY...
ASHLAND HAS NO HEIR TO THE THRONE.
AND I HAVE NO SON.

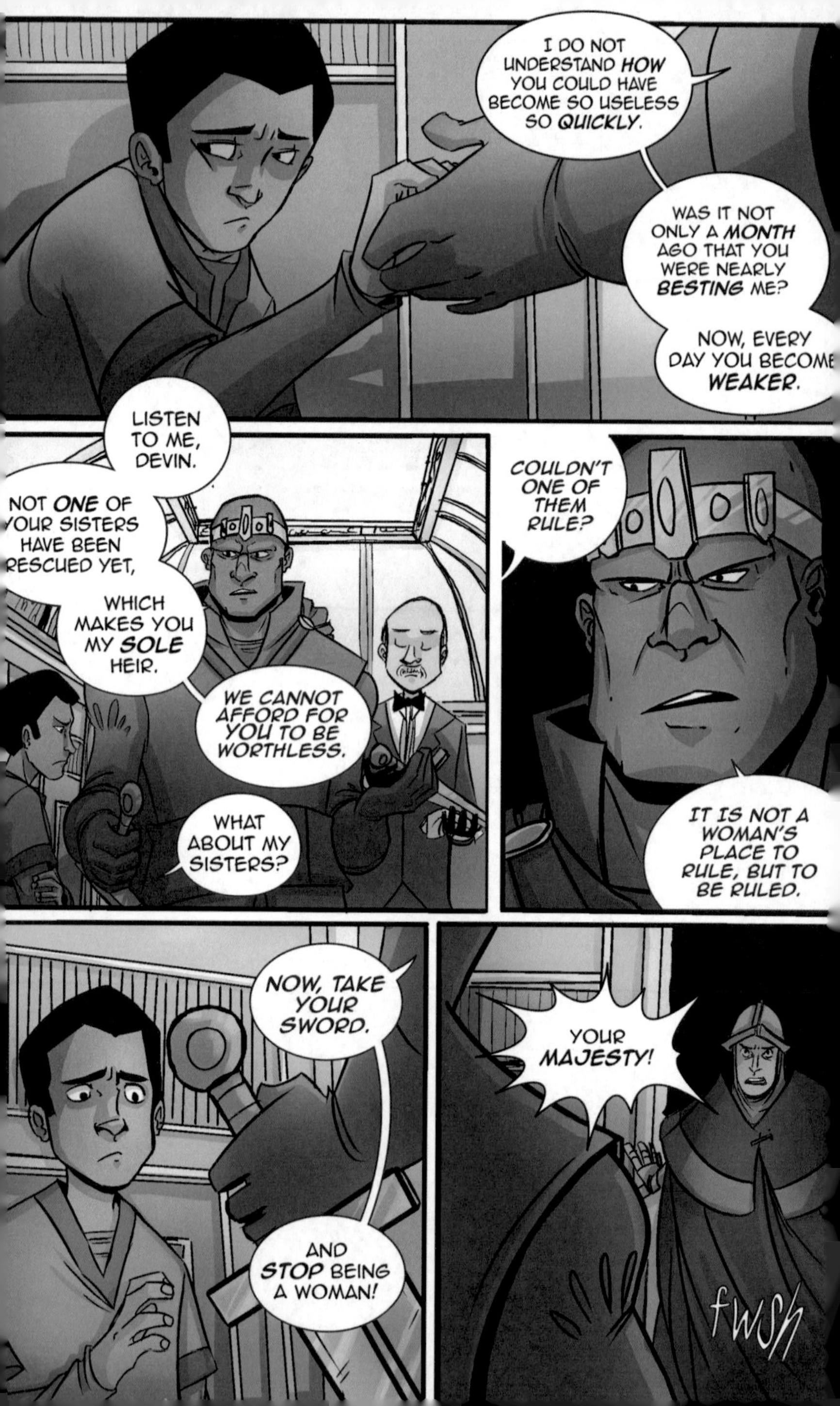
I DO NOT UNDERSTAND HOW YOU COULD HAVE BECOME SO USELESS SO QUICKLY.
WAS IT NOT ONLY A MONTH AGO THAT YOU WERE NEARLY BESTING ME?
NOW, EVERY DAY YOU BECOME WEAKER.
LISTEN TO ME, DEVIN.
NOT ONE OF YOUR SISTERS HAVE BEEN RESCUED YET,
WHICH MAKES YOU MY SOLE HEIR.
WE CANNOT AFFORD FOR YOU TO BE WORTHLESS.
WHAT ABOUT MY SISTERS?
COULDN'T ONE OF THEM RULE?
IT IS NOT A WOMAN'S PLACE TO RULE, BUT TO BE RULED.
NOW, TAKE YOUR SWORD.
AND STOP BEING A WOMAN!
YOUR MAJESTY!
fwsh

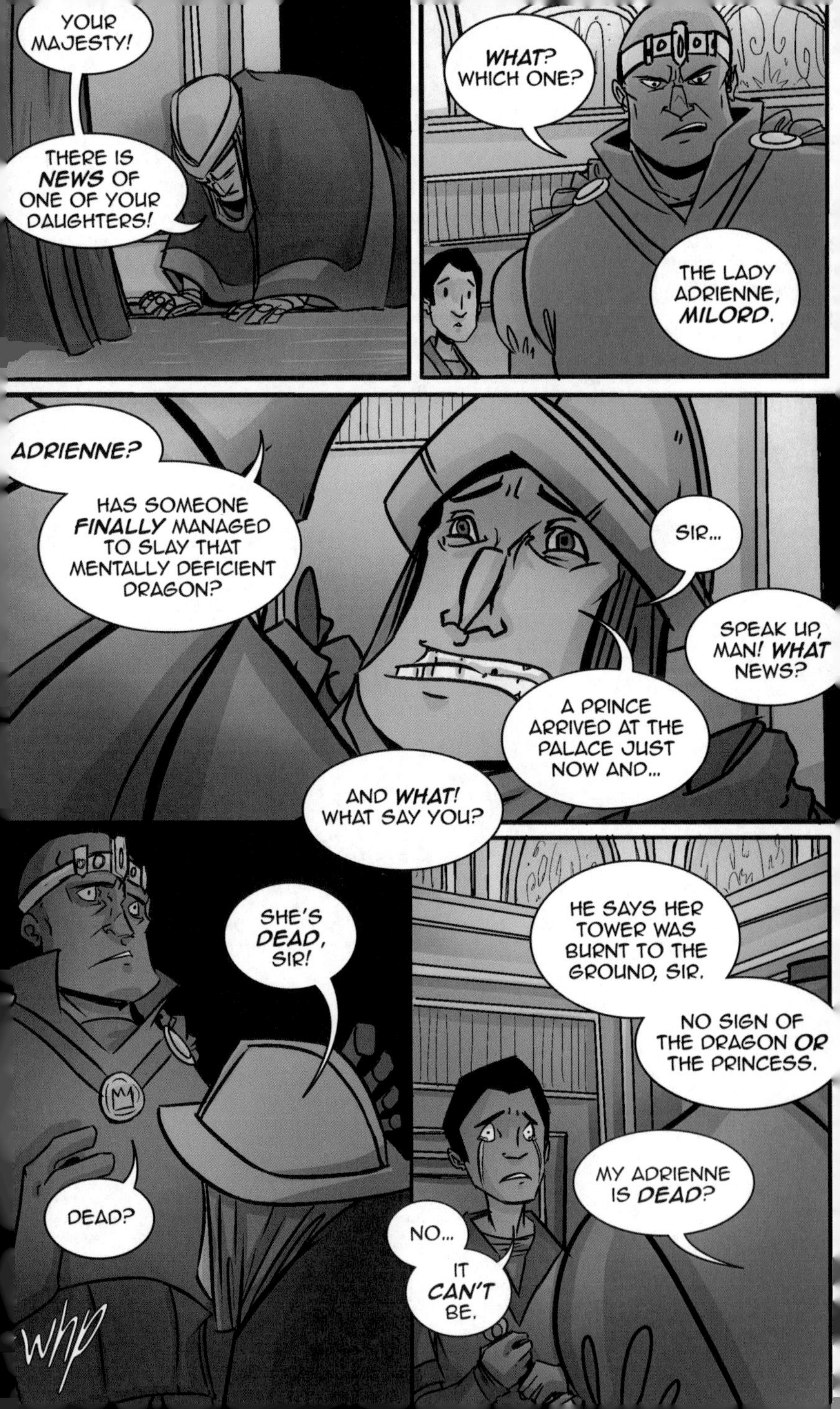
YOUR MAJESTY!
THERE IS NEWS OF ONE OF YOUR DAUGHTERS!
WHAT? WHICH ONE?
THE LADY ADRIENNE, MILORD.
ADRIENNE?
HAS SOMEONE FINALLY MANAGED TO SLAY THAT MENTALLY DEFICIENT DRAGON?
SIR...
SPEAK UP, MAN! WHAT NEWS?
A PRINCE ARRIVED AT THE PALACE JUST NOW AND...
AND WHAT! WHAT SAY YOU?
SHE'S DEAD, SIR!
DEAD?
HE SAYS HER TOWER WAS BURNT TO THE GROUND, SIR.
NO SIGN OF THE DRAGON OR THE PRINCESS.
MY ADRIENNE IS DEAD?
NO...
IT CAN'T BE.

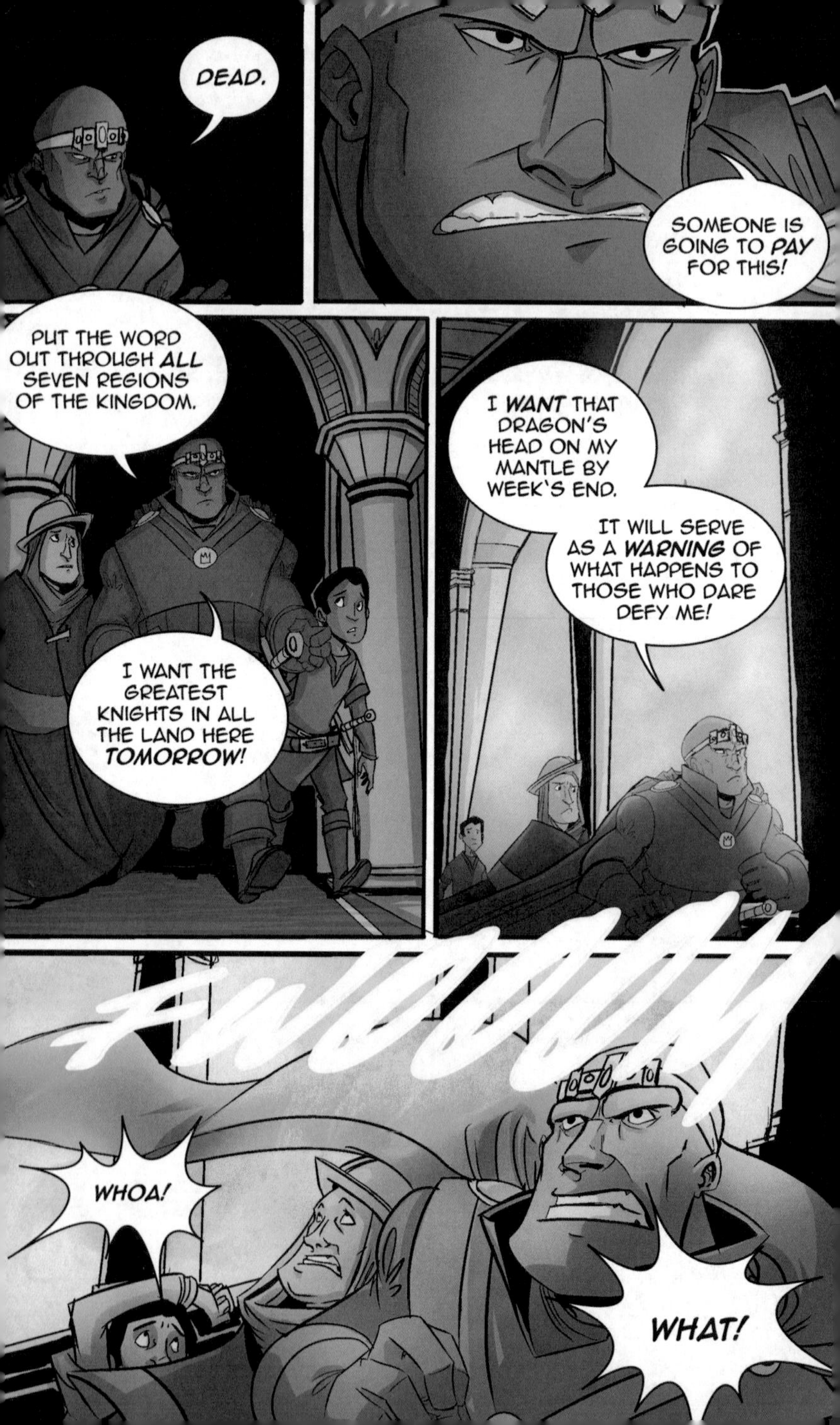
DEAD.
SOMEONE IS GOING TO PAY FOR THIS!
PUT THE WORD OUT THROUGH ALL SEVEN REGIONS OF THE KINGDOM.
I WANT THE GREATEST KNIGHTS IN ALL THE LAND HERE TOMORROW!
I WANT THAT DRAGON'S HEAD ON MY MANTLE BY WEEK'S END.
IT WILL SERVE AS A WARNING OF WHAT HAPPENS TO THOSE WHO DARE DEFY ME!
FWOOOM
WHOA!
WHAT!

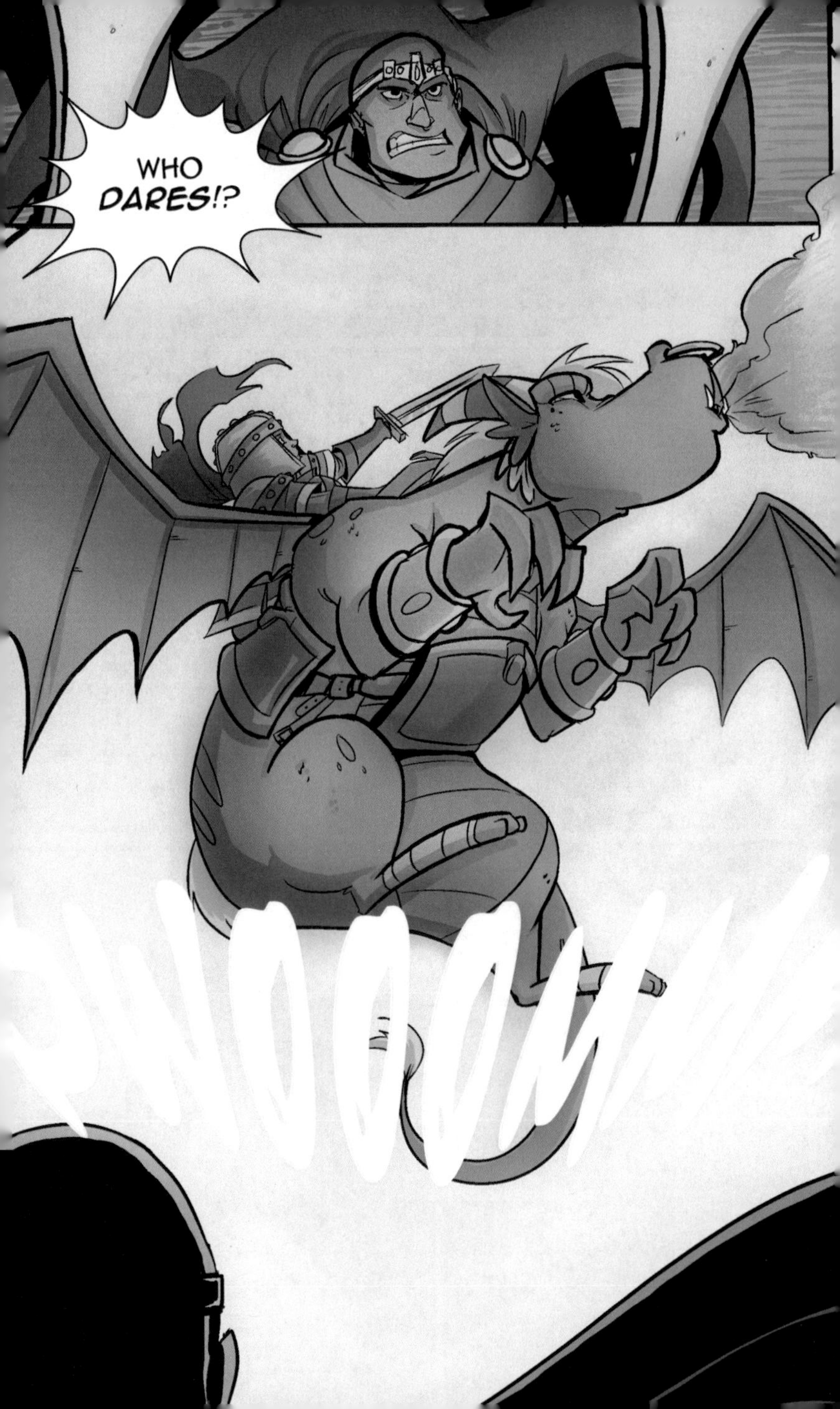
WHO DARES!?

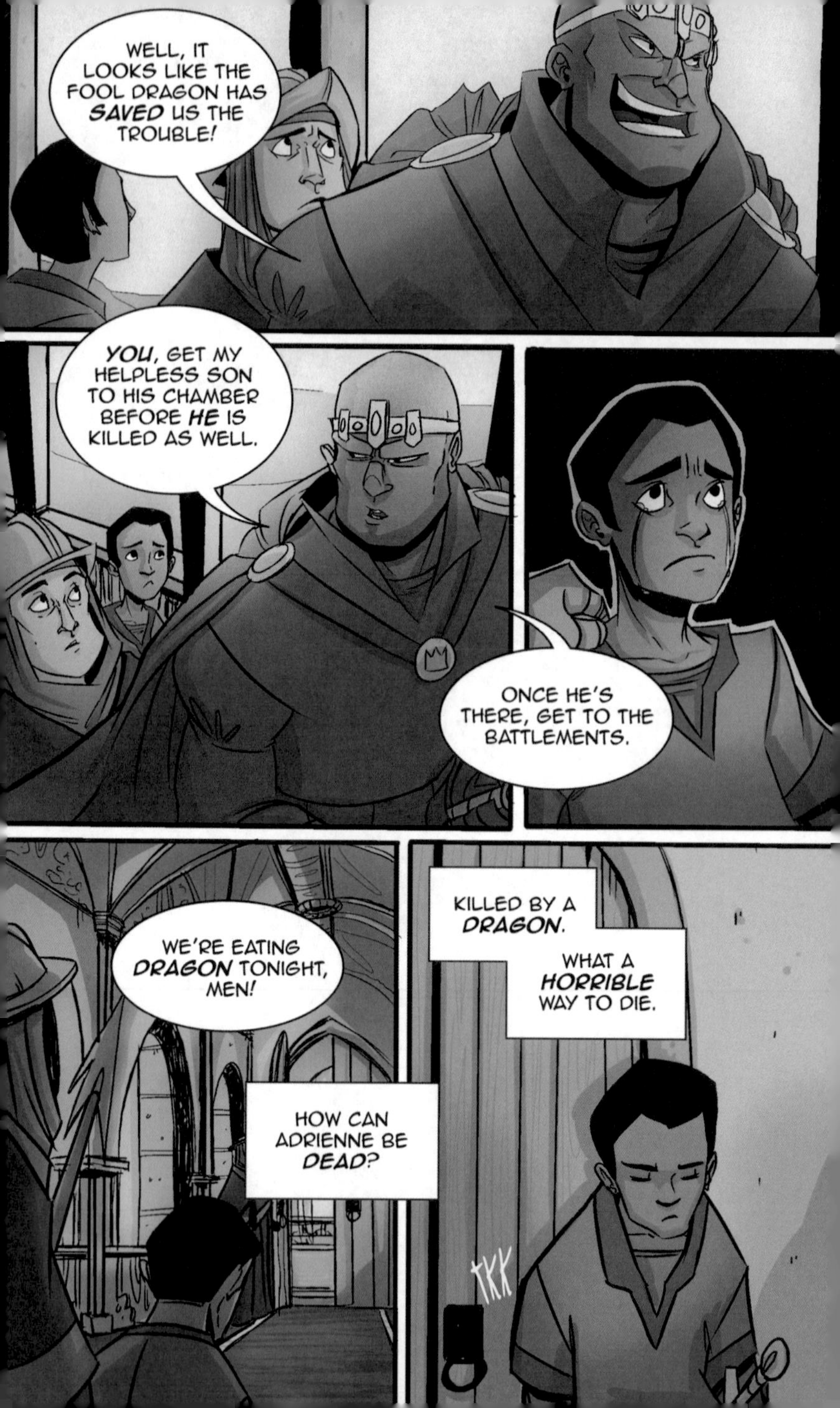
WELL, IT LOOKS LIKE THE FOOL DRAGON HAS *SAVED* US THE TROUBLE!
YOU, GET MY HELPLESS SON TO HIS CHAMBER BEFORE *HE* IS KILLED AS WELL.
ONCE HE'S THERE, GET TO THE BATTLEMENTS.
WE'RE EATING *DRAGON* TONIGHT, MEN!
HOW CAN ADRIENNE BE *DEAD*?
KILLED BY A *DRAGON*.
WHAT A *HORRIBLE* WAY TO DIE.
TKK

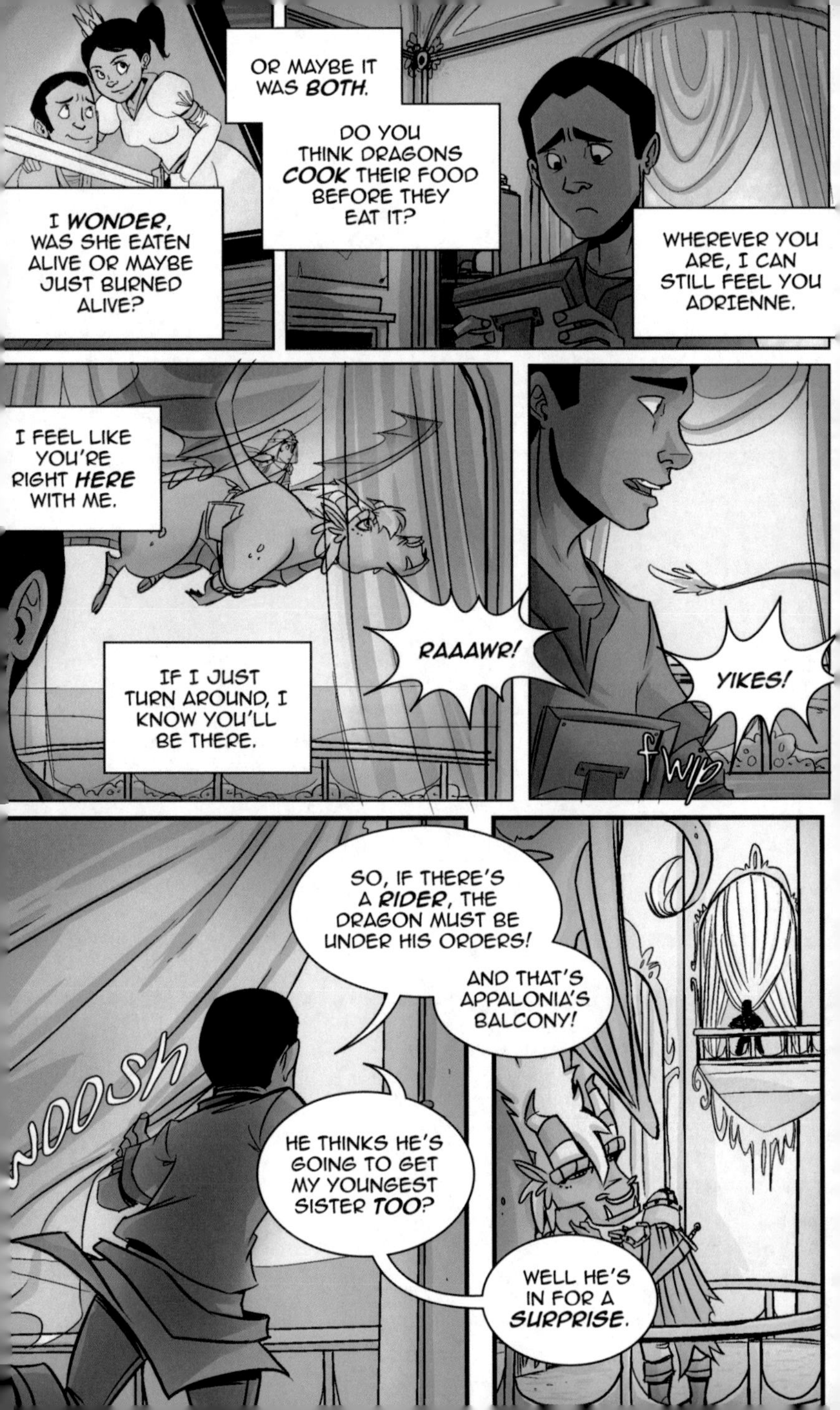

OR MAYBE IT WAS BOTH.
DO YOU THINK DRAGONS COOK THEIR FOOD BEFORE THEY EAT IT?
I WONDER, WAS SHE EATEN ALIVE OR MAYBE JUST BURNED ALIVE?
WHEREVER YOU ARE, I CAN STILL FEEL YOU ADRIENNE.
I FEEL LIKE YOU'RE RIGHT HERE WITH ME.
IF I JUST TURN AROUND, I KNOW YOU'LL BE THERE.
RAAAWR!
YIKES!
fwip
WOOSH
SO, IF THERE'S A RIDER, THE DRAGON MUST BE UNDER HIS ORDERS!
AND THAT'S APPALONIA'S BALCONY!
HE THINKS HE'S GOING TO GET MY YOUNGEST SISTER TOO?
WELL HE'S IN FOR A SURPRISE.

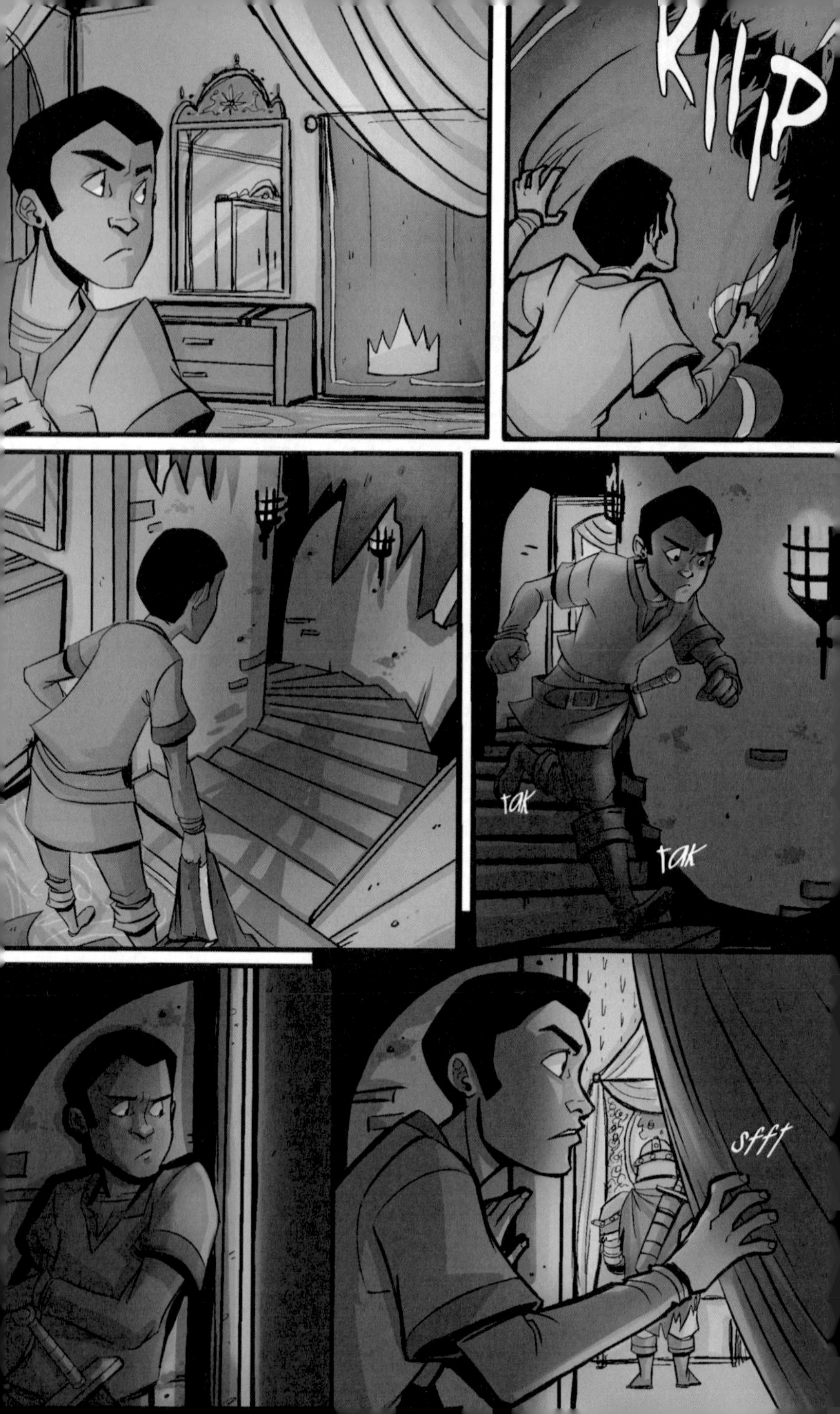
KLIP
tak
tak
sfft

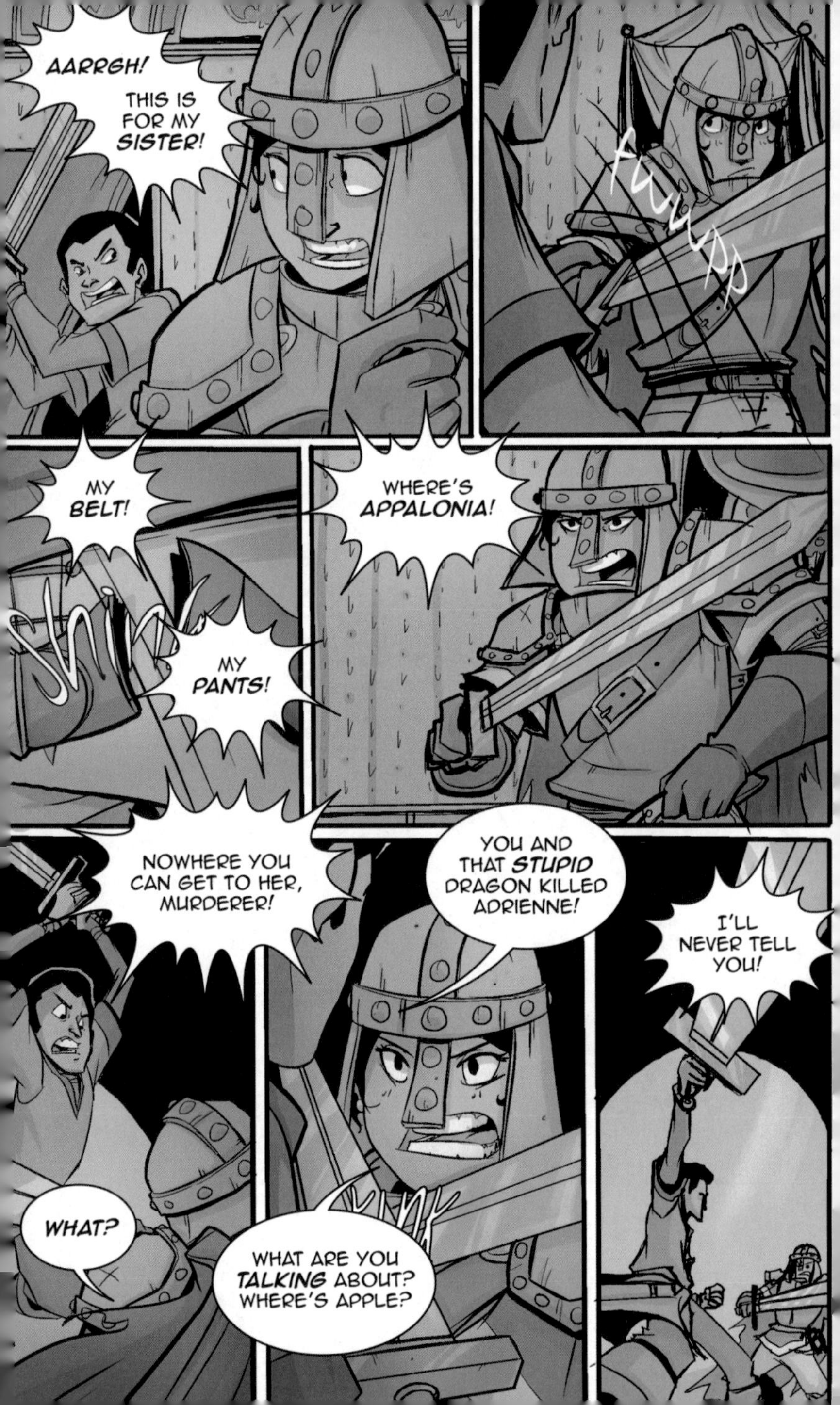
AARRGH!
THIS IS FOR MY SISTER!
FWUPP
MY BELT!
WHERE'S APPALONIA!
SHIK
MY PANTS!
NOWHERE YOU CAN GET TO HER, MURDERER!
YOU AND THAT STUPID DRAGON KILLED ADRIENNE!
I'LL NEVER TELL YOU!
WHAT?
WHAT ARE YOU TALKING ABOUT? WHERE'S APPLE?

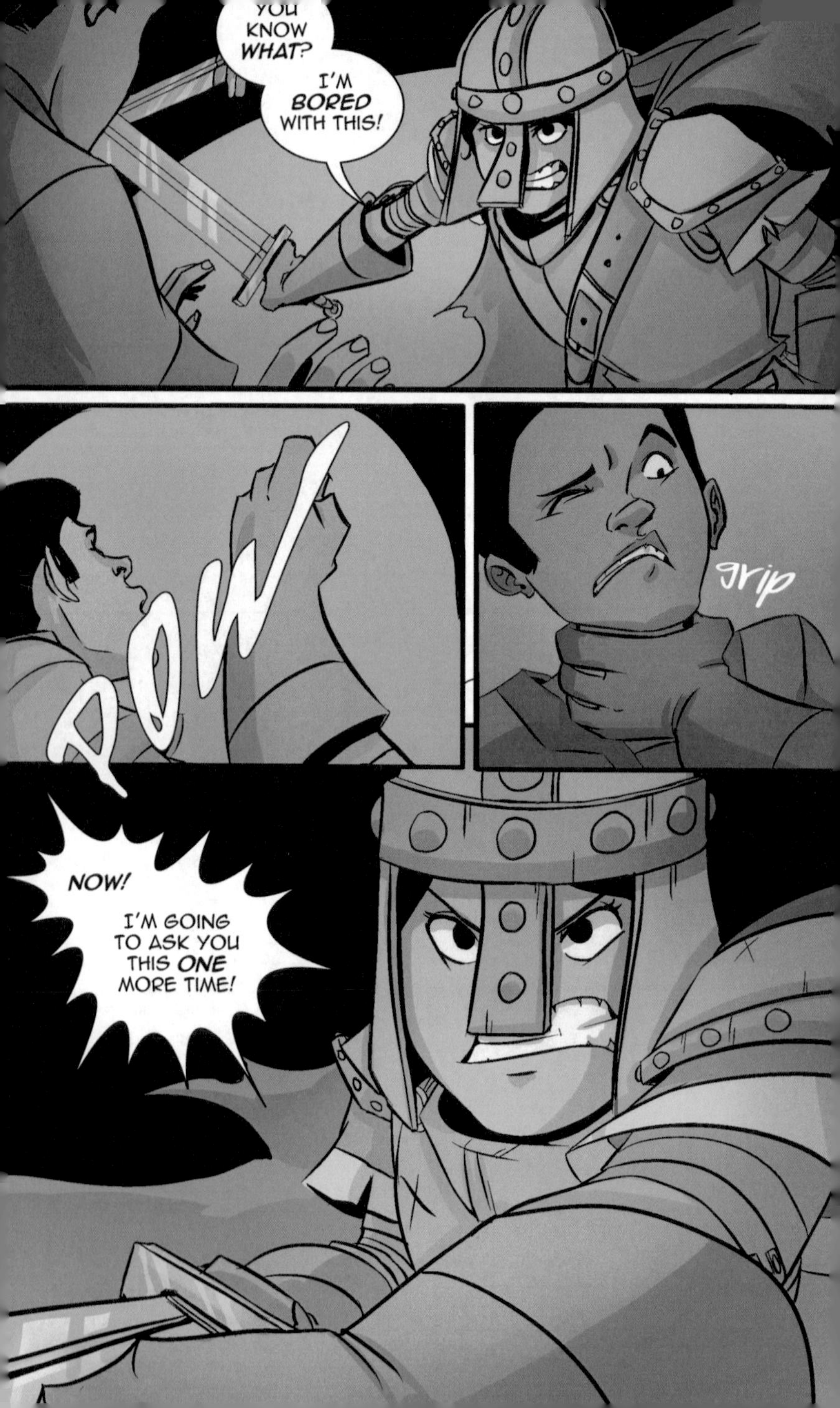
YOU KNOW WHAT?
I'M BORED WITH THIS!
POW
grip
NOW!
I'M GOING TO ASK YOU THIS ONE MORE TIME!

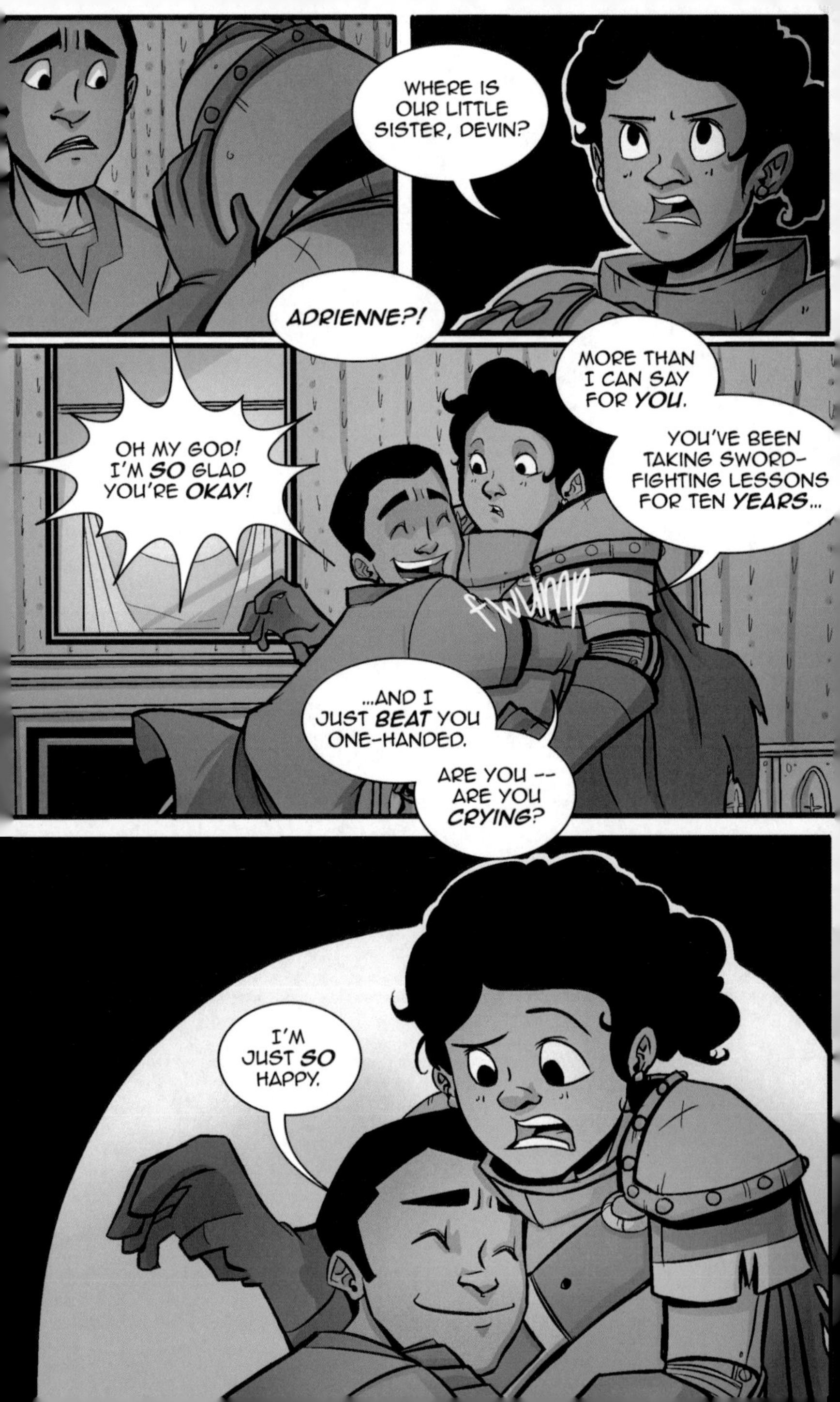
WHERE IS OUR LITTLE SISTER, DEVIN?
ADRIENNE?!
OH MY GOD! I'M SO GLAD YOU'RE OKAY!
MORE THAN I CAN SAY FOR YOU.
YOU'VE BEEN TAKING SWORD-FIGHTING LESSONS FOR TEN YEARS...
fwump
...AND I JUST BEAT YOU ONE-HANDED.
ARE YOU -- ARE YOU CRYING?
I'M JUST SO HAPPY.

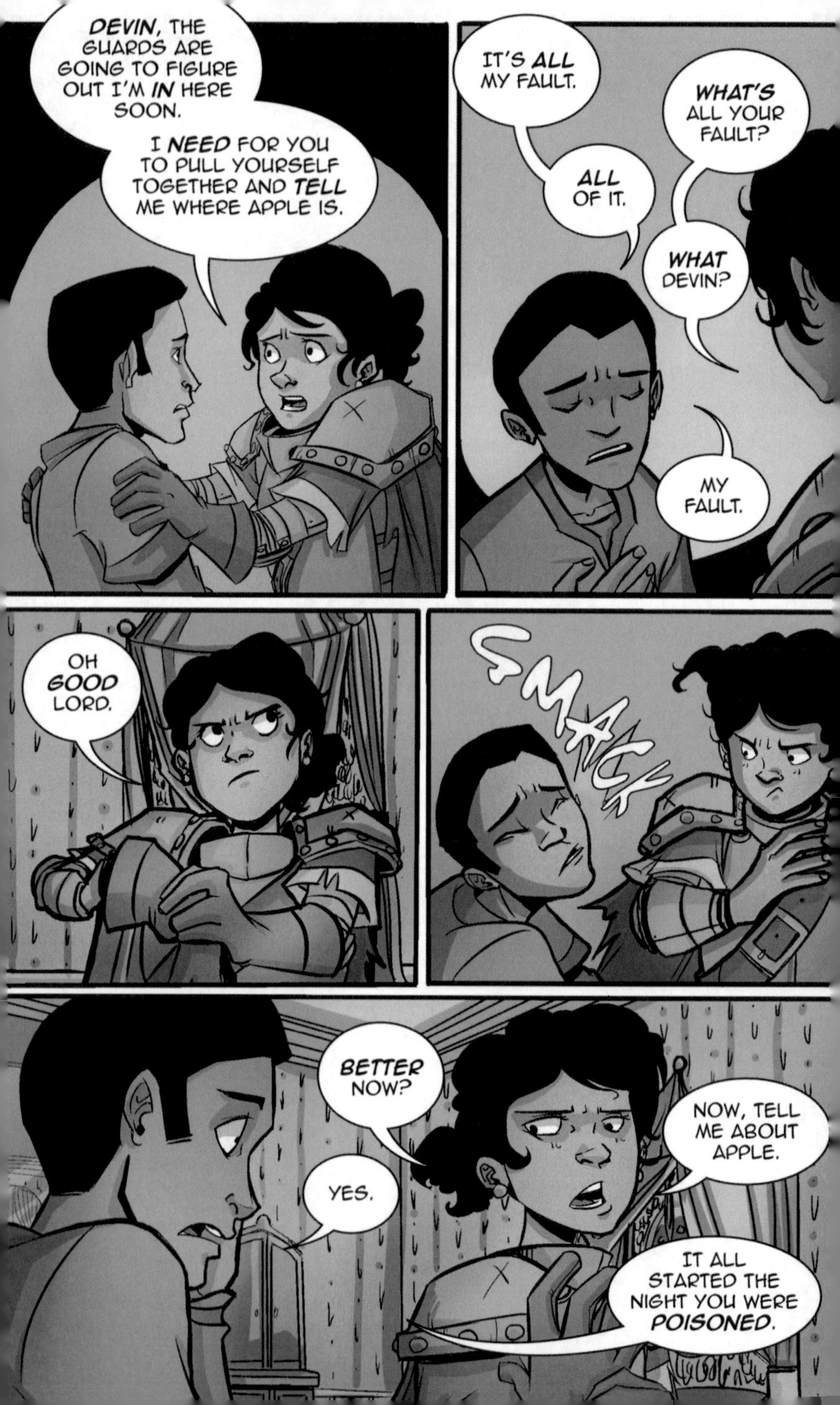
DEVIN, THE GUARDS ARE GOING TO FIGURE OUT I'M IN HERE SOON.
I NEED FOR YOU TO PULL YOURSELF TOGETHER AND TELL ME WHERE APPLE IS.
IT'S ALL MY FAULT.
WHAT'S ALL YOUR FAULT?
ALL OF IT.
WHAT DEVIN?
MY FAULT.
OH GOOD LORD.
SMACK
BETTER NOW?
YES.
NOW, TELL ME ABOUT APPLE.
IT ALL STARTED THE NIGHT YOU WERE POISONED.

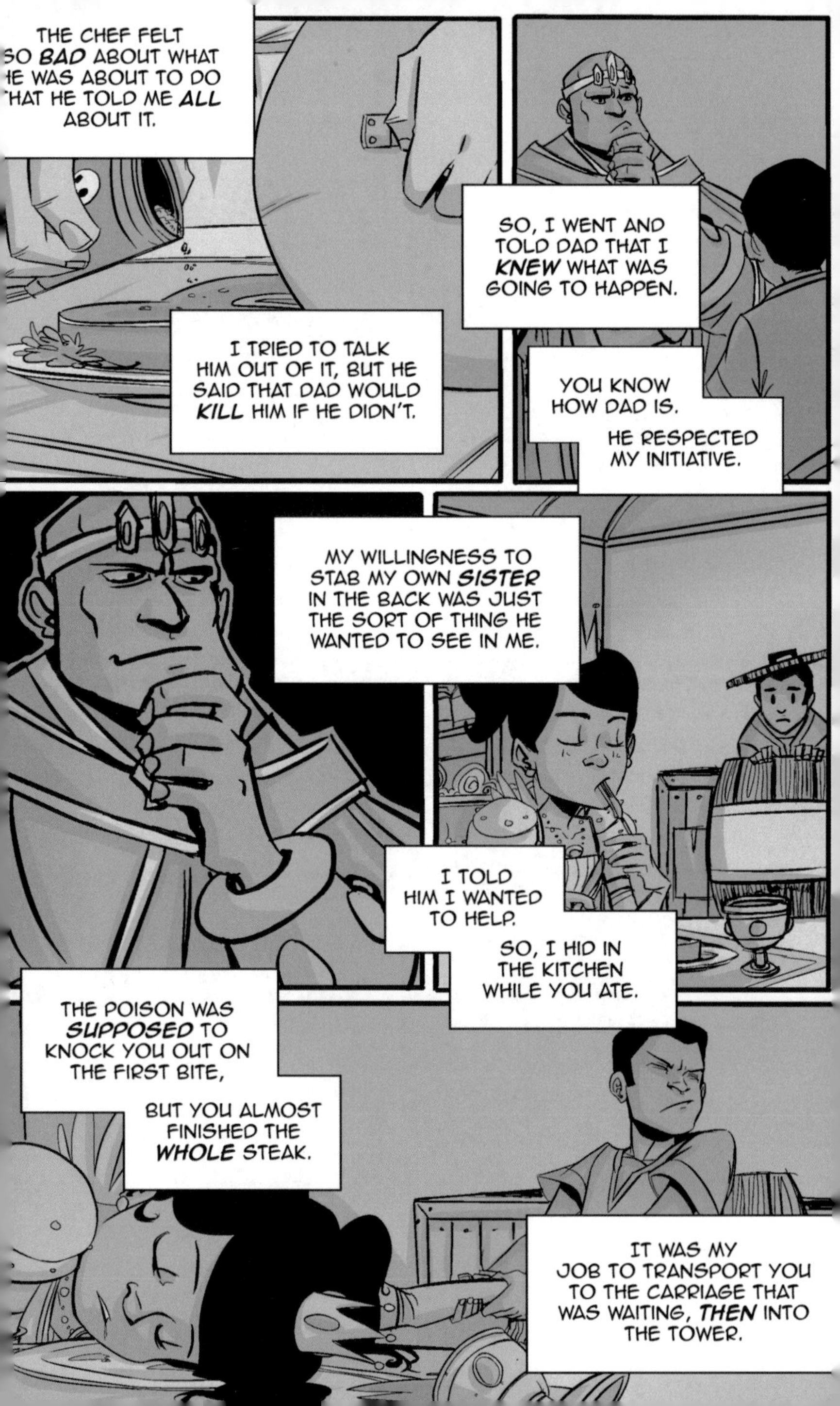
THE CHEF FELT SO BAD ABOUT WHAT HE WAS ABOUT TO DO THAT HE TOLD ME ALL ABOUT IT.
I TRIED TO TALK HIM OUT OF IT, BUT HE SAID THAT DAD WOULD KILL HIM IF HE DIDN'T.
SO, I WENT AND TOLD DAD THAT I KNEW WHAT WAS GOING TO HAPPEN.
YOU KNOW HOW DAD IS.
HE RESPECTED MY INITIATIVE.
MY WILLINGNESS TO STAB MY OWN SISTER IN THE BACK WAS JUST THE SORT OF THING HE WANTED TO SEE IN ME.
I TOLD HIM I WANTED TO HELP.
SO, I HID IN THE KITCHEN WHILE YOU ATE.
THE POISON WAS SUPPOSED TO KNOCK YOU OUT ON THE FIRST BITE,
BUT YOU ALMOST FINISHED THE WHOLE STEAK.
IT WAS MY JOB TO TRANSPORT YOU TO THE CARRIAGE THAT WAS WAITING, THEN INTO THE TOWER.

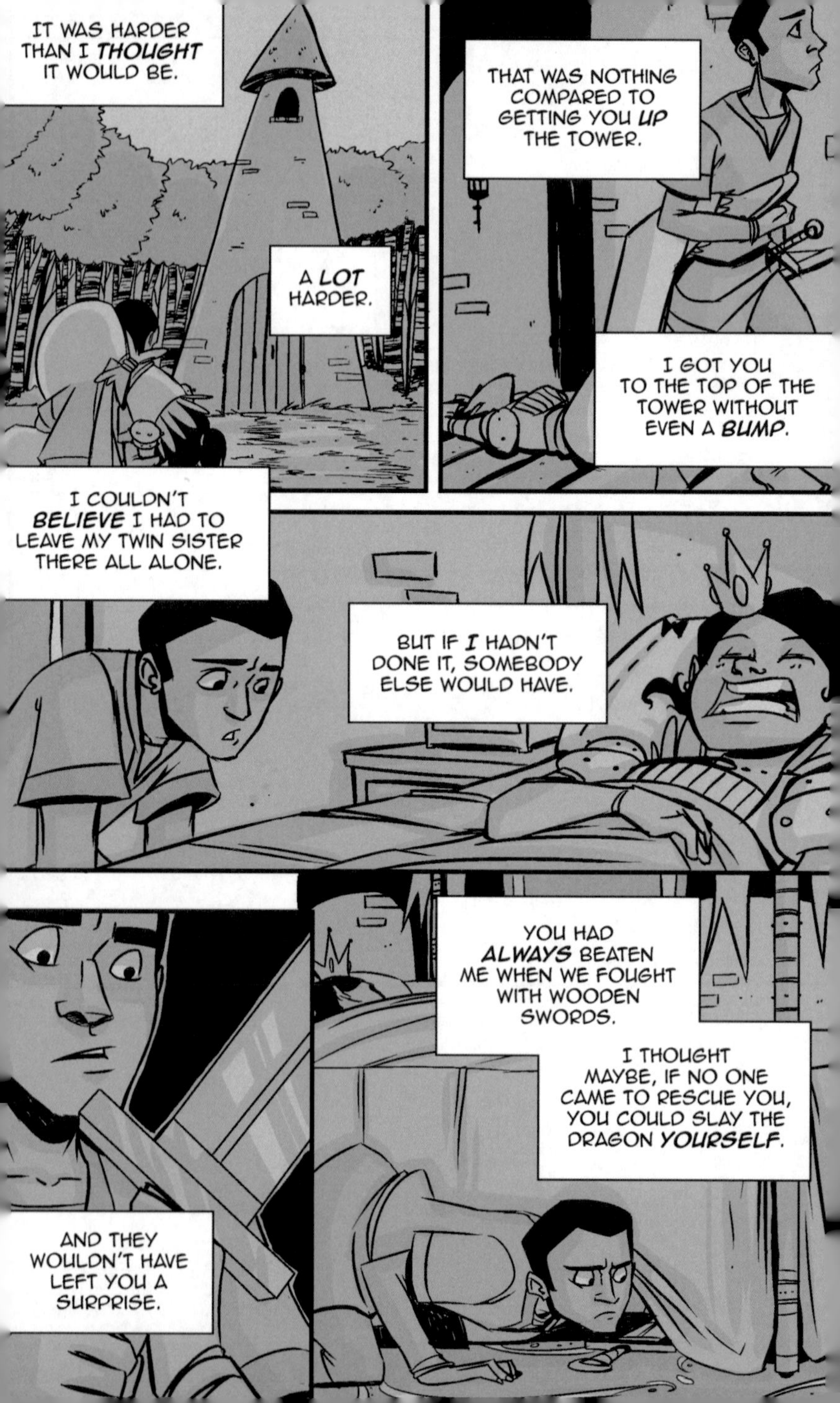
IT WAS HARDER THAN I THOUGHT IT WOULD BE.
A LOT HARDER.
THAT WAS NOTHING COMPARED TO GETTING YOU UP THE TOWER.
I GOT YOU TO THE TOP OF THE TOWER WITHOUT EVEN A BUMP.
I COULDN'T BELIEVE I HAD TO LEAVE MY TWIN SISTER THERE ALL ALONE.
BUT IF I HADN'T DONE IT, SOMEBODY ELSE WOULD HAVE.
AND THEY WOULDN'T HAVE LEFT YOU A SURPRISE.
YOU HAD ALWAYS BEATEN ME WHEN WE FOUGHT WITH WOODEN SWORDS.
I THOUGHT MAYBE, IF NO ONE CAME TO RESCUE YOU, YOU COULD SLAY THE DRAGON YOURSELF.

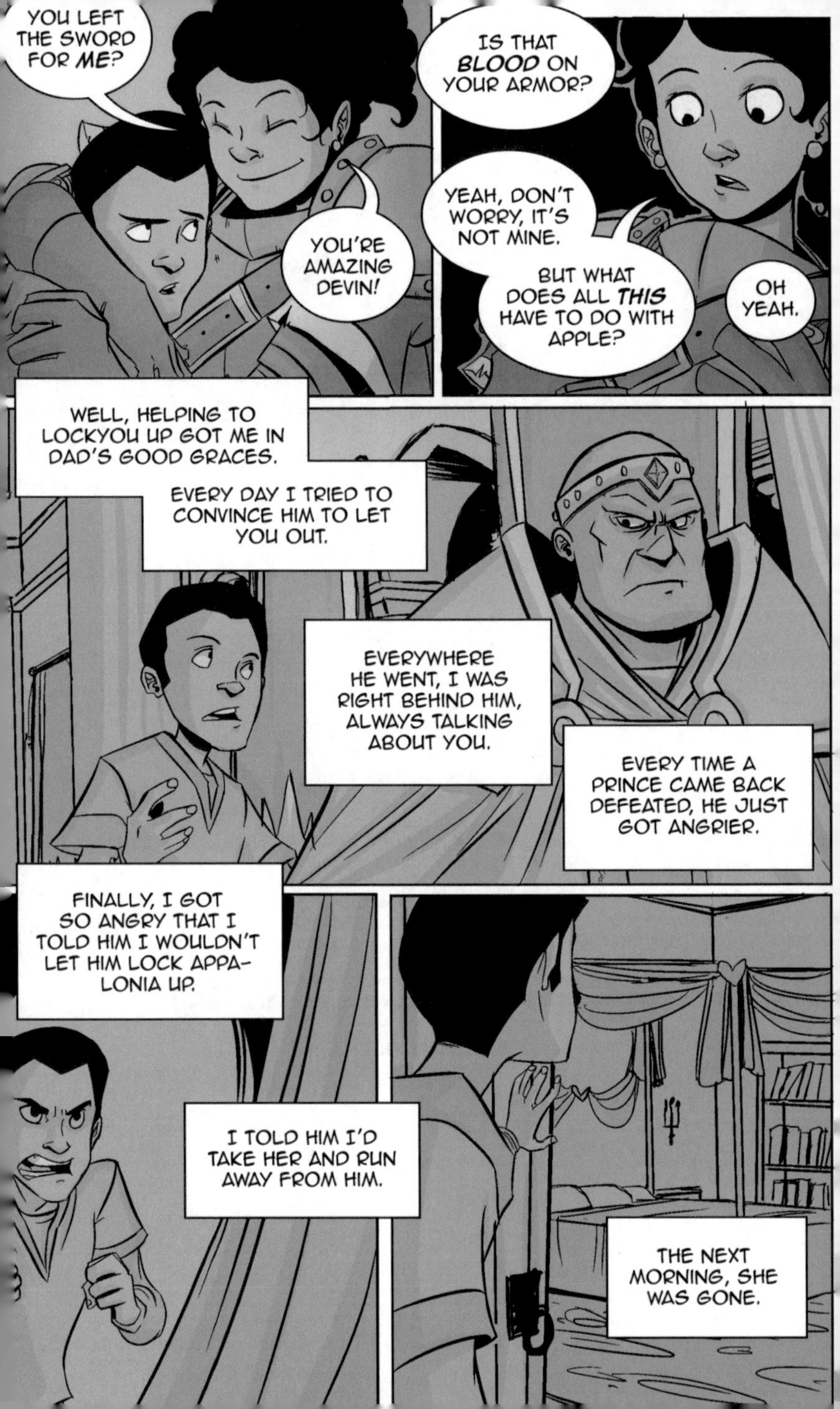
YOU LEFT THE SWORD FOR *ME*?
YOU'RE AMAZING DEVIN!
IS THAT *BLOOD* ON YOUR ARMOR?
YEAH, DON'T WORRY, IT'S NOT MINE.
BUT WHAT DOES ALL *THIS* HAVE TO DO WITH APPLE?
OH YEAH.
WELL, HELPING TO LOCKYOU UP GOT ME IN DAD'S GOOD GRACES.
EVERY DAY I TRIED TO CONVINCE HIM TO LET YOU OUT.
EVERYWHERE HE WENT, I WAS RIGHT BEHIND HIM, ALWAYS TALKING ABOUT YOU.
EVERY TIME A PRINCE CAME BACK DEFEATED, HE JUST GOT ANGRIER.
FINALLY, I GOT SO ANGRY THAT I TOLD HIM I WOULDN'T LET HIM LOCK APPA-LONIA UP.
I TOLD HIM I'D TAKE HER AND RUN AWAY FROM HIM.
THE NEXT MORNING, SHE WAS GONE.

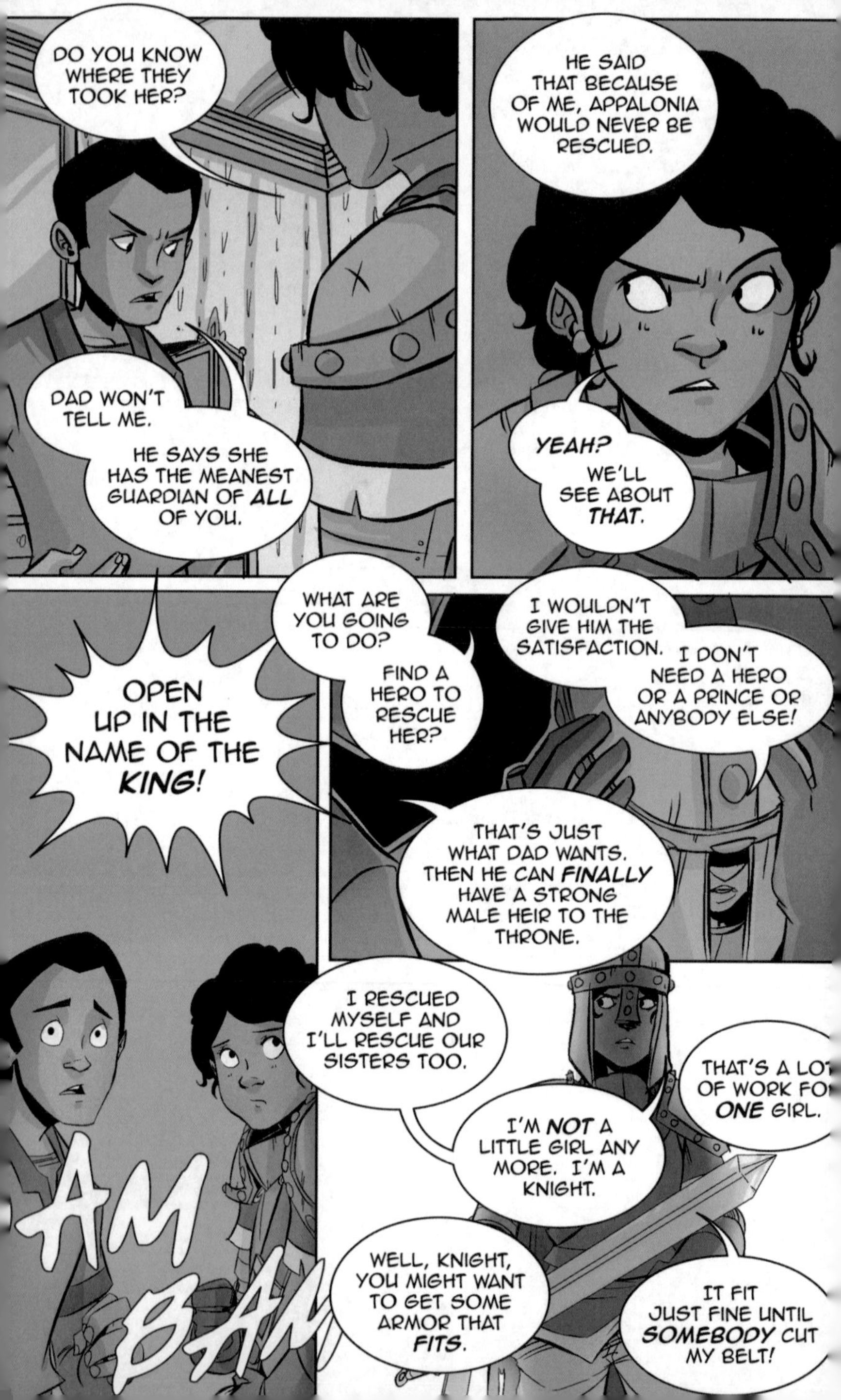
DO YOU KNOW WHERE THEY TOOK HER?
DAD WON'T TELL ME.
HE SAYS SHE HAS THE MEANEST GUARDIAN OF ALL OF YOU.
HE SAID THAT BECAUSE OF ME, APPALONIA WOULD NEVER BE RESCUED.
YEAH?
WE'LL SEE ABOUT THAT.
WHAT ARE YOU GOING TO DO?
FIND A HERO TO RESCUE HER?
I WOULDN'T GIVE HIM THE SATISFACTION.
I DON'T NEED A HERO OR A PRINCE OR ANYBODY ELSE!
THAT'S JUST WHAT DAD WANTS. THEN HE CAN FINALLY HAVE A STRONG MALE HEIR TO THE THRONE.
OPEN UP IN THE NAME OF THE KING!
I RESCUED MYSELF AND I'LL RESCUE OUR SISTERS TOO.
THAT'S A LOT OF WORK FOR ONE GIRL.
I'M NOT A LITTLE GIRL ANY MORE. I'M A KNIGHT.
WELL, KNIGHT, YOU MIGHT WANT TO GET SOME ARMOR THAT FITS.
IT FIT JUST FINE UNTIL SOMEBODY CUT MY BELT!

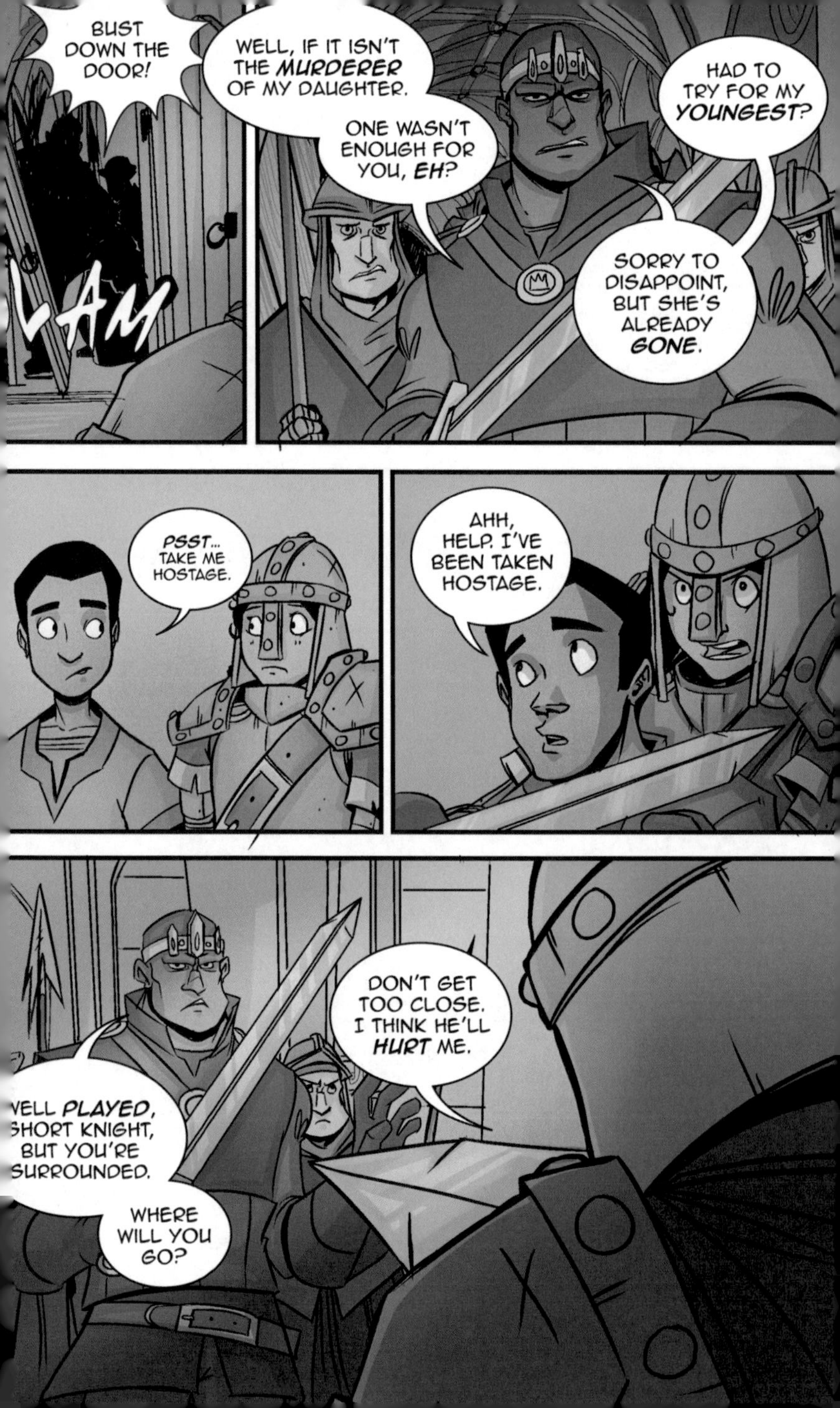
BUST DOWN THE DOOR!
SLAM
WELL, IF IT ISN'T THE MURDERER OF MY DAUGHTER.
ONE WASN'T ENOUGH FOR YOU, EH?
HAD TO TRY FOR MY YOUNGEST?
SORRY TO DISAPPOINT, BUT SHE'S ALREADY GONE.
PSST... TAKE ME HOSTAGE.
AHH, HELP. I'VE BEEN TAKEN HOSTAGE.
DON'T GET TOO CLOSE. I THINK HE'LL HURT ME.
WELL PLAYED, SHORT KNIGHT, BUT YOU'RE SURROUNDED.
WHERE WILL YOU GO?

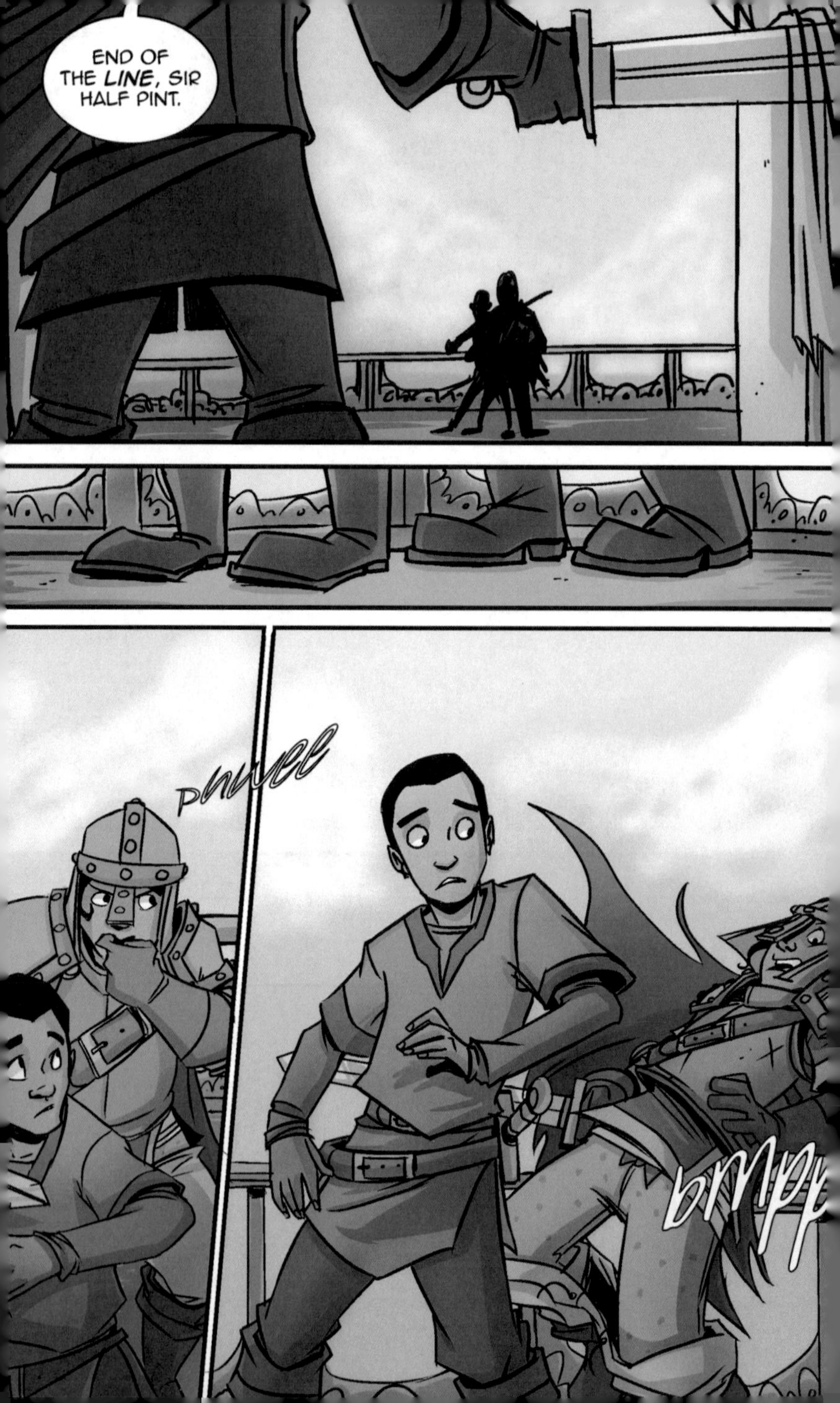
END OF THE LINE, SIR HALF PINT.
phweel
bmpf

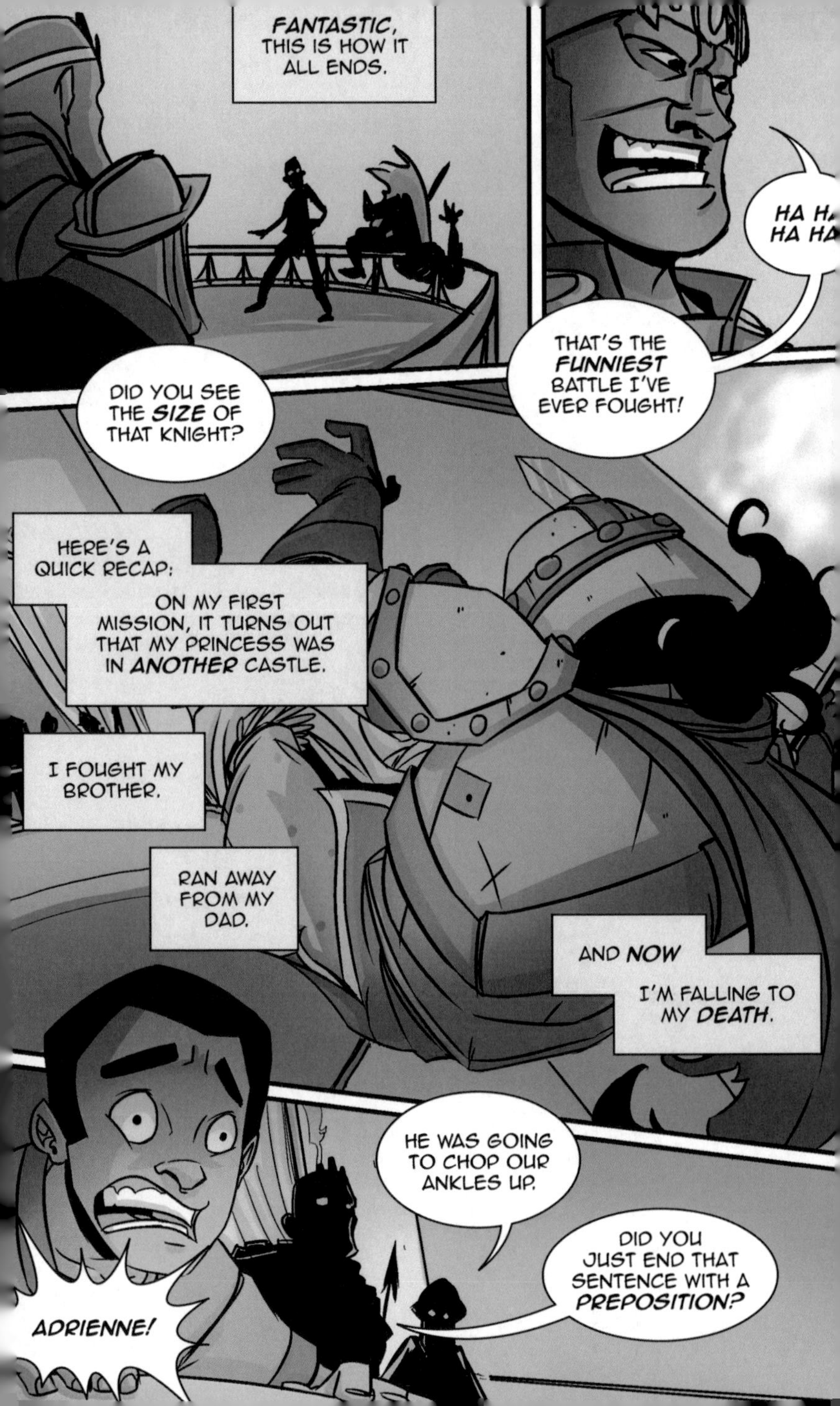

FANTASTIC, THIS IS HOW IT ALL ENDS.
HA HA HA HA
THAT'S THE FUNNIEST BATTLE I'VE EVER FOUGHT!
DID YOU SEE THE SIZE OF THAT KNIGHT?
HERE'S A QUICK RECAP:
ON MY FIRST MISSION, IT TURNS OUT THAT MY PRINCESS WAS IN ANOTHER CASTLE.
I FOUGHT MY BROTHER.
RAN AWAY FROM MY DAD.
AND NOW
I'M FALLING TO MY DEATH.
ADRIENNE!
HE WAS GOING TO CHOP OUR ANKLES UP.
DID YOU JUST END THAT SENTENCE WITH A PREPOSITION?

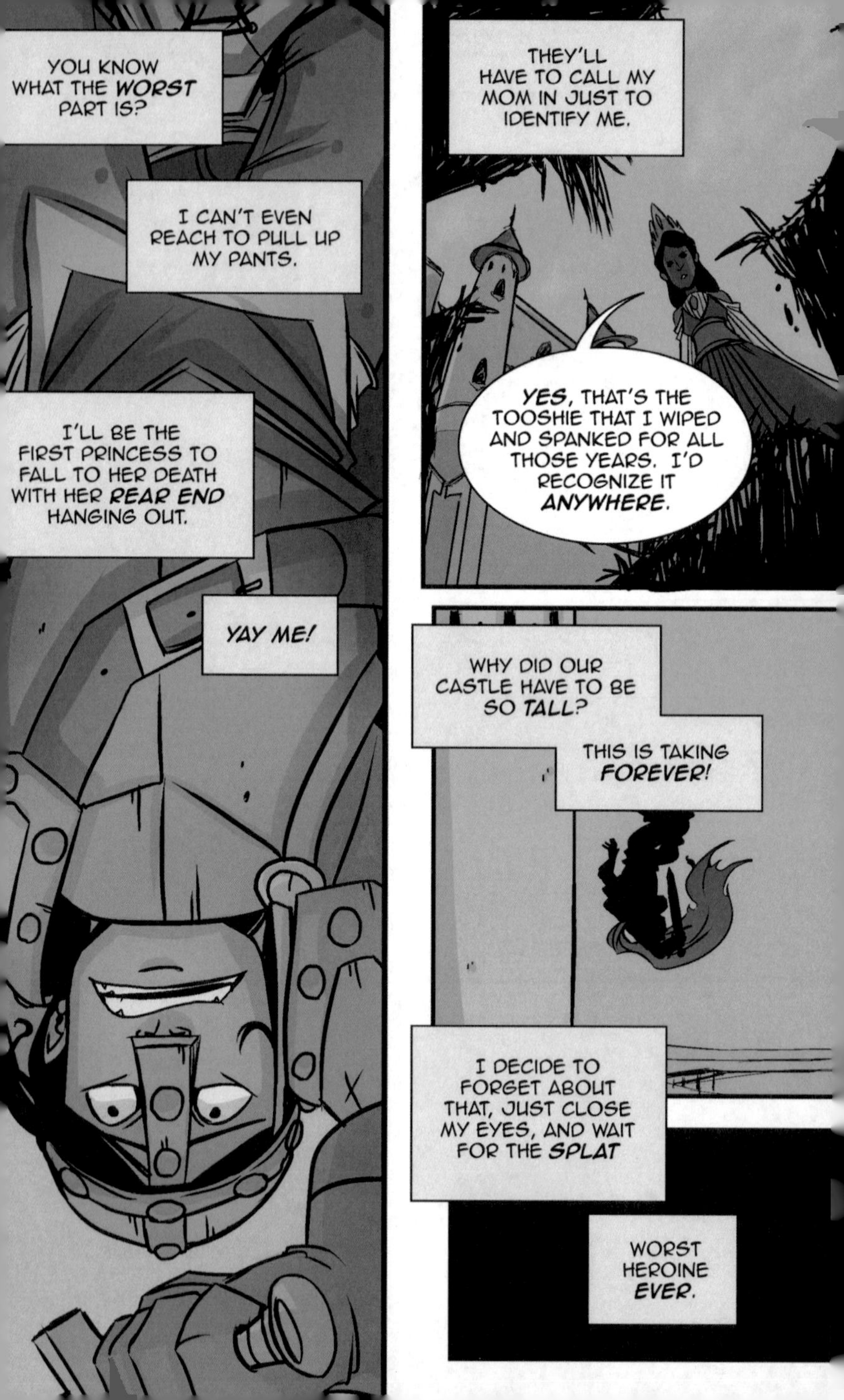
YOU KNOW WHAT THE WORST PART IS?
I CAN'T EVEN REACH TO PULL UP MY PANTS.
I'LL BE THE FIRST PRINCESS TO FALL TO HER DEATH WITH HER REAR END HANGING OUT.
YAY ME!
THEY'LL HAVE TO CALL MY MOM IN JUST TO IDENTIFY ME.
YES, THAT'S THE TOOSHIE THAT I WIPED AND SPANKED FOR ALL THOSE YEARS. I'D RECOGNIZE IT ANYWHERE.
WHY DID OUR CASTLE HAVE TO BE SO TALL?
THIS IS TAKING FOREVER!
I DECIDE TO FORGET ABOUT THAT, JUST CLOSE MY EYES, AND WAIT FOR THE SPLAT
WORST HEROINE EVER.

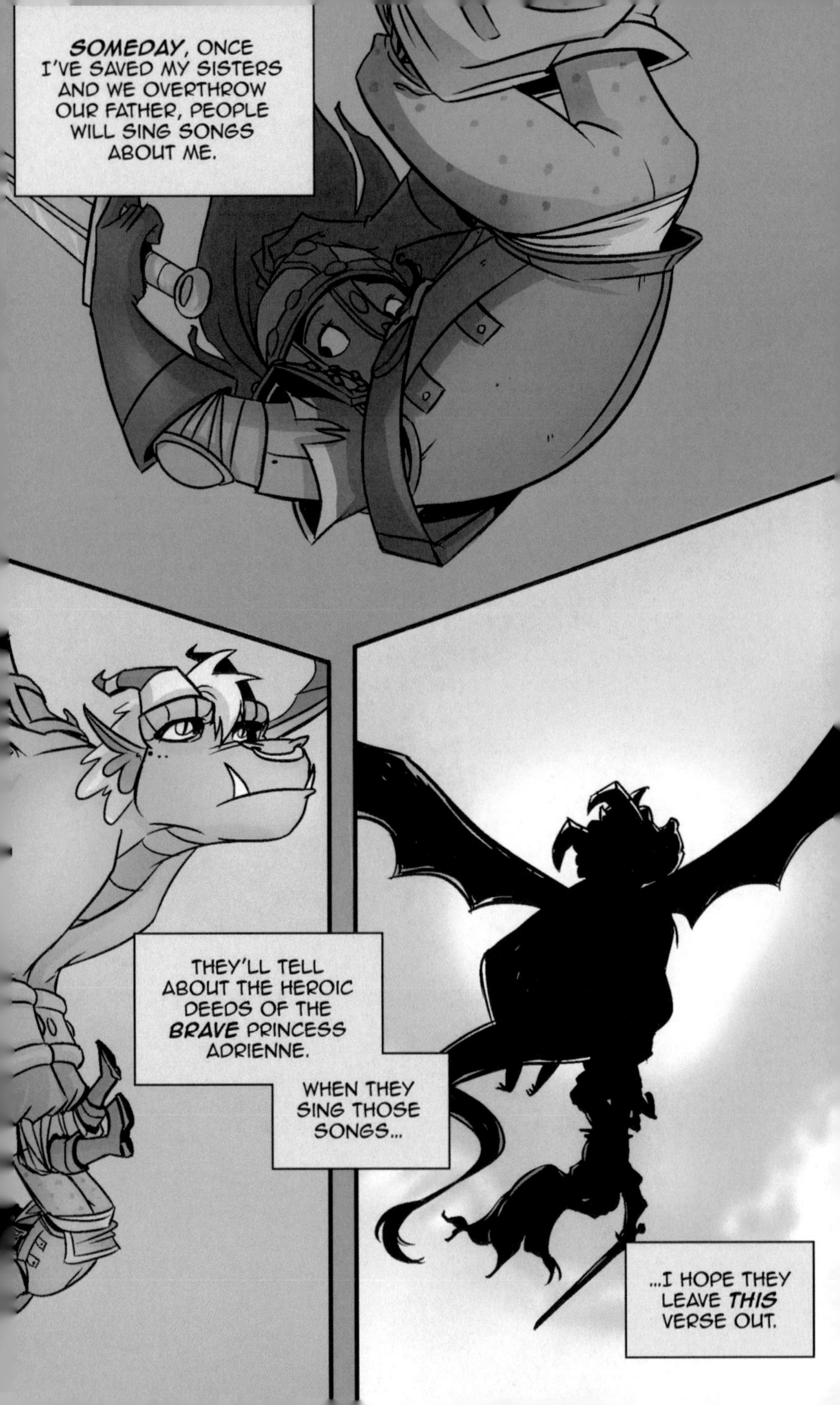
SOMEDAY, ONCE I'VE SAVED MY SISTERS AND WE OVERTHROW OUR FATHER, PEOPLE WILL SING SONGS ABOUT ME.
THEY'LL TELL ABOUT THE HEROIC DEEDS OF THE BRAVE PRINCESS ADRIENNE.
WHEN THEY SING THOSE SONGS...
...I HOPE THEY LEAVE THIS VERSE OUT.

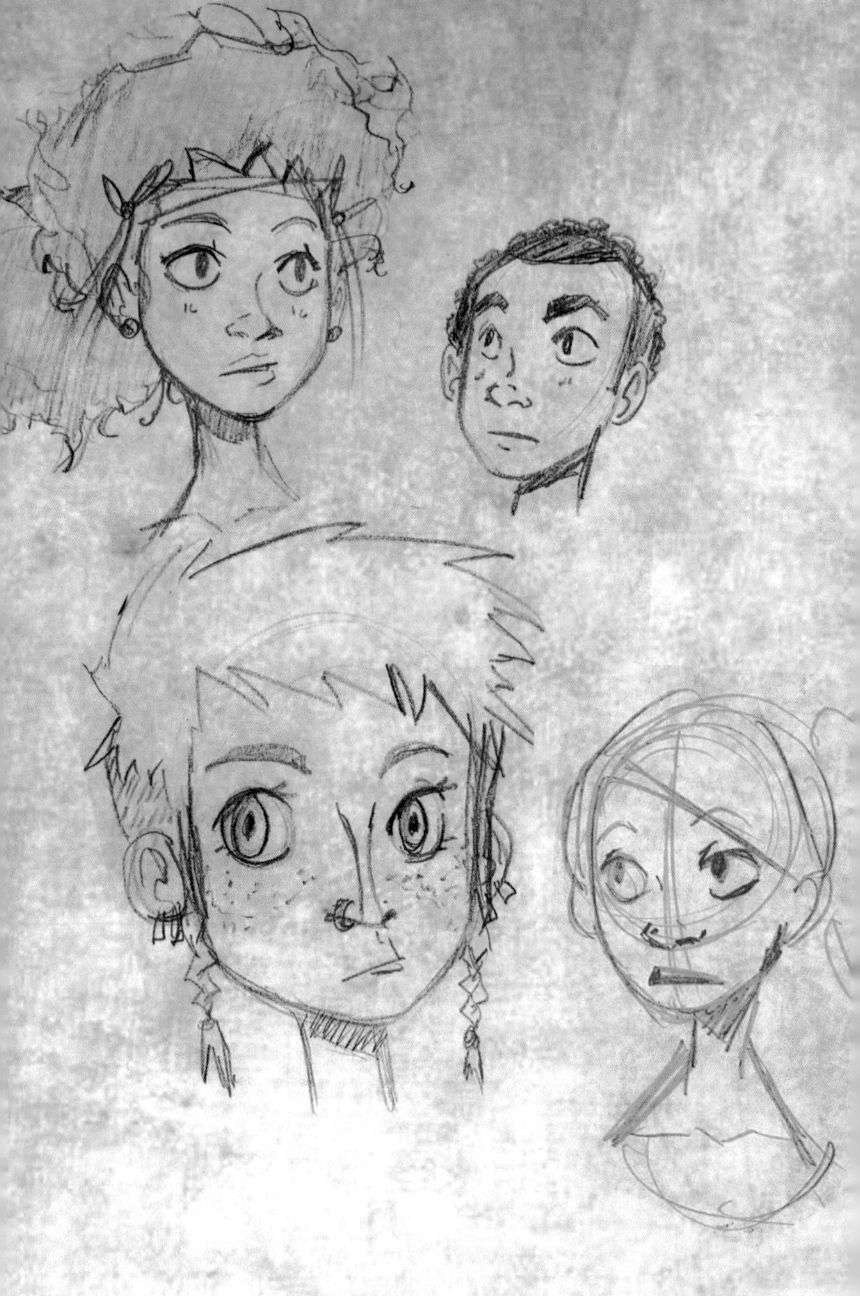

3: On Sexism in the Armor Industry

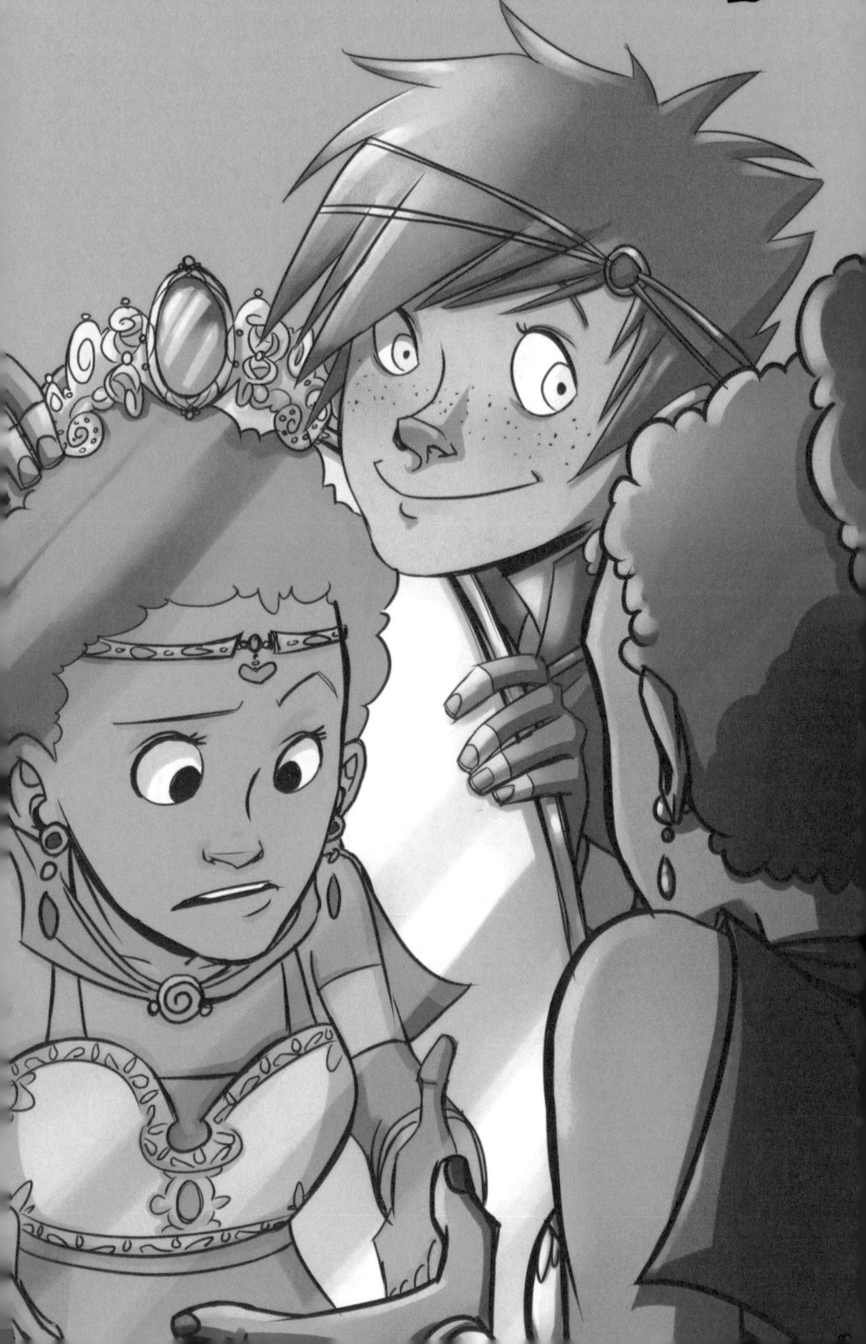

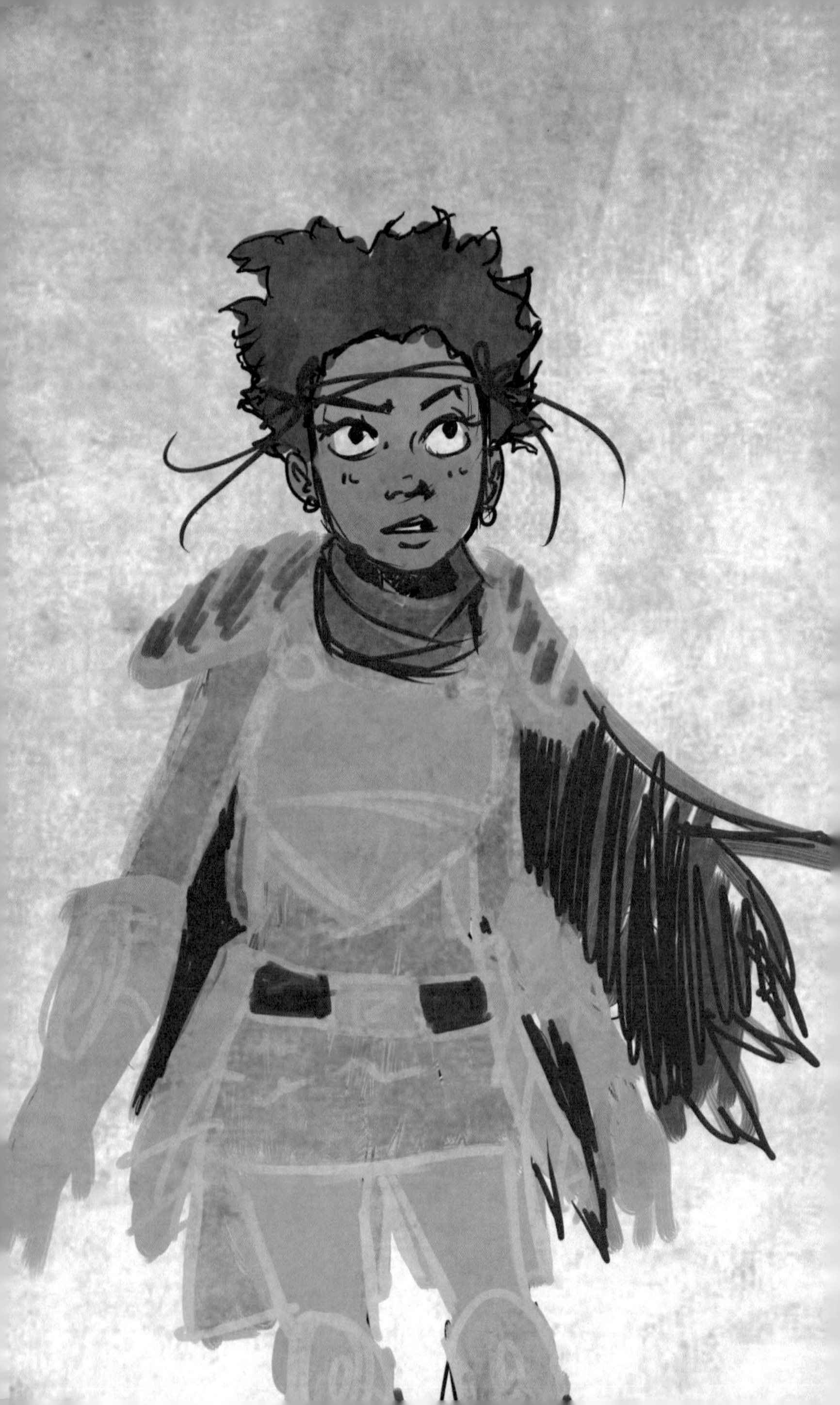

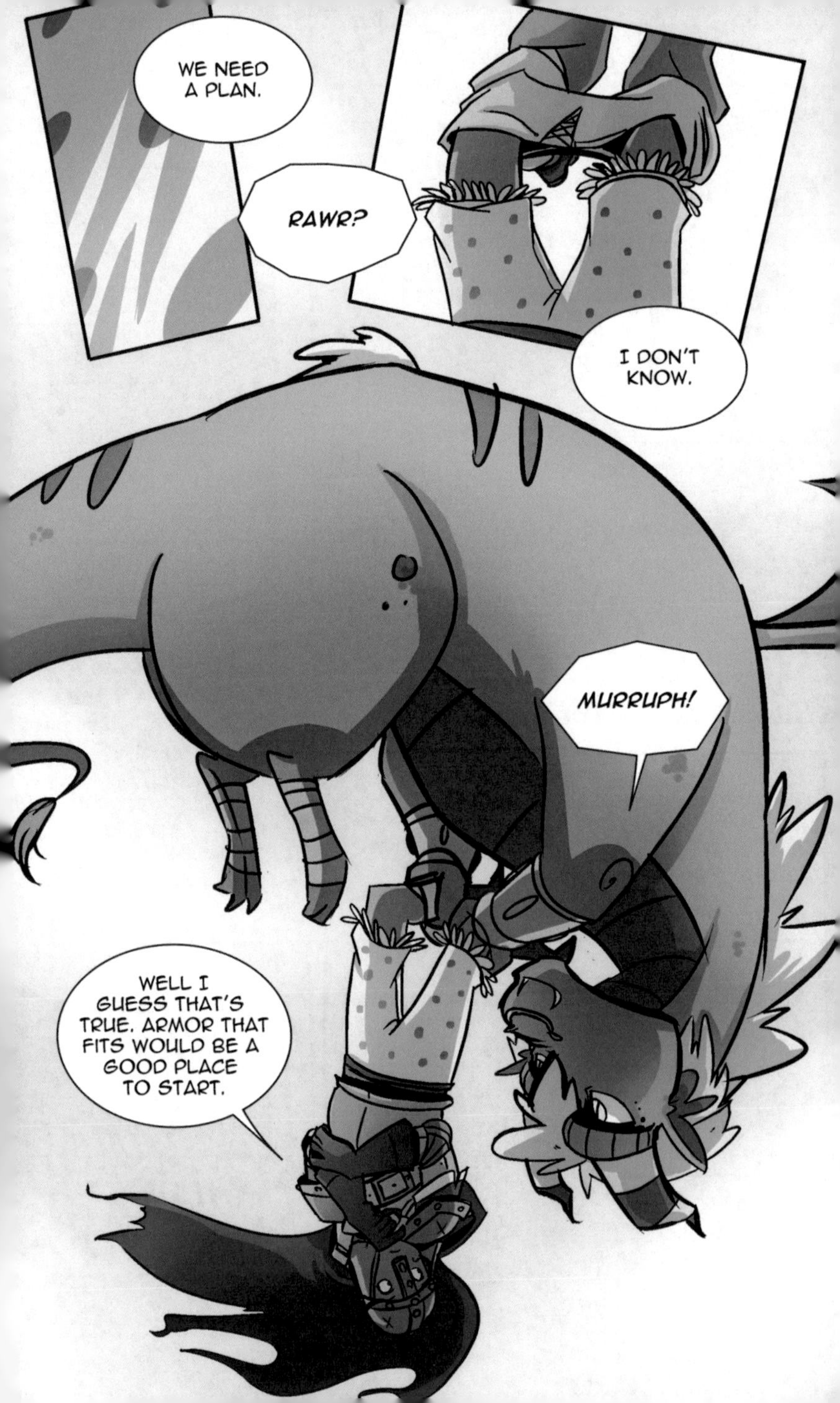
WE NEED A PLAN.
RAWR?
I DON'T KNOW.
MURRUPH!
WELL I GUESS THAT'S TRUE. ARMOR THAT FITS WOULD BE A GOOD PLACE TO START.

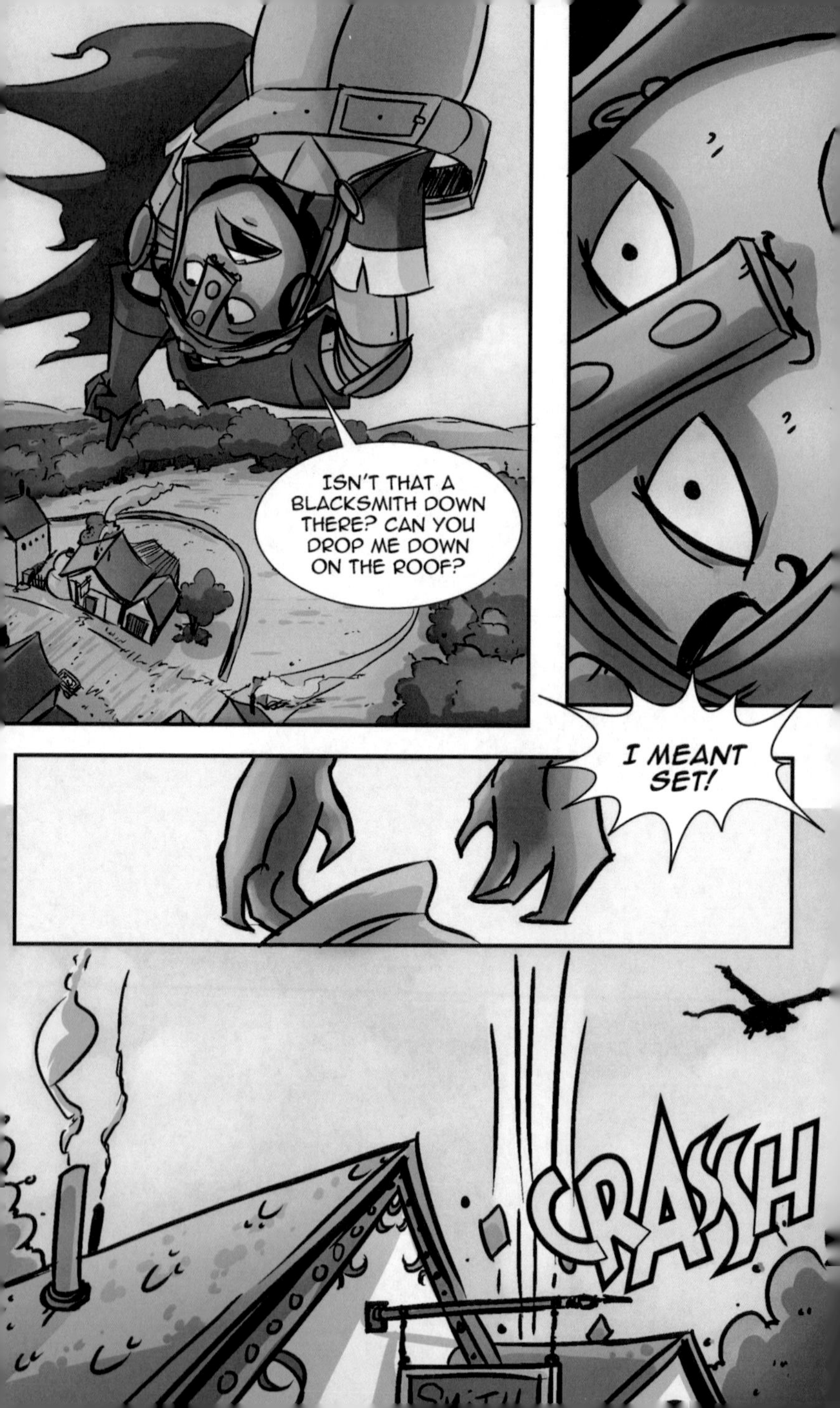
ISN'T THAT A BLACKSMITH DOWN THERE? CAN YOU DROP ME DOWN ON THE ROOF?
I MEANT SET!
CRASH

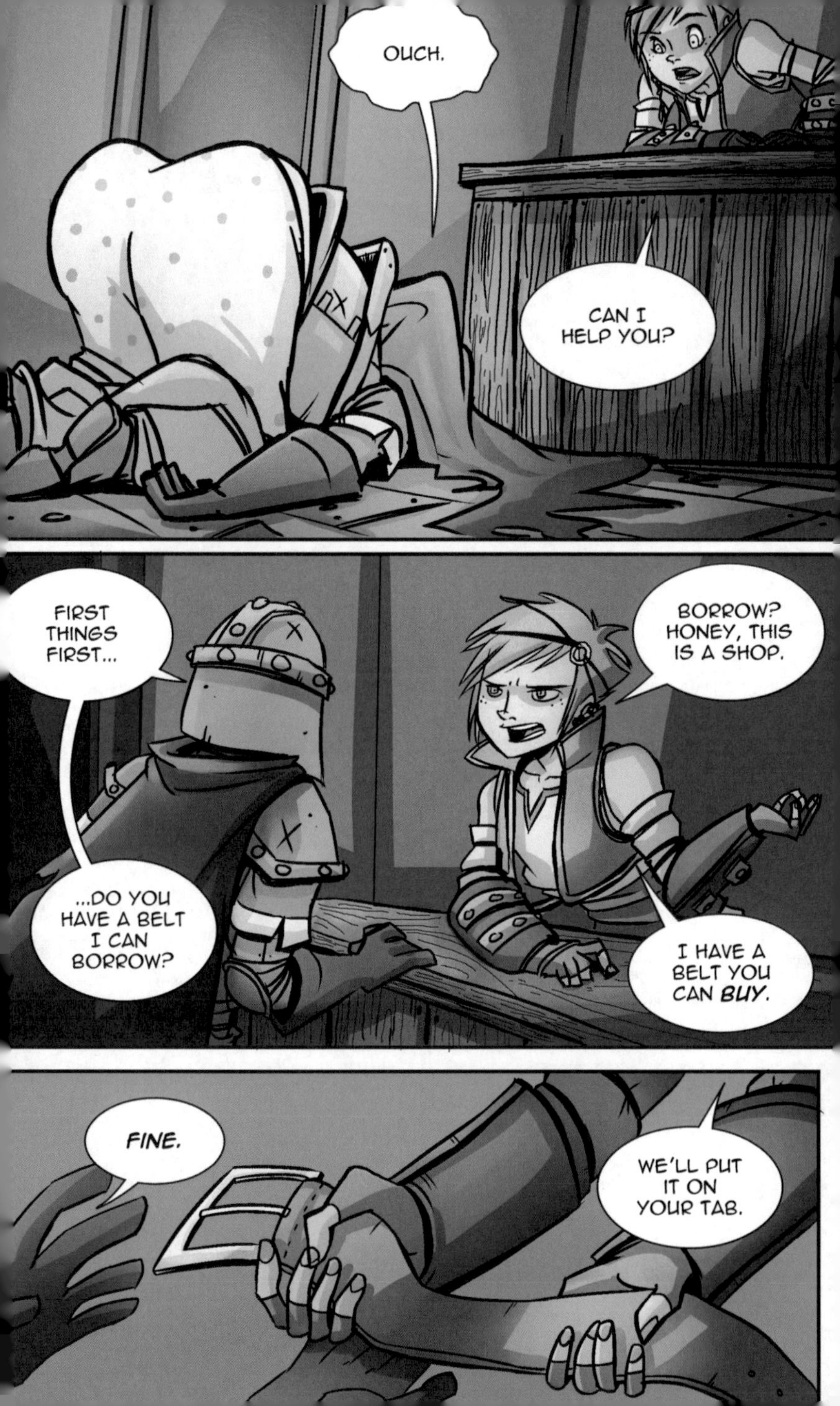
OUCH.
CAN I HELP YOU?
FIRST THINGS FIRST...
...DO YOU HAVE A BELT I CAN BORROW?
BORROW? HONEY, THIS IS A SHOP.
I HAVE A BELT YOU CAN *BUY*.
FINE.
WE'LL PUT IT ON YOUR TAB.

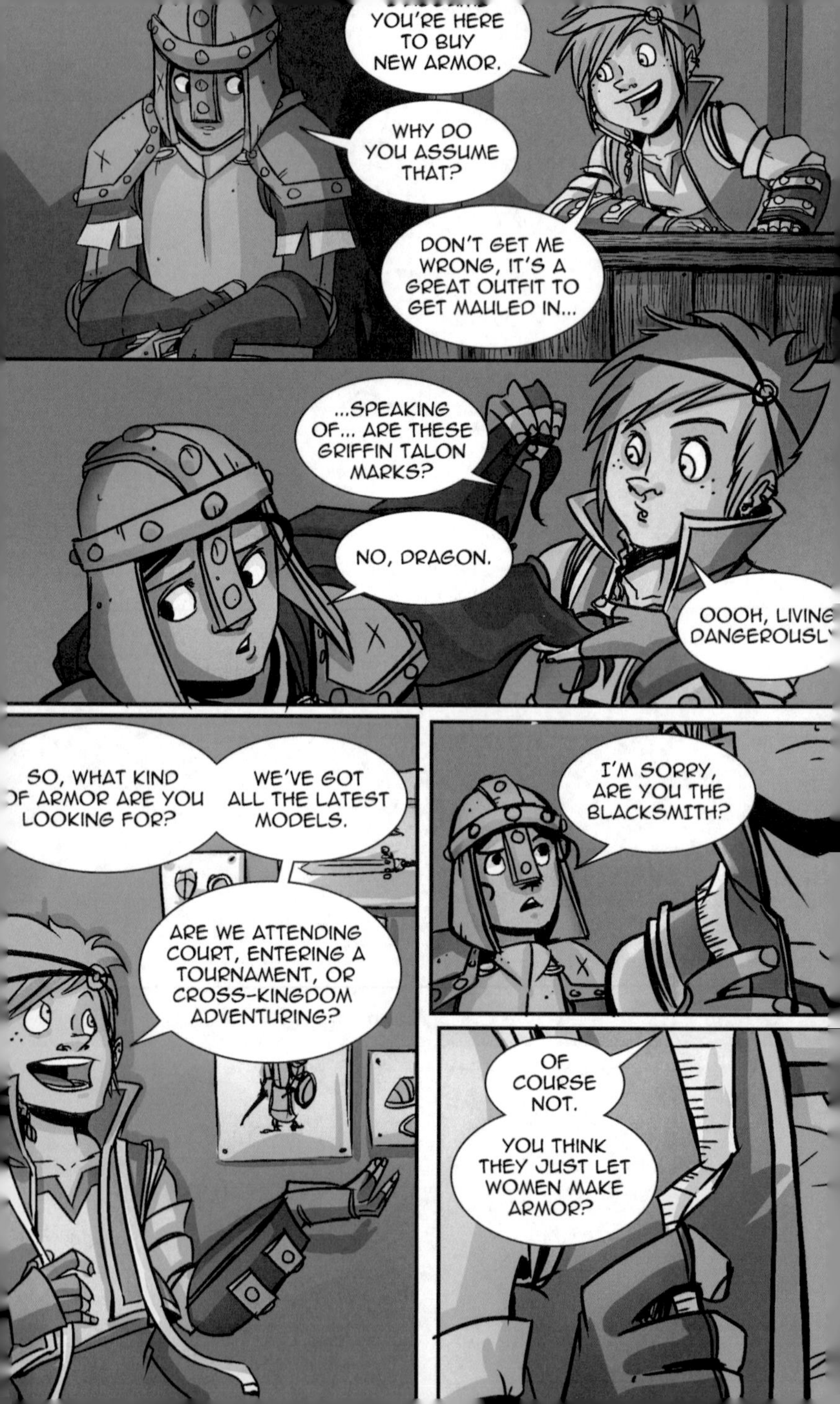
YOU'RE HERE TO BUY NEW ARMOR.
WHY DO YOU ASSUME THAT?
DON'T GET ME WRONG, IT'S A GREAT OUTFIT TO GET MAULED IN...
...SPEAKING OF... ARE THESE GRIFFIN TALON MARKS?
NO, DRAGON.
OOOH, LIVING DANGEROUSL
SO, WHAT KIND OF ARMOR ARE YOU LOOKING FOR?
WE'VE GOT ALL THE LATEST MODELS.
ARE WE ATTENDING COURT, ENTERING A TOURNAMENT, OR CROSS-KINGDOM ADVENTURING?
I'M SORRY, ARE YOU THE BLACKSMITH?
OF COURSE NOT.
YOU THINK THEY JUST LET WOMEN MAKE ARMOR?

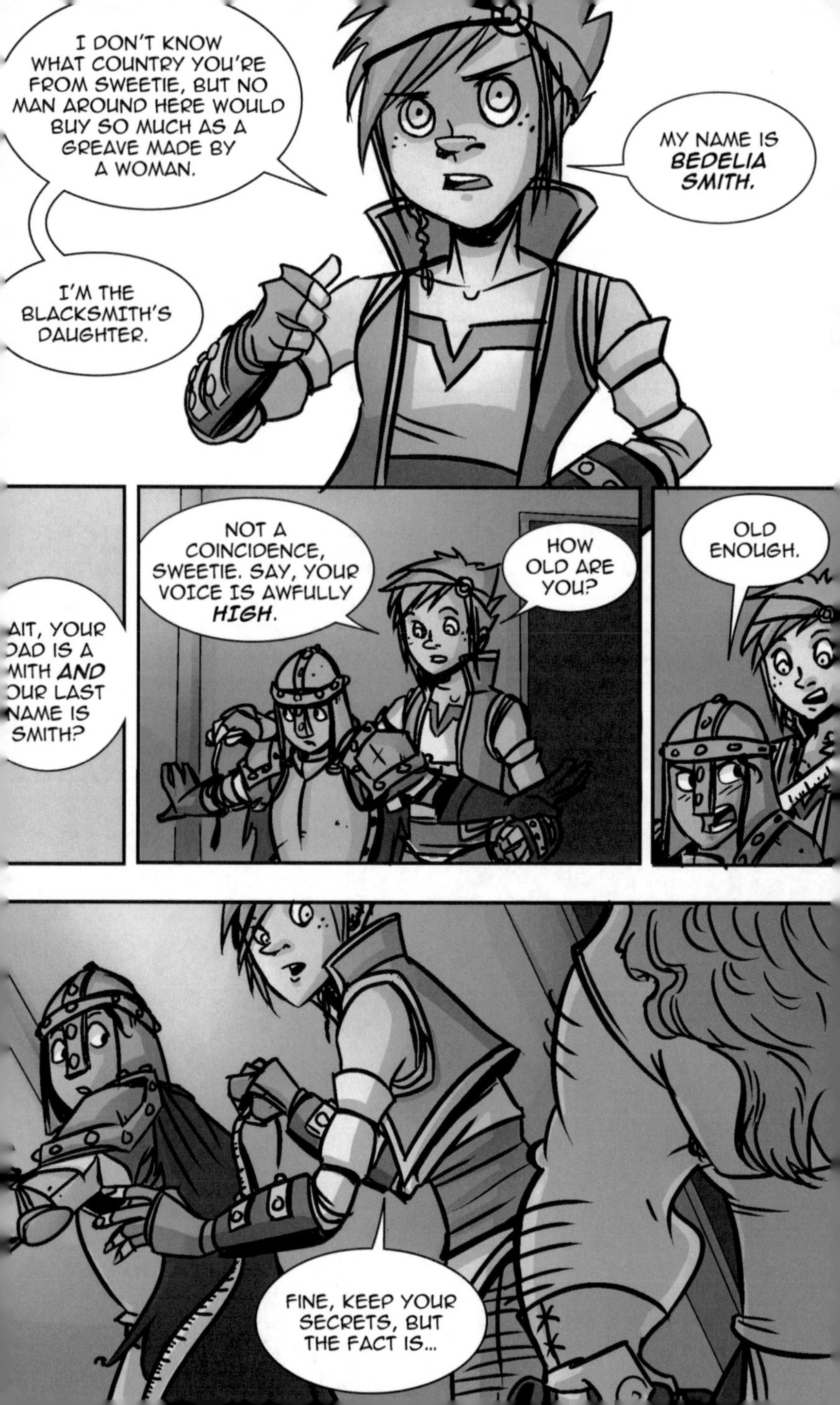
I DON'T KNOW WHAT COUNTRY YOU'RE FROM SWEETIE, BUT NO MAN AROUND HERE WOULD BUY SO MUCH AS A GREAVE MADE BY A WOMAN.
MY NAME IS BEDELIA SMITH.
I'M THE BLACKSMITH'S DAUGHTER.
AIT, YOUR DAD IS A MITH AND OUR LAST NAME IS SMITH?
NOT A COINCIDENCE, SWEETIE. SAY, YOUR VOICE IS AWFULLY HIGH.
HOW OLD ARE YOU?
OLD ENOUGH.
FINE, KEEP YOUR SECRETS, BUT THE FACT IS...

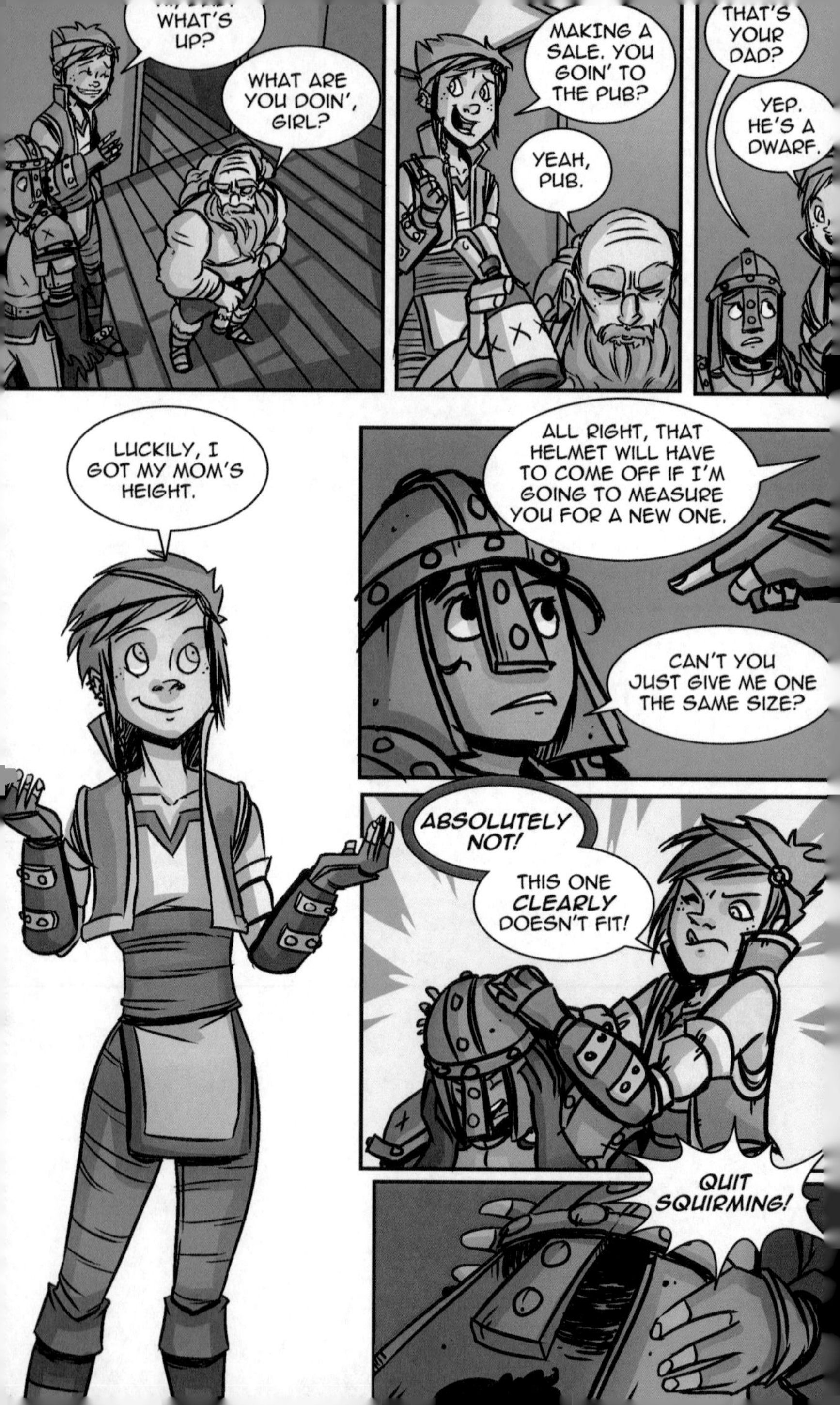

WHAT'S UP?
WHAT ARE YOU DOIN', GIRL?
MAKING A SALE. YOU GOIN' TO THE PUB?
YEAH, PUB.
THAT'S YOUR DAD?
YEP. HE'S A DWARF.
LUCKILY, I GOT MY MOM'S HEIGHT.
ALL RIGHT, THAT HELMET WILL HAVE TO COME OFF IF I'M GOING TO MEASURE YOU FOR A NEW ONE.
CAN'T YOU JUST GIVE ME ONE THE SAME SIZE?
ABSOLUTELY NOT!
THIS ONE CLEARLY DOESN'T FIT!
QUIT SQUIRMING!

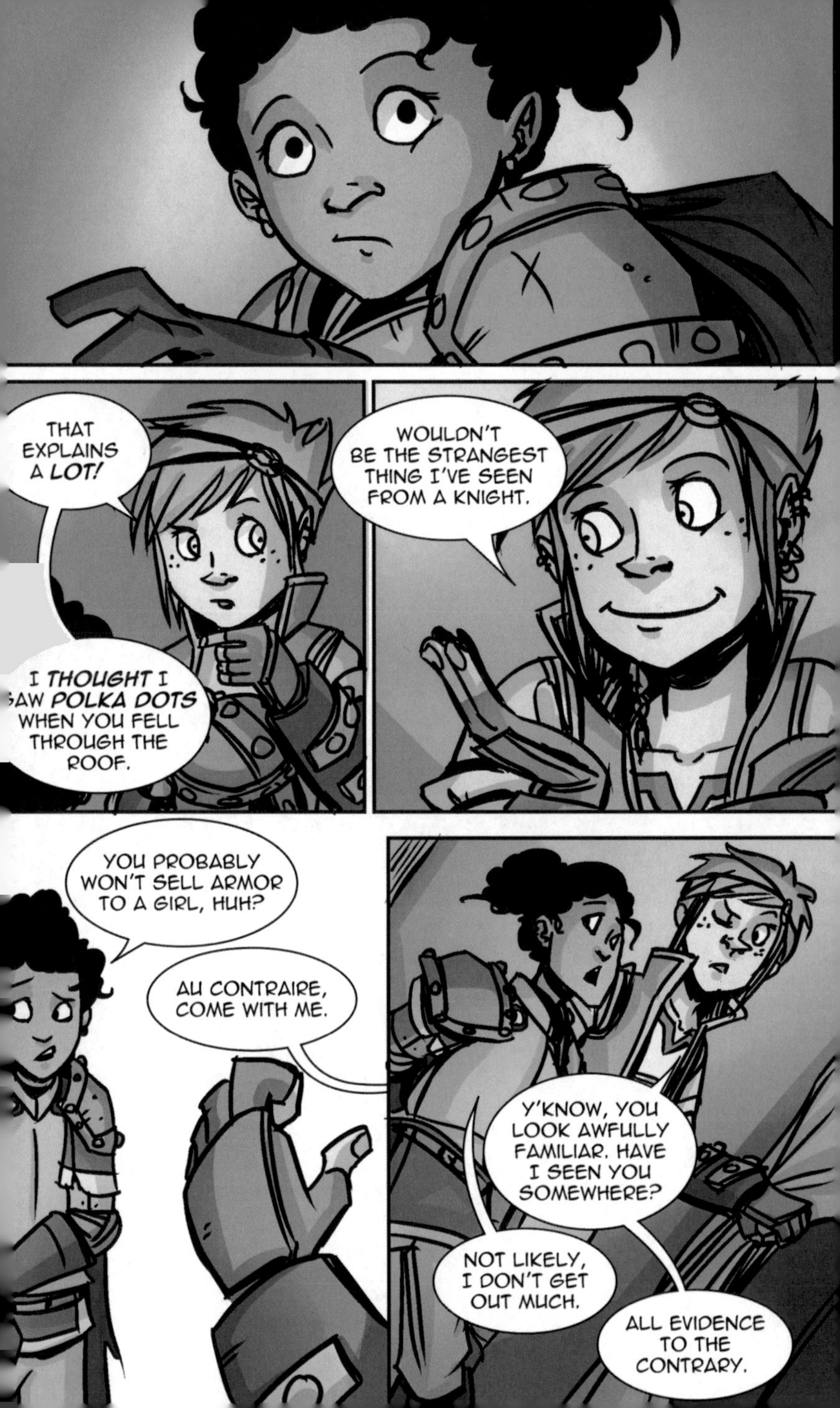
THAT EXPLAINS A *LOT!*
I *THOUGHT* I SAW *POLKA DOTS* WHEN YOU FELL THROUGH THE ROOF.
WOULDN'T BE THE STRANGEST THING I'VE SEEN FROM A KNIGHT.
YOU PROBABLY WON'T SELL ARMOR TO A GIRL, HUH?
AU CONTRAIRE, COME WITH ME.
Y'KNOW, YOU LOOK AWFULLY FAMILIAR. HAVE I SEEN YOU SOMEWHERE?
NOT LIKELY, I DON'T GET OUT MUCH.
ALL EVIDENCE TO THE CONTRARY.

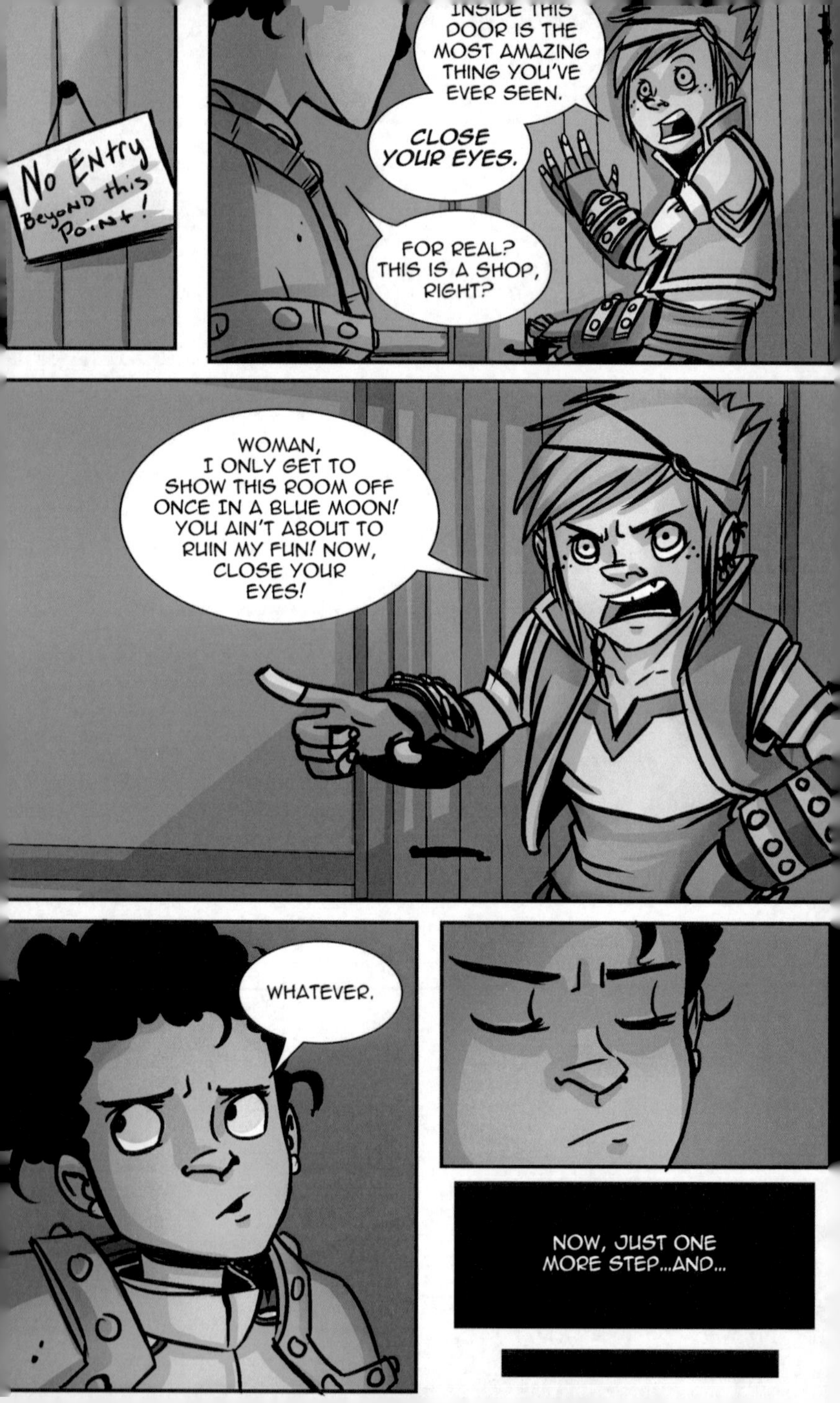
No Entry Beyond this Point!
INSIDE THIS DOOR IS THE MOST AMAZING THING YOU'VE EVER SEEN.
CLOSE YOUR EYES.
FOR REAL? THIS IS A SHOP, RIGHT?
WOMAN, I ONLY GET TO SHOW THIS ROOM OFF ONCE IN A BLUE MOON! YOU AIN'T ABOUT TO RUIN MY FUN! NOW, CLOSE YOUR EYES!
WHATEVER.
NOW, JUST ONE MORE STEP...AND...

BEHOLD, THE *WOMEN WARRIORS COLLECTION!*

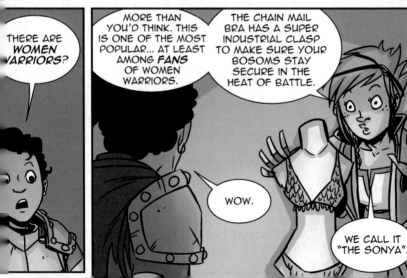

THERE ARE *WOMEN WARRIORS?*

MORE THAN YOU'D THINK. THIS IS ONE OF THE MOST POPULAR... AT LEAST AMONG *FANS* OF WOMEN WARRIORS.

THE CHAIN MAIL BRA HAS A SUPER INDUSTRIAL CLASP TO MAKE SURE YOUR BOSOMS STAY SECURE IN THE HEAT OF BATTLE.

WOW.

WE CALL IT "THE SONYA".

WOULDN'T *THAT* GIVE YOU A WEDGIE?

THE SHORT ANSWER? *YES.*

THE LONG ANSWER IS ALSO YES, BUT THAT'S THE LEAST PAINFUL THING IT DOES.

BUT WHAT'S MORE IMPORTANT, COMFORT OR LOOKING GOOD?

MOVING ON. THIS IS "THE DIANA".

IT COMES WITH A METAL BREAST PLATE, CLOTH SHIRT, AND MINI-TIGHTS.

THE TIGHTS COME WITH OR WITHOUT LIMITED METAL PLATING. OH, AND THESE DARLING BANGLES.

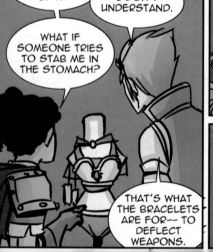

SO, IF THE CHEST IS PLATED WITH ARMOR, WHY NOT THE REST OF IT?

I DON'T UNDERSTAND.

WHAT IF SOMEONE TRIES TO STAB ME IN THE STOMACH?

THAT'S WHAT THE BRACELETS ARE FOR-- TO DEFLECT WEAPONS.

BUT WHAT IF SOMEONE TRIES TO STAB ME WHILE I'M TRYING TO STAB THEM?

OH, THERE'S NO SWORD WITH THIS ONE... JUST A ROPE.

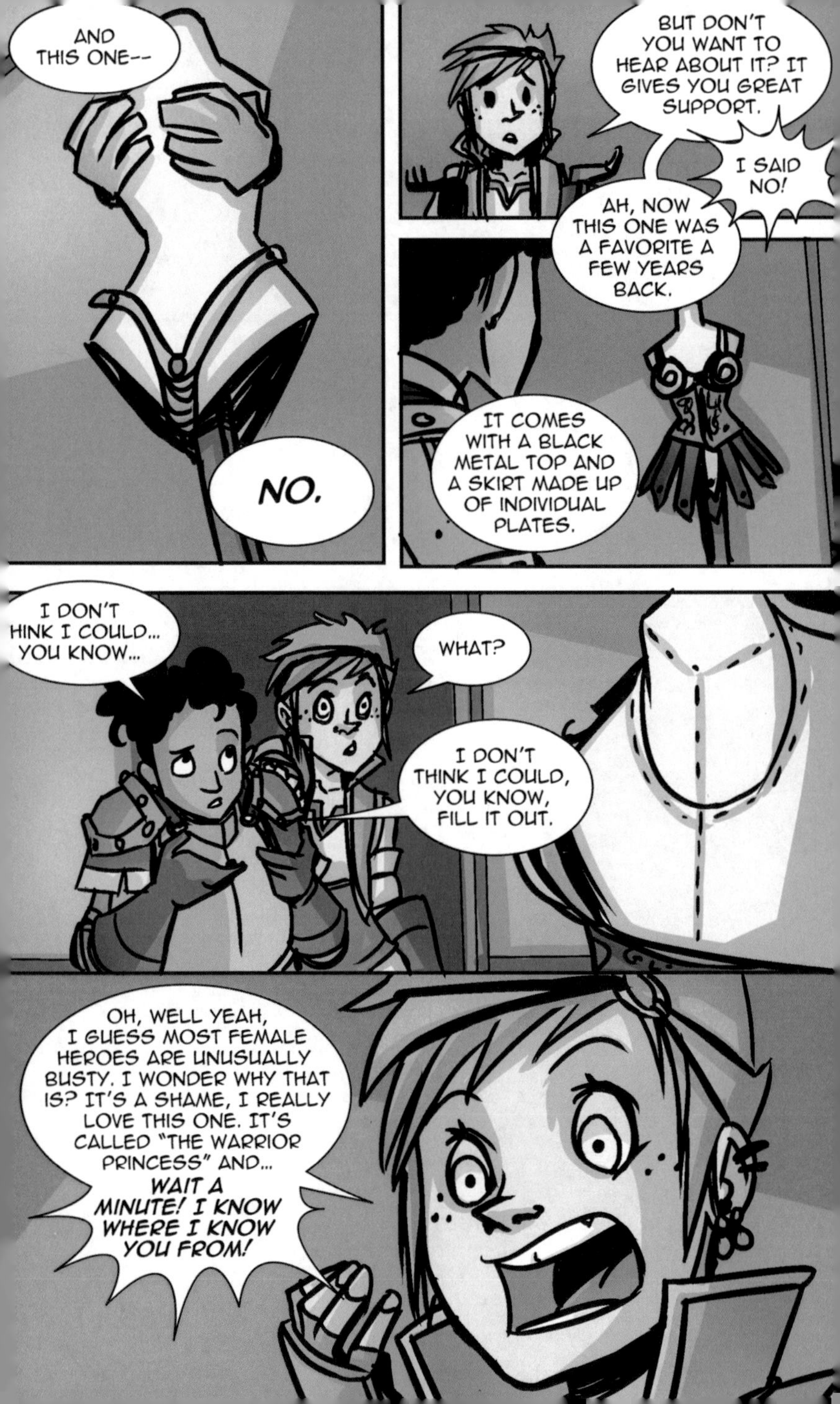
AND THIS ONE--
BUT DON'T YOU WANT TO HEAR ABOUT IT? IT GIVES YOU GREAT SUPPORT.
I SAID NO!
AH, NOW THIS ONE WAS A FAVORITE A FEW YEARS BACK.
IT COMES WITH A BLACK METAL TOP AND A SKIRT MADE UP OF INDIVIDUAL PLATES.
NO.
I DON'T HINK I COULD... YOU KNOW...
WHAT?
I DON'T THINK I COULD, YOU KNOW, FILL IT OUT.
OH, WELL YEAH, I GUESS MOST FEMALE HEROES ARE UNUSUALLY BUSTY. I WONDER WHY THAT IS? IT'S A SHAME, I REALLY LOVE THIS ONE. IT'S CALLED "THE WARRIOR PRINCESS" AND... WAIT A MINUTE! I KNOW WHERE I KNOW YOU FROM!

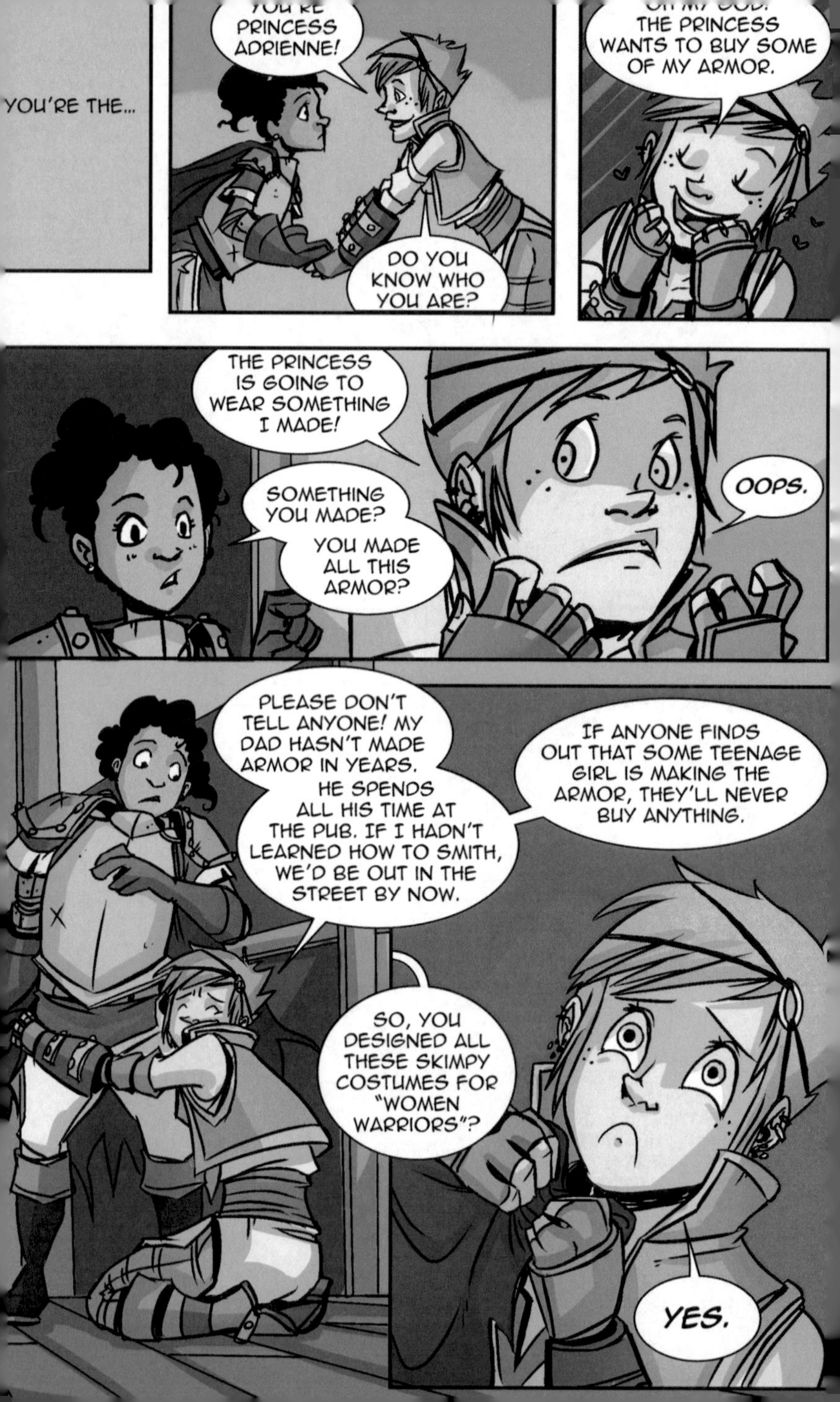

YOU'RE THE...
PRINCESS ADRIENNE!
DO YOU KNOW WHO YOU ARE?
THE PRINCESS WANTS TO BUY SOME OF MY ARMOR.
THE PRINCESS IS GOING TO WEAR SOMETHING I MADE!
SOMETHING YOU MADE?
YOU MADE ALL THIS ARMOR?
OOPS.
PLEASE DON'T TELL ANYONE! MY DAD HASN'T MADE ARMOR IN YEARS.
HE SPENDS ALL HIS TIME AT THE PUB. IF I HADN'T LEARNED HOW TO SMITH, WE'D BE OUT IN THE STREET BY NOW.
IF ANYONE FINDS OUT THAT SOME TEENAGE GIRL IS MAKING THE ARMOR, THEY'LL NEVER BUY ANYTHING.
SO, YOU DESIGNED ALL THESE SKIMPY COSTUMES FOR "WOMEN WARRIORS"?
YES.

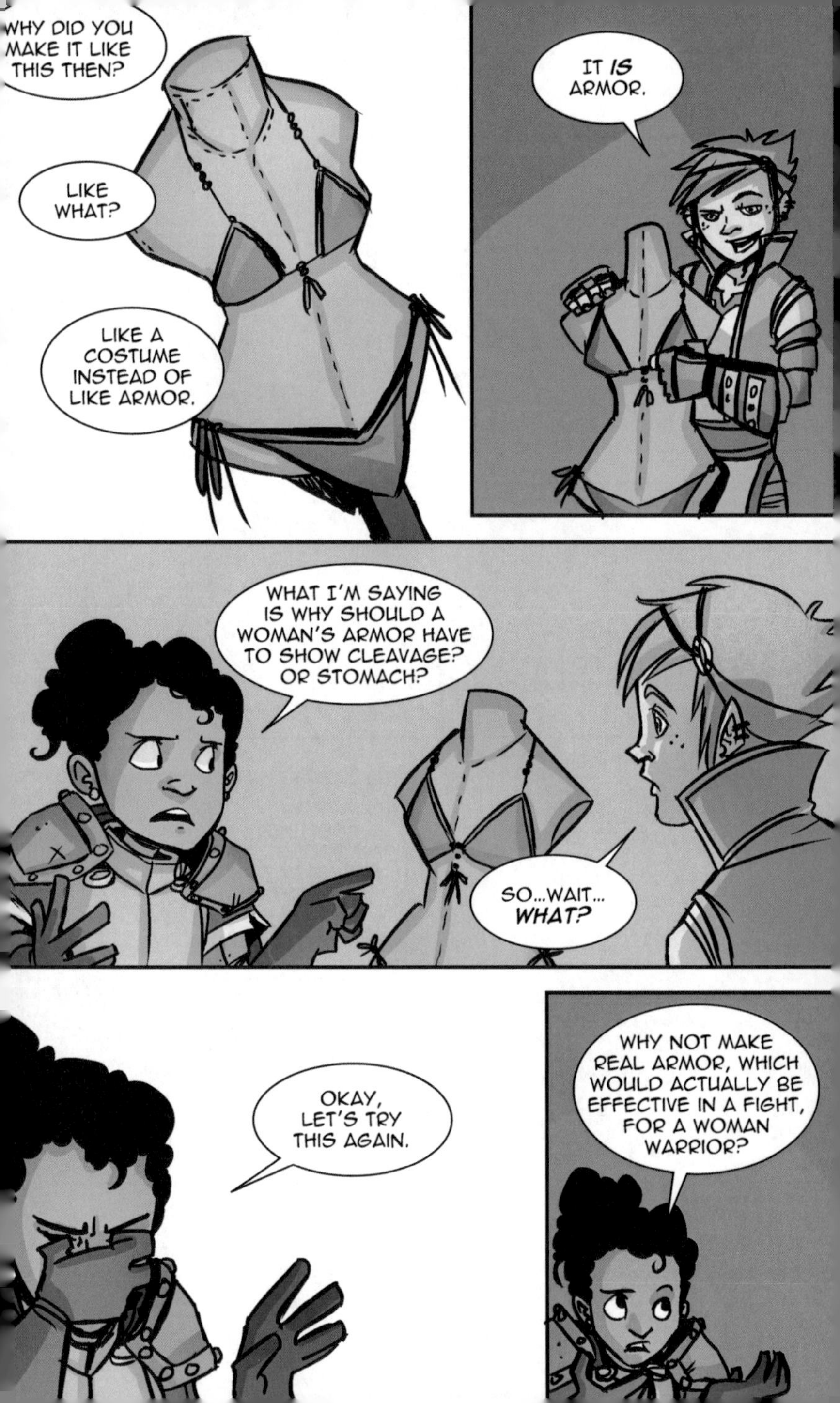
WHY DID YOU MAKE IT LIKE THIS THEN?
LIKE WHAT?
LIKE A COSTUME INSTEAD OF LIKE ARMOR.
IT *IS* ARMOR.
WHAT I'M SAYING IS WHY SHOULD A WOMAN'S ARMOR HAVE TO SHOW CLEAVAGE? OR STOMACH?
SO...WAIT... *WHAT?*
OKAY, LET'S TRY THIS AGAIN.
WHY NOT MAKE REAL ARMOR, WHICH WOULD ACTUALLY BE EFFECTIVE IN A FIGHT, FOR A WOMAN WARRIOR?

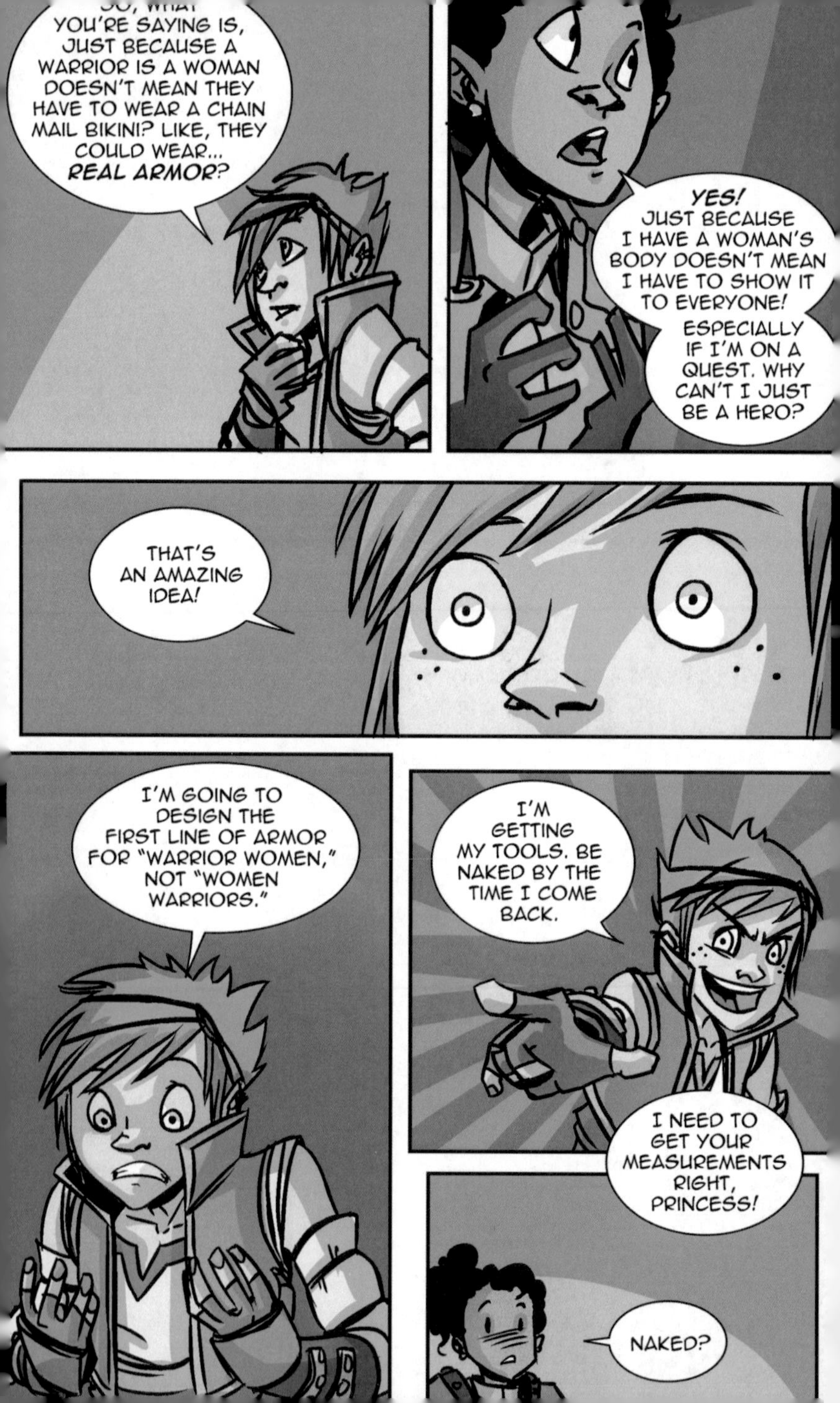
SO, WHAT YOU'RE SAYING IS, JUST BECAUSE A WARRIOR IS A WOMAN DOESN'T MEAN THEY HAVE TO WEAR A CHAIN MAIL BIKINI? LIKE, THEY COULD WEAR... *REAL ARMOR*?
YES! JUST BECAUSE I HAVE A WOMAN'S BODY DOESN'T MEAN I HAVE TO SHOW IT TO EVERYONE!
ESPECIALLY IF I'M ON A QUEST. WHY CAN'T I JUST BE A HERO?
THAT'S AN AMAZING IDEA!
I'M GOING TO DESIGN THE FIRST LINE OF ARMOR FOR "WARRIOR WOMEN," NOT "WOMEN WARRIORS."
I'M GETTING MY TOOLS. BE NAKED BY THE TIME I COME BACK.
I NEED TO GET YOUR MEASUREMENTS RIGHT, PRINCESS!
NAKED?

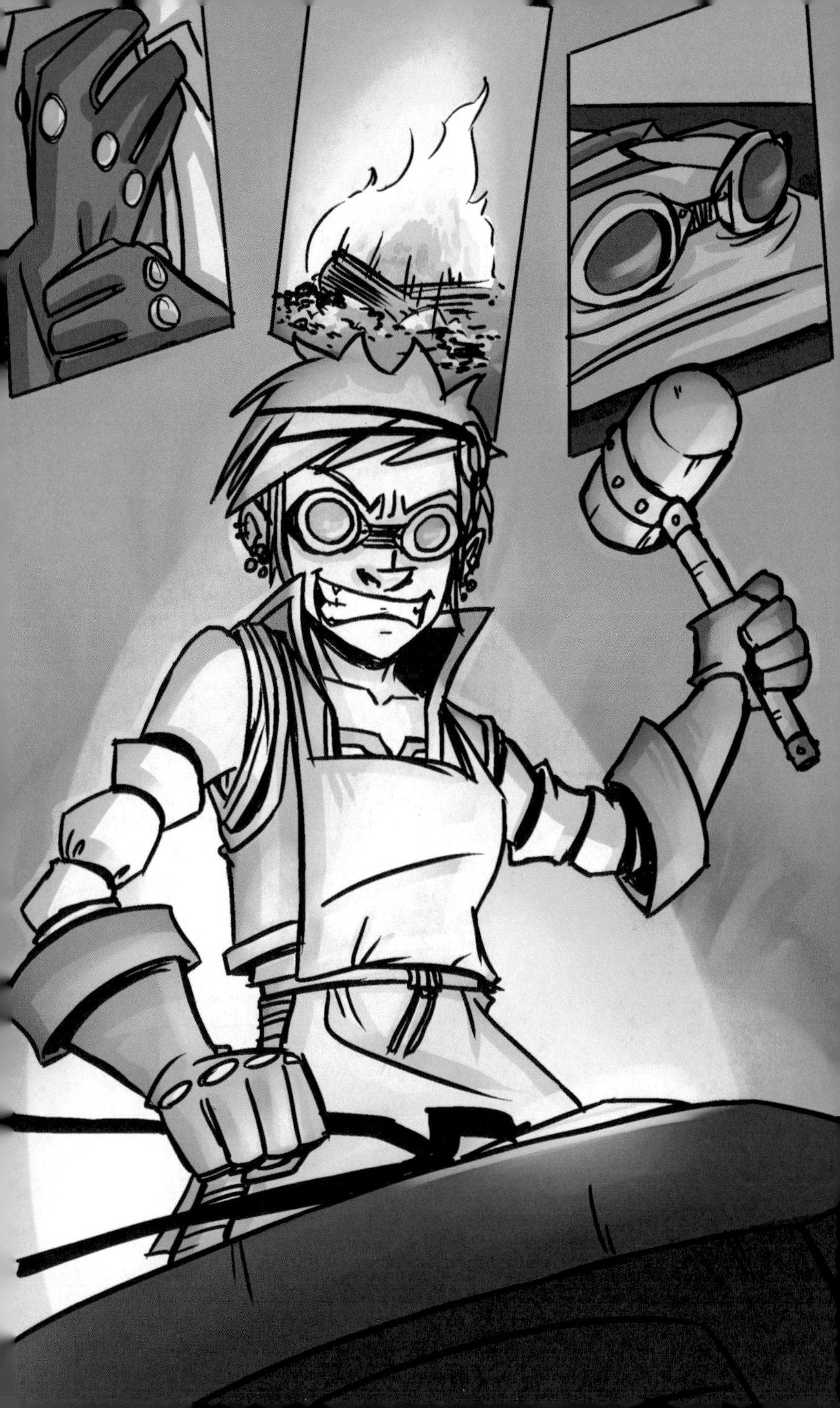

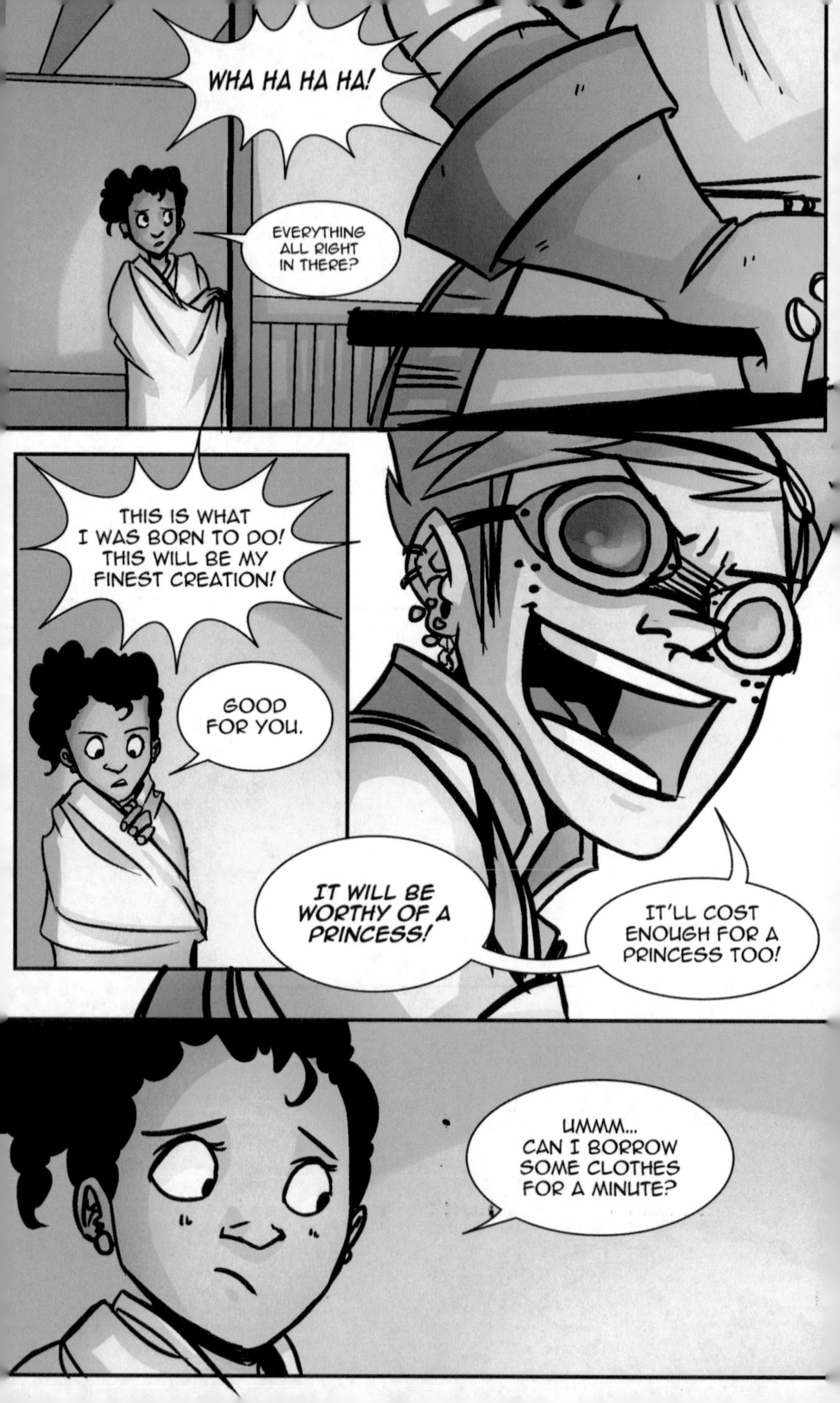
WHA HA HA HA!
EVERYTHING ALL RIGHT IN THERE?
THIS IS WHAT I WAS BORN TO DO! THIS WILL BE MY FINEST CREATION!
GOOD FOR YOU.
IT WILL BE WORTHY OF A PRINCESS!
IT'LL COST ENOUGH FOR A PRINCESS TOO!
UMMM... CAN I BORROW SOME CLOTHES FOR A MINUTE?

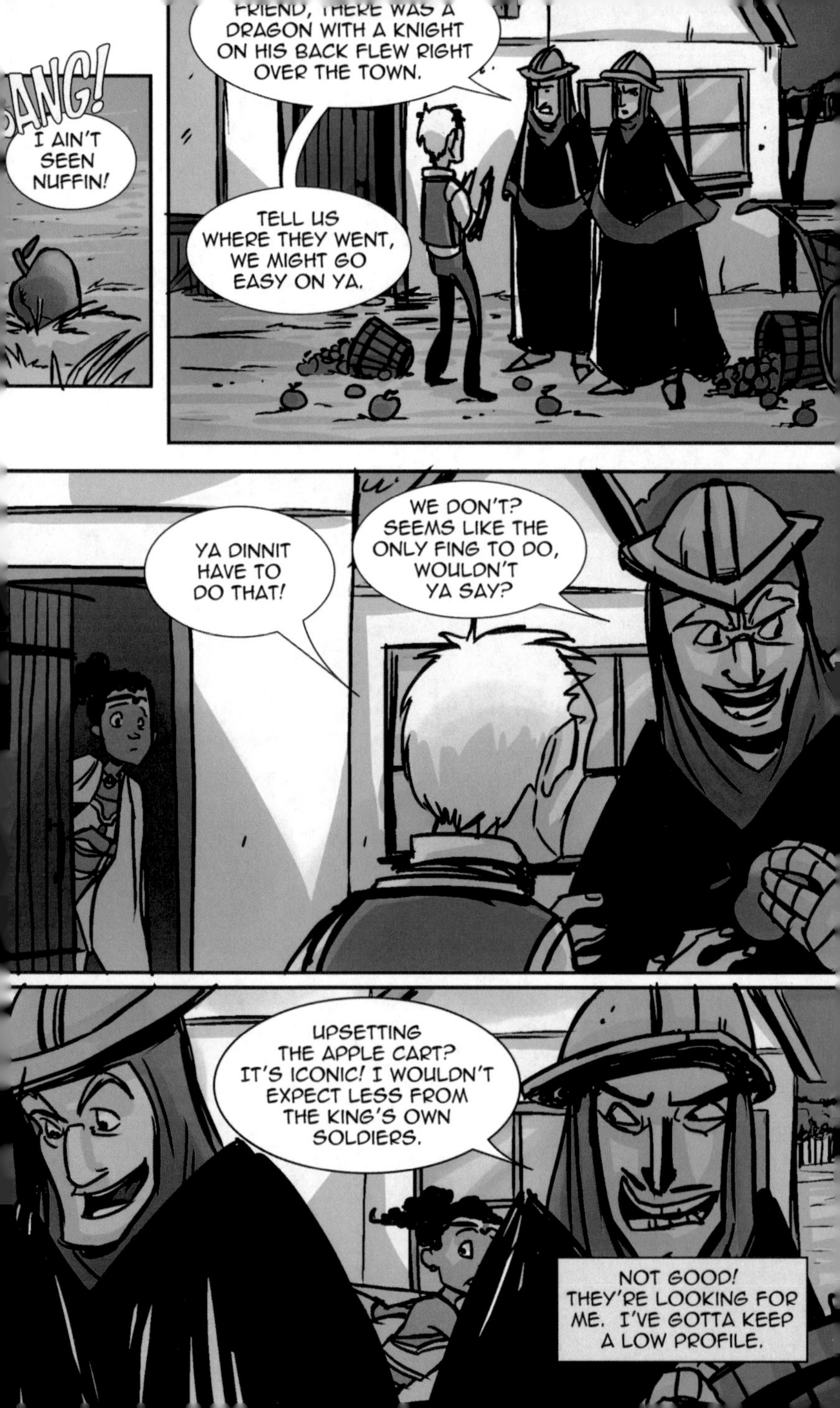

...ANG!
I AIN'T SEEN NUFFIN!
FRIEND, THERE WAS A DRAGON WITH A KNIGHT ON HIS BACK FLEW RIGHT OVER THE TOWN.
TELL US WHERE THEY WENT, WE MIGHT GO EASY ON YA.
YA DINNIT HAVE TO DO THAT!
WE DON'T? SEEMS LIKE THE ONLY FING TO DO, WOULDN'T YA SAY?
UPSETTING THE APPLE CART? IT'S ICONIC! I WOULDN'T EXPECT LESS FROM THE KING'S OWN SOLDIERS.
NOT GOOD! THEY'RE LOOKING FOR ME. I'VE GOTTA KEEP A LOW PROFILE.

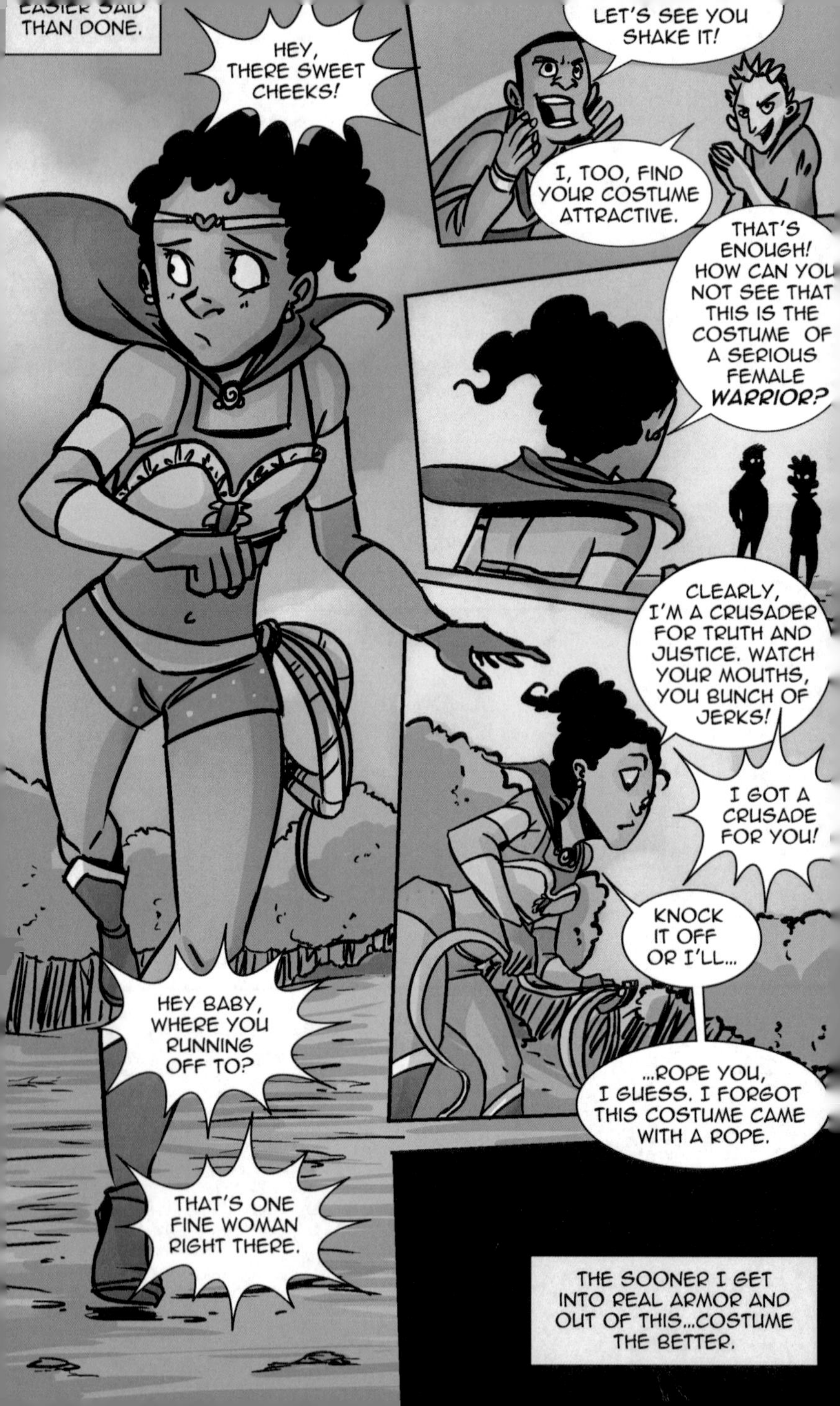
EASIER SAID THAN DONE.
HEY, THERE SWEET CHEEKS!
LET'S SEE YOU SHAKE IT!
I, TOO, FIND YOUR COSTUME ATTRACTIVE.
THAT'S ENOUGH! HOW CAN YOU NOT SEE THAT THIS IS THE COSTUME OF A SERIOUS FEMALE *WARRIOR?*
CLEARLY, I'M A CRUSADER FOR TRUTH AND JUSTICE. WATCH YOUR MOUTHS, YOU BUNCH OF JERKS!
I GOT A CRUSADE FOR YOU!
KNOCK IT OFF OR I'LL...
...ROPE YOU, I GUESS. I FORGOT THIS COSTUME CAME WITH A ROPE.
HEY BABY, WHERE YOU RUNNING OFF TO?
THAT'S ONE FINE WOMAN RIGHT THERE.
THE SOONER I GET INTO REAL ARMOR AND OUT OF THIS...COSTUME THE BETTER.

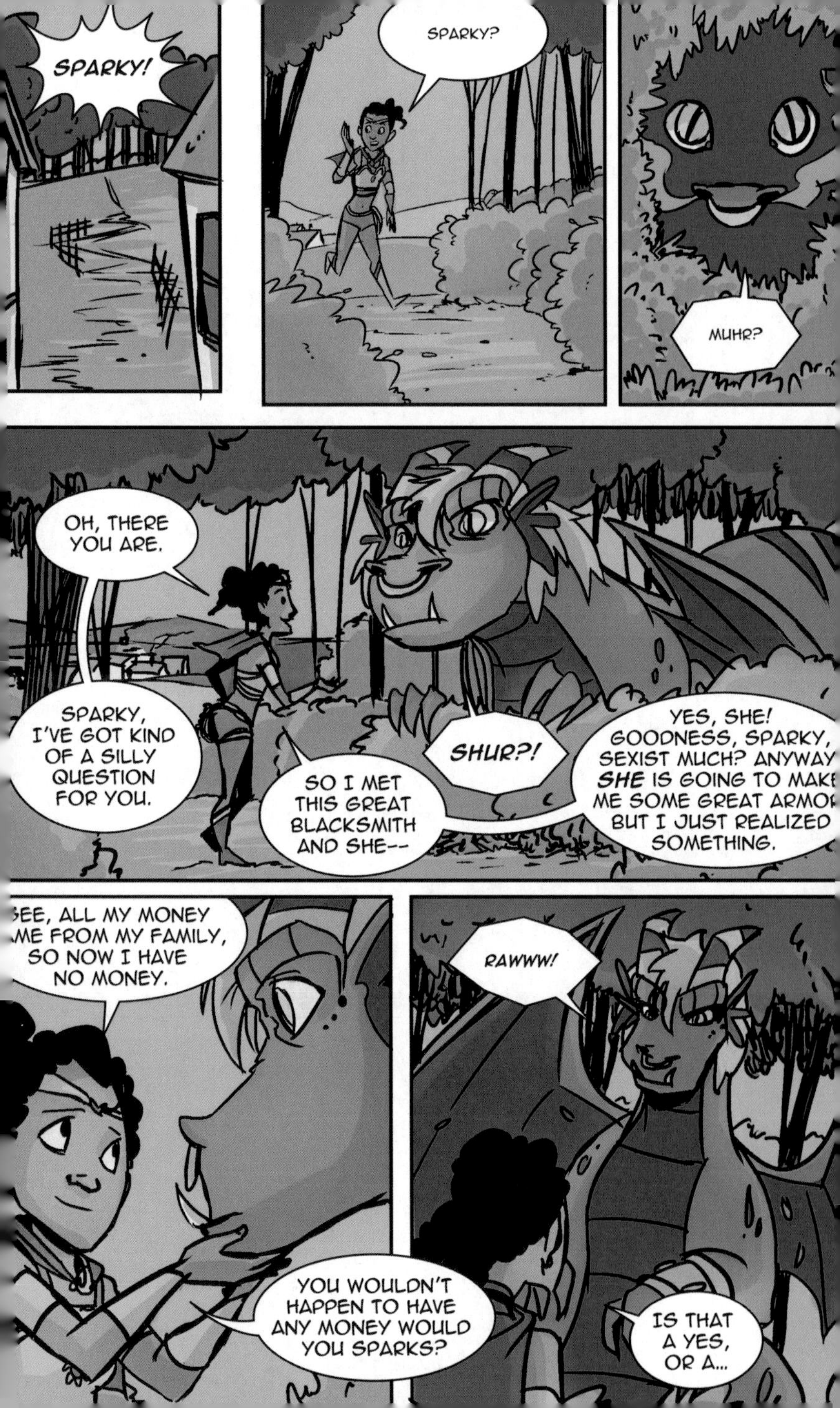

SPARKY!
SPARKY?
MUHR?
OH, THERE YOU ARE.
SPARKY, I'VE GOT KIND OF A SILLY QUESTION FOR YOU.
SO I MET THIS GREAT BLACKSMITH AND SHE--
SHUR?!
YES, SHE! GOODNESS, SPARKY, SEXIST MUCH? ANYWAY SHE IS GOING TO MAKE ME SOME GREAT ARMOR BUT I JUST REALIZED SOMETHING.
SEE, ALL MY MONEY CAME FROM MY FAMILY, SO NOW I HAVE NO MONEY.
YOU WOULDN'T HAPPEN TO HAVE ANY MONEY WOULD YOU SPARKS?
RAWWW!
IS THAT A YES, OR A...

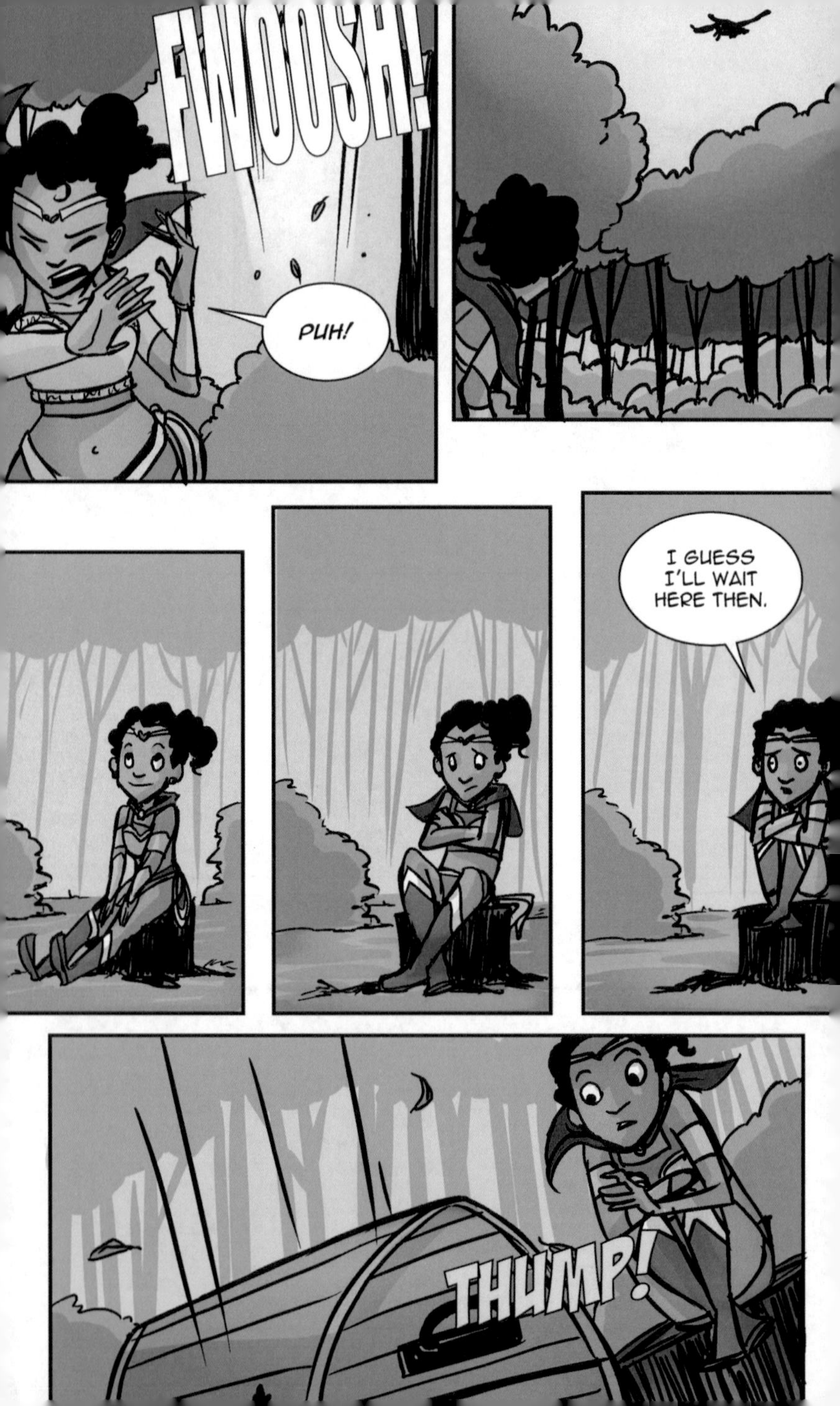
FWOOSH!
PUH!
I GUESS I'LL WAIT HERE THEN.
THUMP!

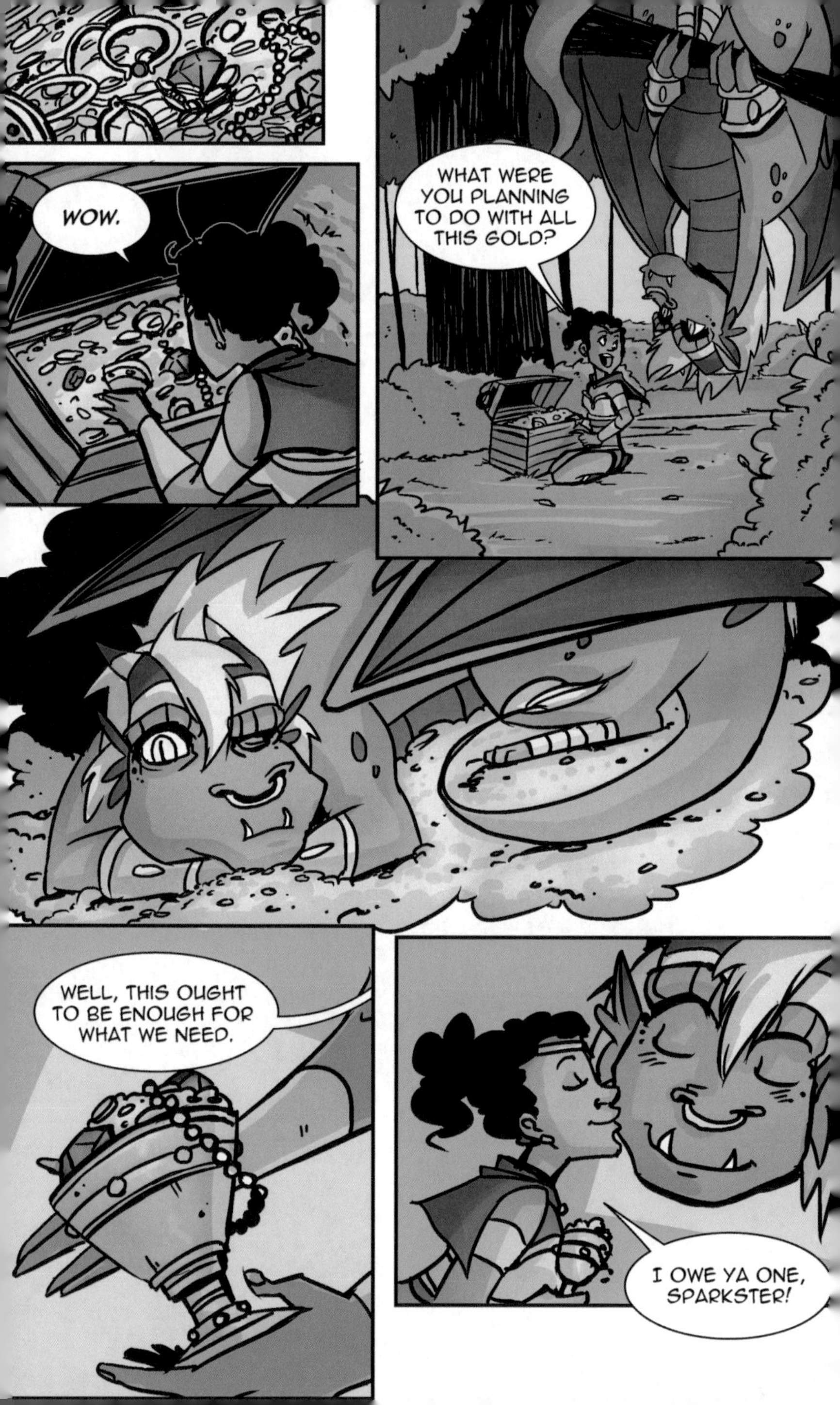
WOW.
WHAT WERE YOU PLANNING TO DO WITH ALL THIS GOLD?
WELL, THIS OUGHT TO BE ENOUGH FOR WHAT WE NEED.
I OWE YA ONE, SPARKSTER!

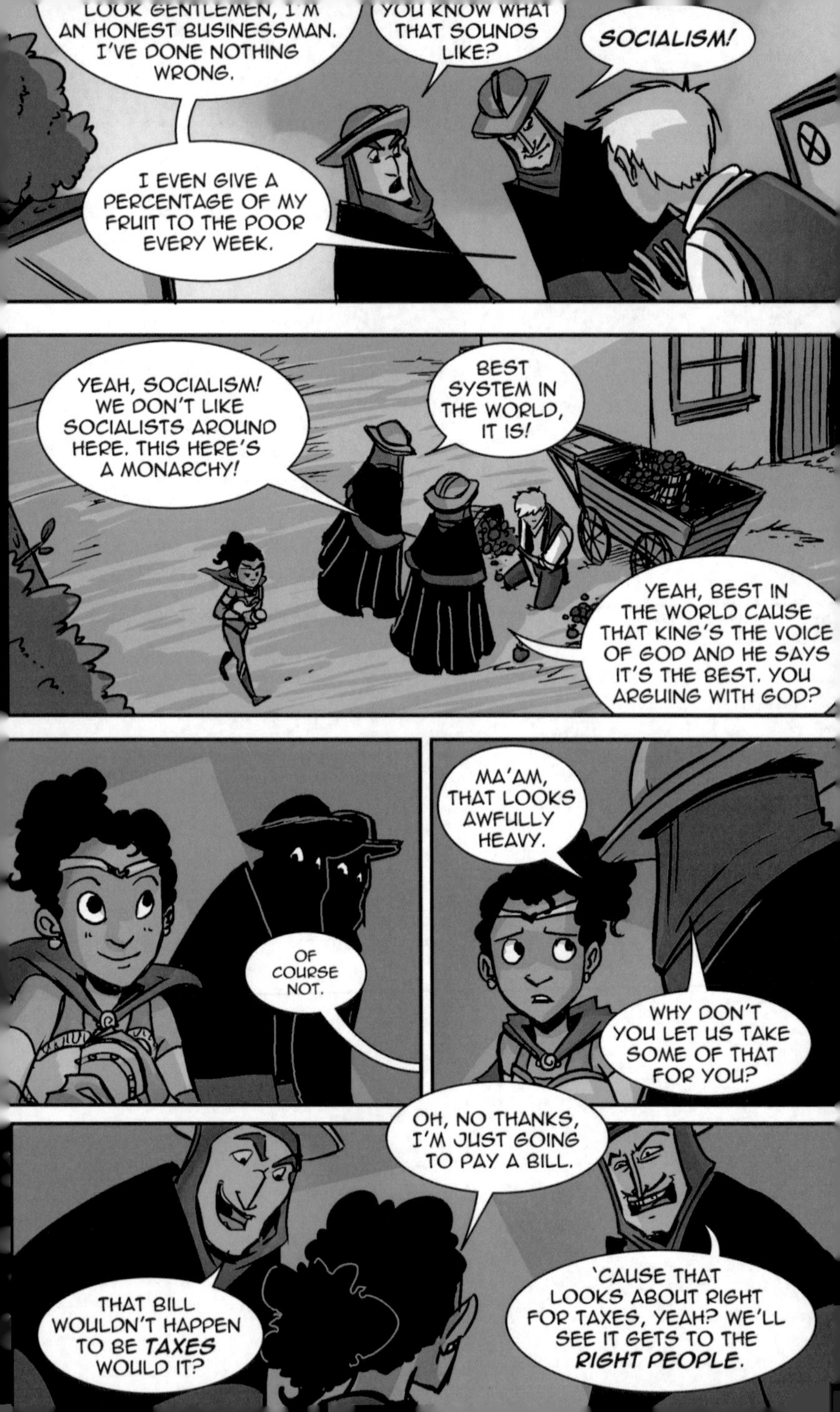
LOOK GENTLEMEN, I'M AN HONEST BUSINESSMAN. I'VE DONE NOTHING WRONG.
I EVEN GIVE A PERCENTAGE OF MY FRUIT TO THE POOR EVERY WEEK.
YOU KNOW WHAT THAT SOUNDS LIKE?
SOCIALISM!
YEAH, SOCIALISM! WE DON'T LIKE SOCIALISTS AROUND HERE. THIS HERE'S A MONARCHY!
BEST SYSTEM IN THE WORLD, IT IS!
YEAH, BEST IN THE WORLD CAUSE THAT KING'S THE VOICE OF GOD AND HE SAYS IT'S THE BEST. YOU ARGUING WITH GOD?
OF COURSE NOT.
MA'AM, THAT LOOKS AWFULLY HEAVY.
WHY DON'T YOU LET US TAKE SOME OF THAT FOR YOU?
OH, NO THANKS, I'M JUST GOING TO PAY A BILL.
THAT BILL WOULDN'T HAPPEN TO BE TAXES WOULD IT?
'CAUSE THAT LOOKS ABOUT RIGHT FOR TAXES, YEAH? WE'LL SEE IT GETS TO THE RIGHT PEOPLE.

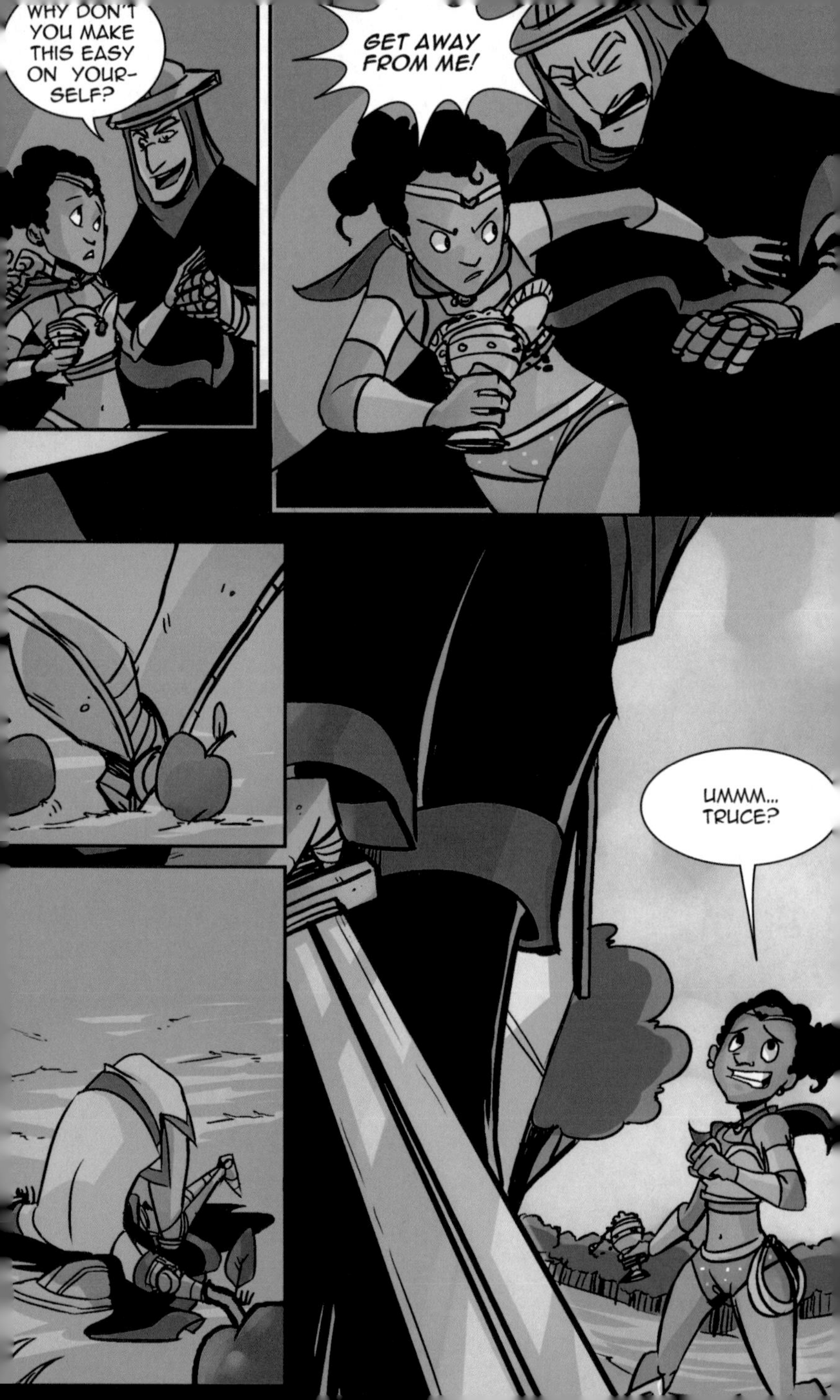
WHY DON'T YOU MAKE THIS EASY ON YOUR-SELF?
GET AWAY FROM ME!
UMMM... TRUCE?

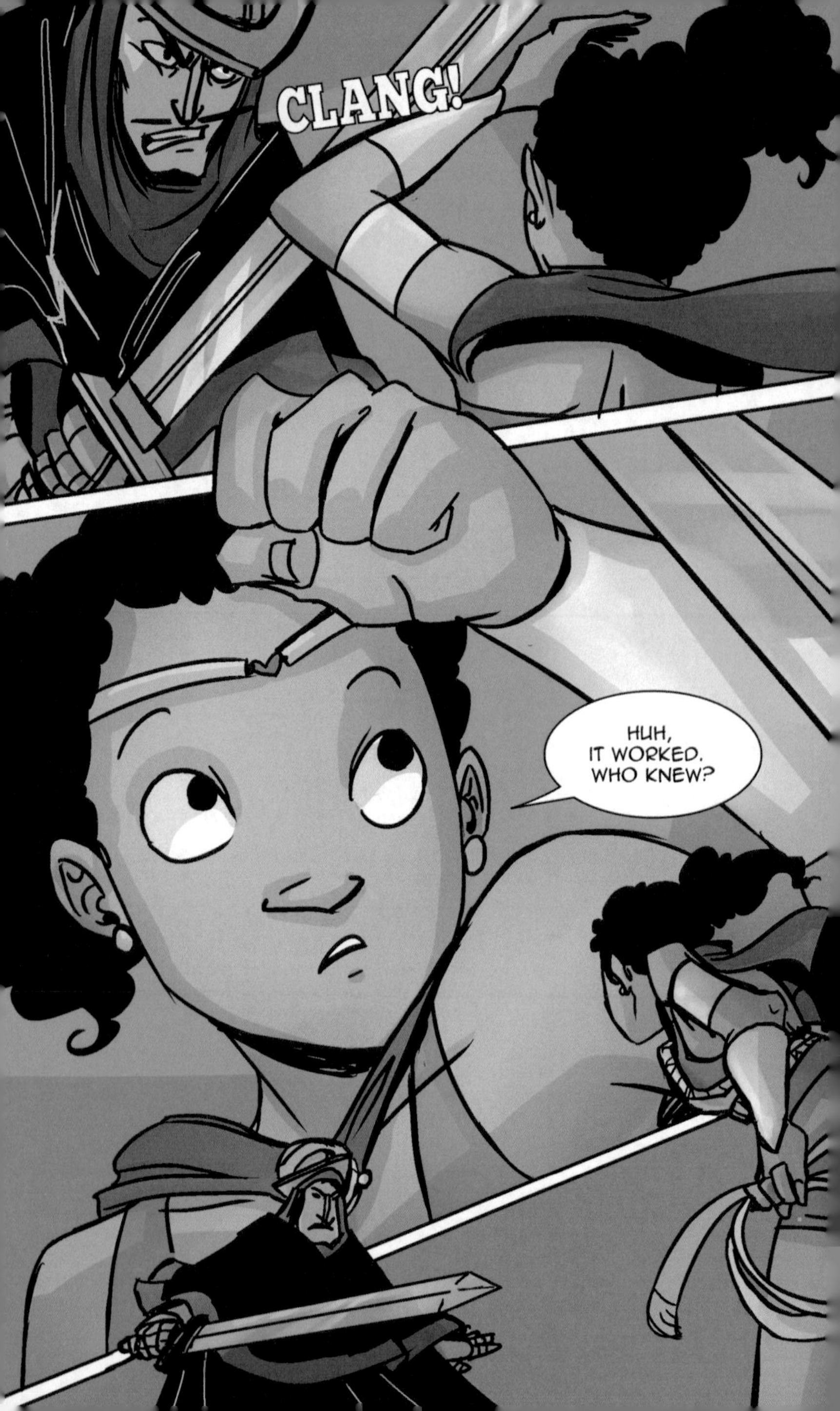
CLANG!
HUH,
IT WORKED.
WHO KNEW?

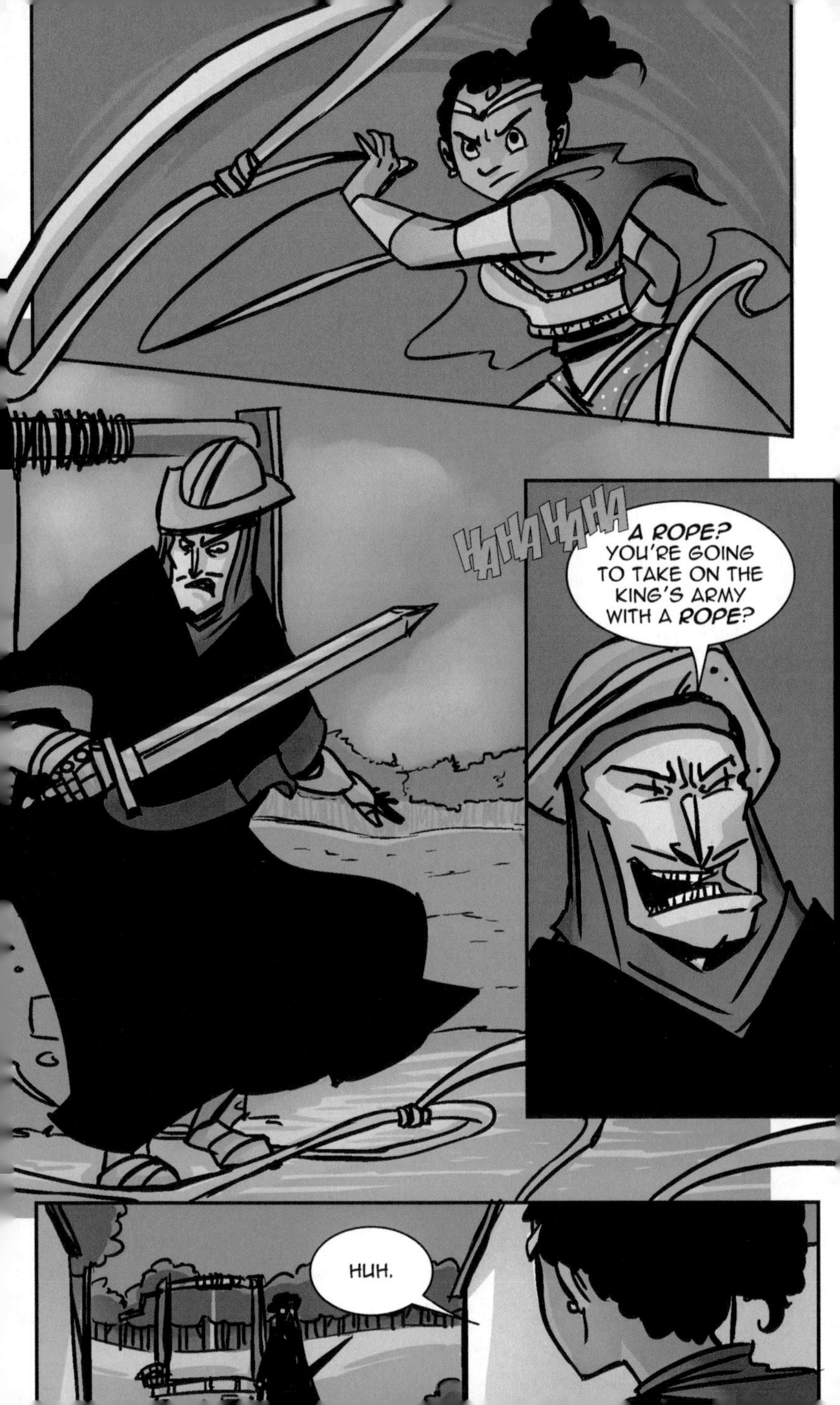
HAHAHAHA
A ROPE? YOU'RE GOING TO TAKE ON THE KING'S ARMY WITH A ROPE?
HUH.

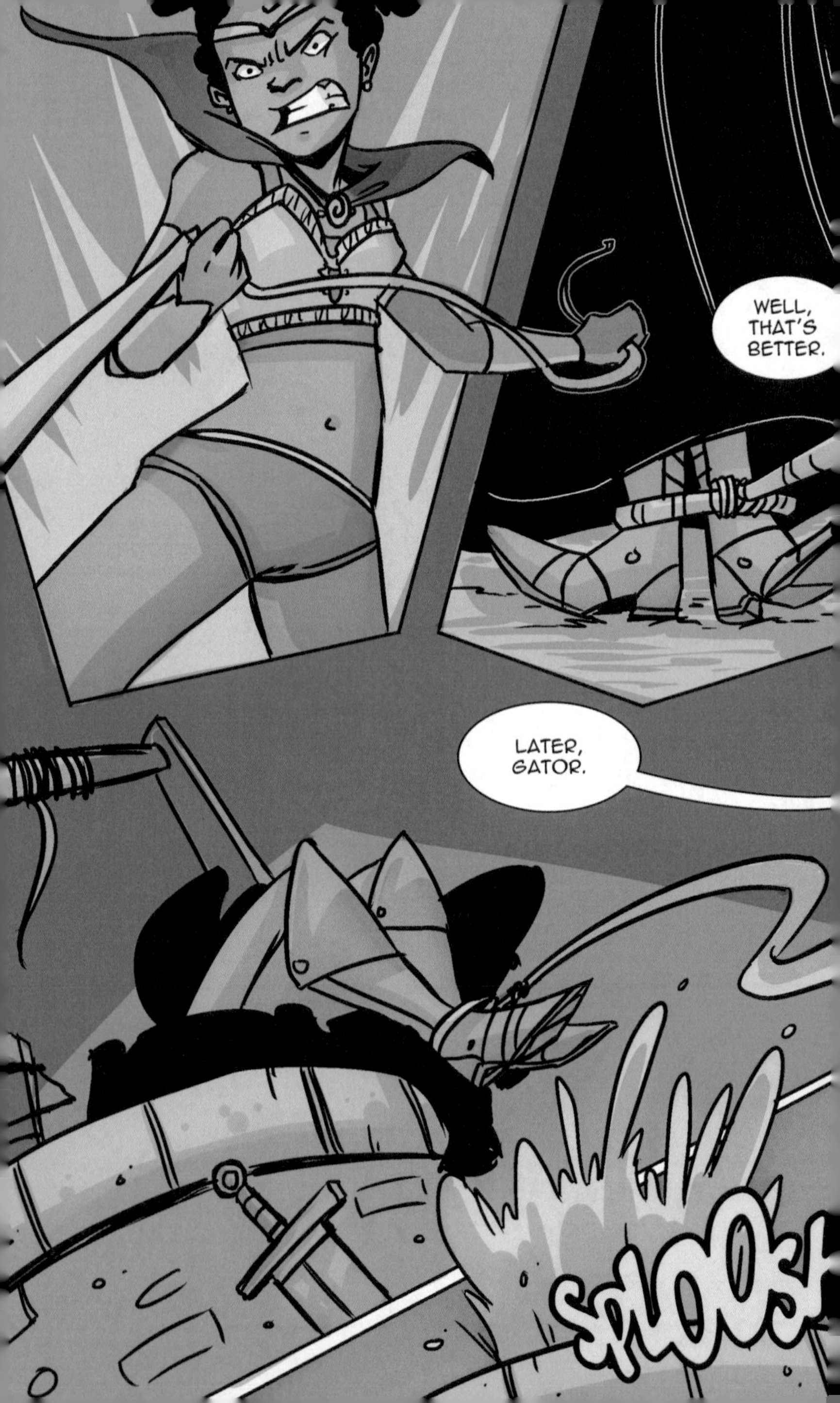
WELL, THAT'S BETTER.
LATER, GATOR.
SPLOOSH

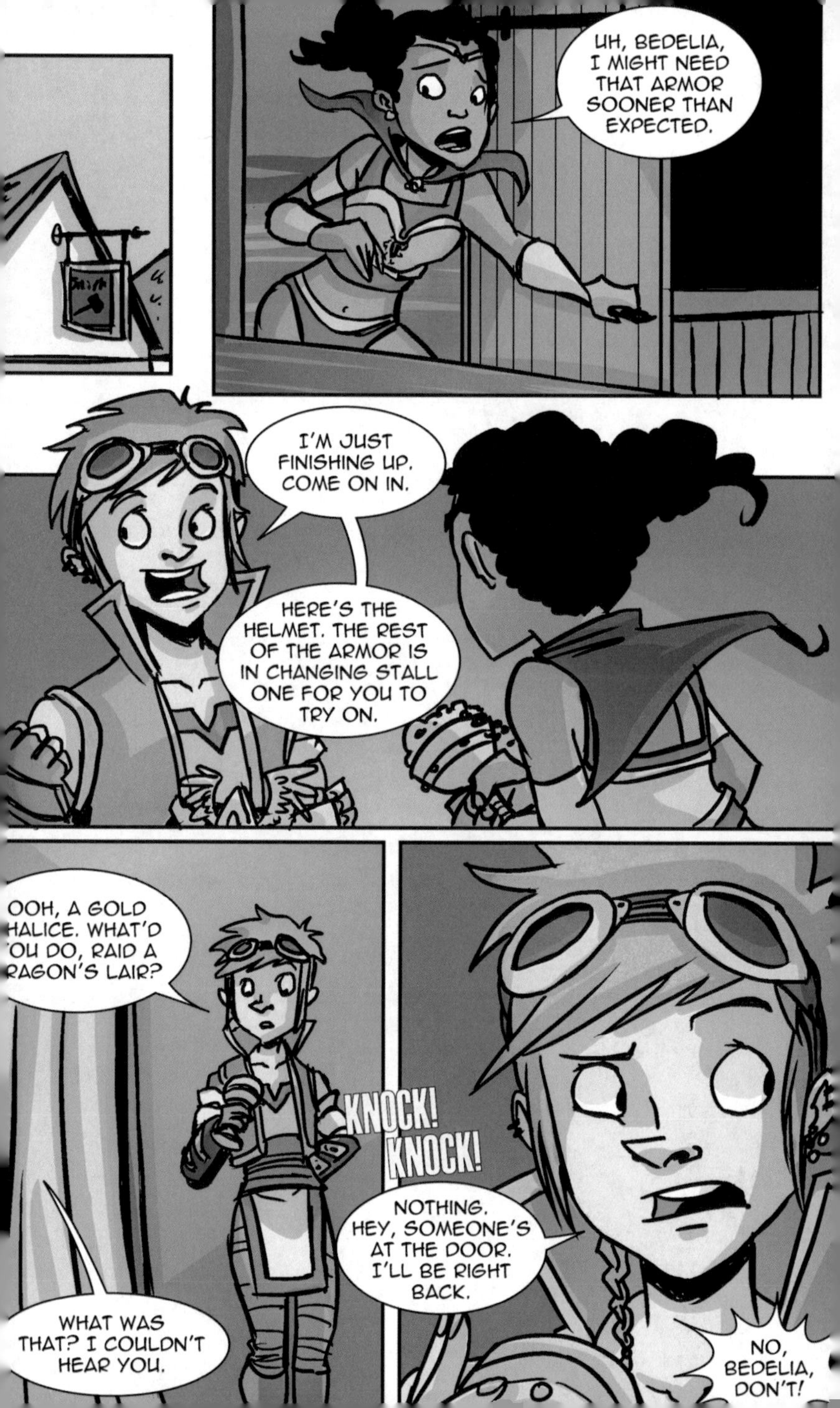

UH, BEDELIA, I MIGHT NEED THAT ARMOR SOONER THAN EXPECTED.
I'M JUST FINISHING UP. COME ON IN.
HERE'S THE HELMET. THE REST OF THE ARMOR IS IN CHANGING STALL ONE FOR YOU TO TRY ON.
OOH, A GOLD HALICE. WHAT'D OU DO, RAID A RAGON'S LAIR?
KNOCK! KNOCK!
WHAT WAS THAT? I COULDN'T HEAR YOU.
NOTHING. HEY, SOMEONE'S AT THE DOOR. I'LL BE RIGHT BACK.
NO, BEDELIA, DON'T!

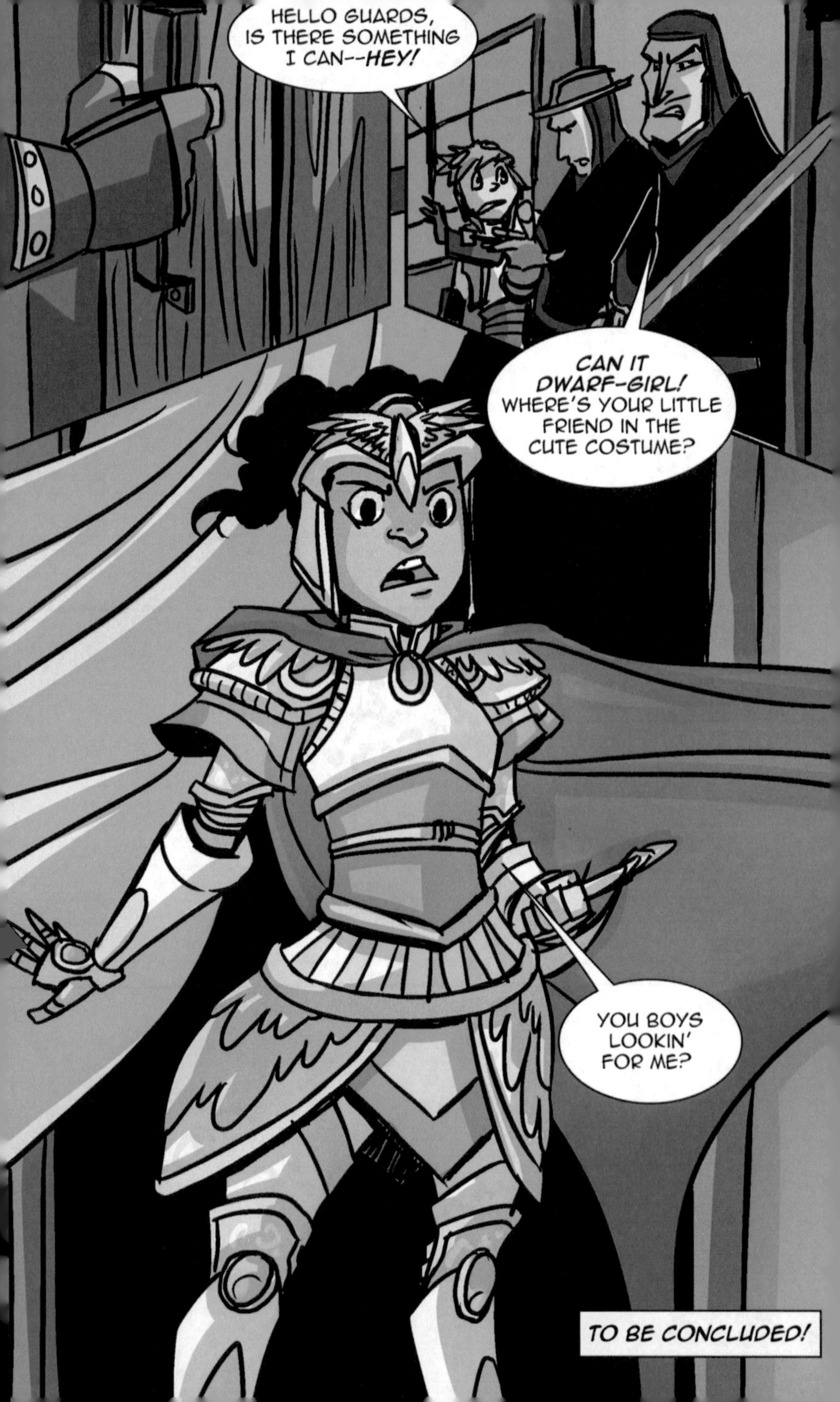
HELLO GUARDS, IS THERE SOMETHING I CAN--*HEY!*
CAN IT DWARF-GIRL! WHERE'S YOUR LITTLE FRIEND IN THE CUTE COSTUME?
YOU BOYS LOOKIN' FOR ME?
TO BE CONCLUDED!

4: Correct Dueling Procedure in Case of Fire

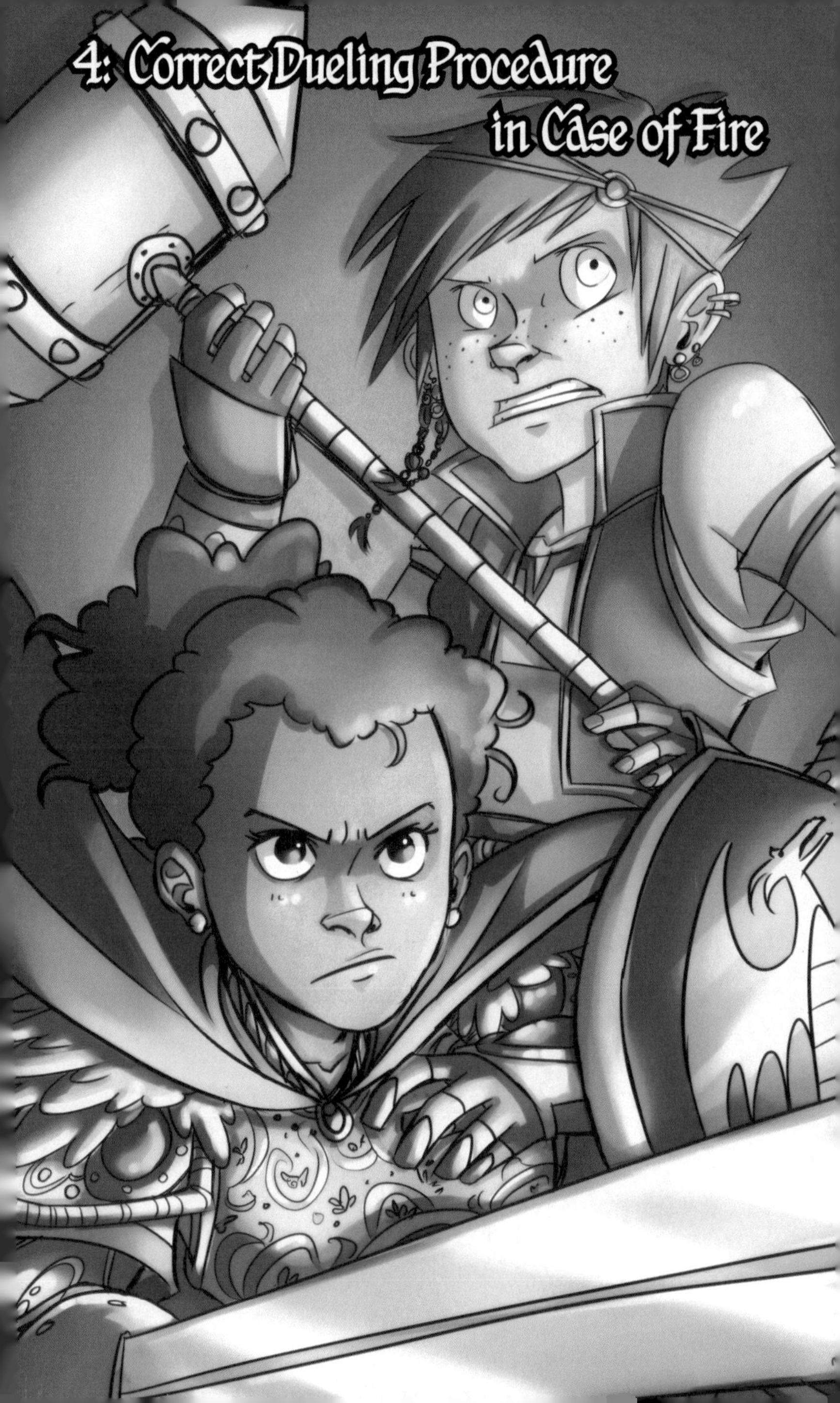

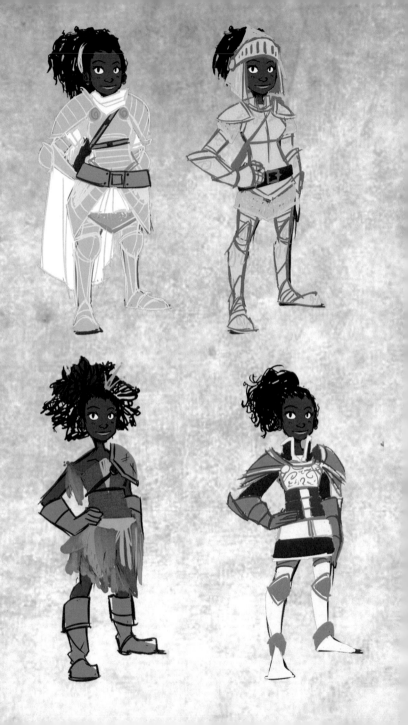

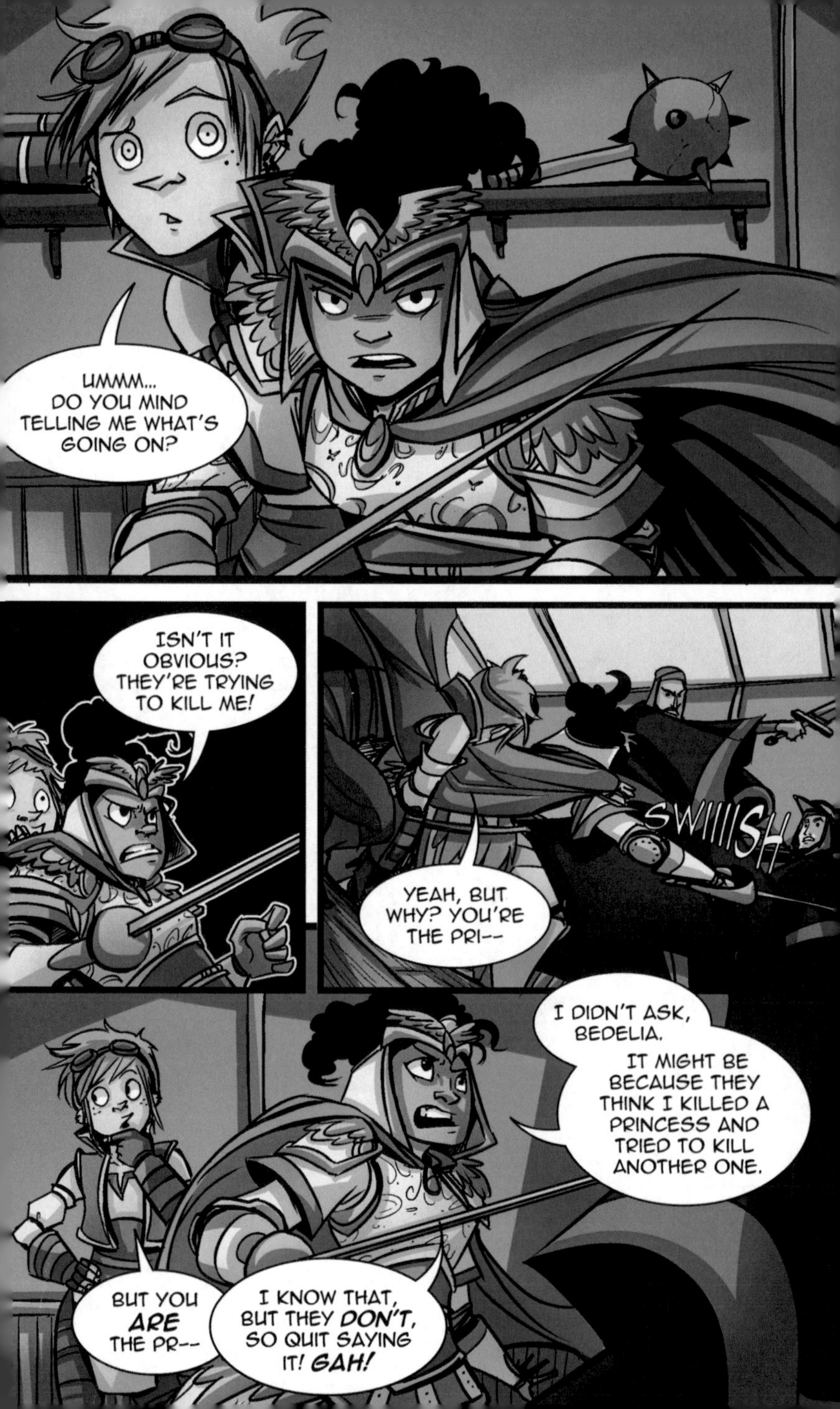
UMMM...
DO YOU MIND
TELLING ME WHAT'S
GOING ON?
ISN'T IT
OBVIOUS?
THEY'RE TRYING
TO KILL ME!
YEAH, BUT
WHY? YOU'RE
THE PRI--
SWIIIISH
I DIDN'T ASK,
BEDELIA.
IT MIGHT BE
BECAUSE THEY
THINK I KILLED A
PRINCESS AND
TRIED TO KILL
ANOTHER ONE.
BUT YOU
ARE
THE PR--
I KNOW THAT,
BUT THEY *DON'T*,
SO QUIT SAYING
IT! *GAH!*

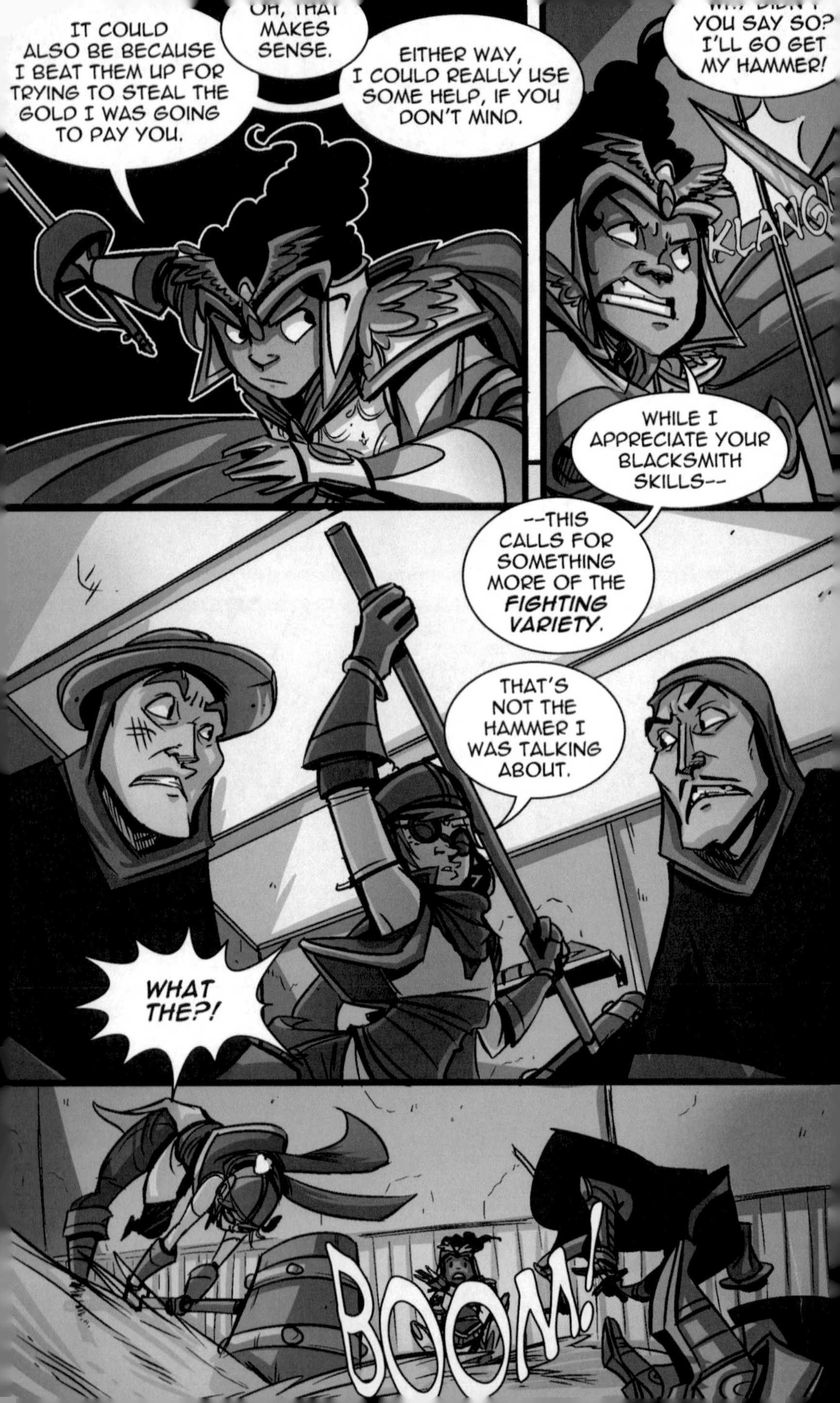

IT COULD ALSO BE BECAUSE I BEAT THEM UP FOR TRYING TO STEAL THE GOLD I WAS GOING TO PAY YOU.
MAKES SENSE.
EITHER WAY, I COULD REALLY USE SOME HELP, IF YOU DON'T MIND.
YOU SAY SO? I'LL GO GET MY HAMMER!
KLANG!
WHILE I APPRECIATE YOUR BLACKSMITH SKILLS--
--THIS CALLS FOR SOMETHING MORE OF THE FIGHTING VARIETY.
THAT'S NOT THE HAMMER I WAS TALKING ABOUT.
WHAT THE?!
BOOM!

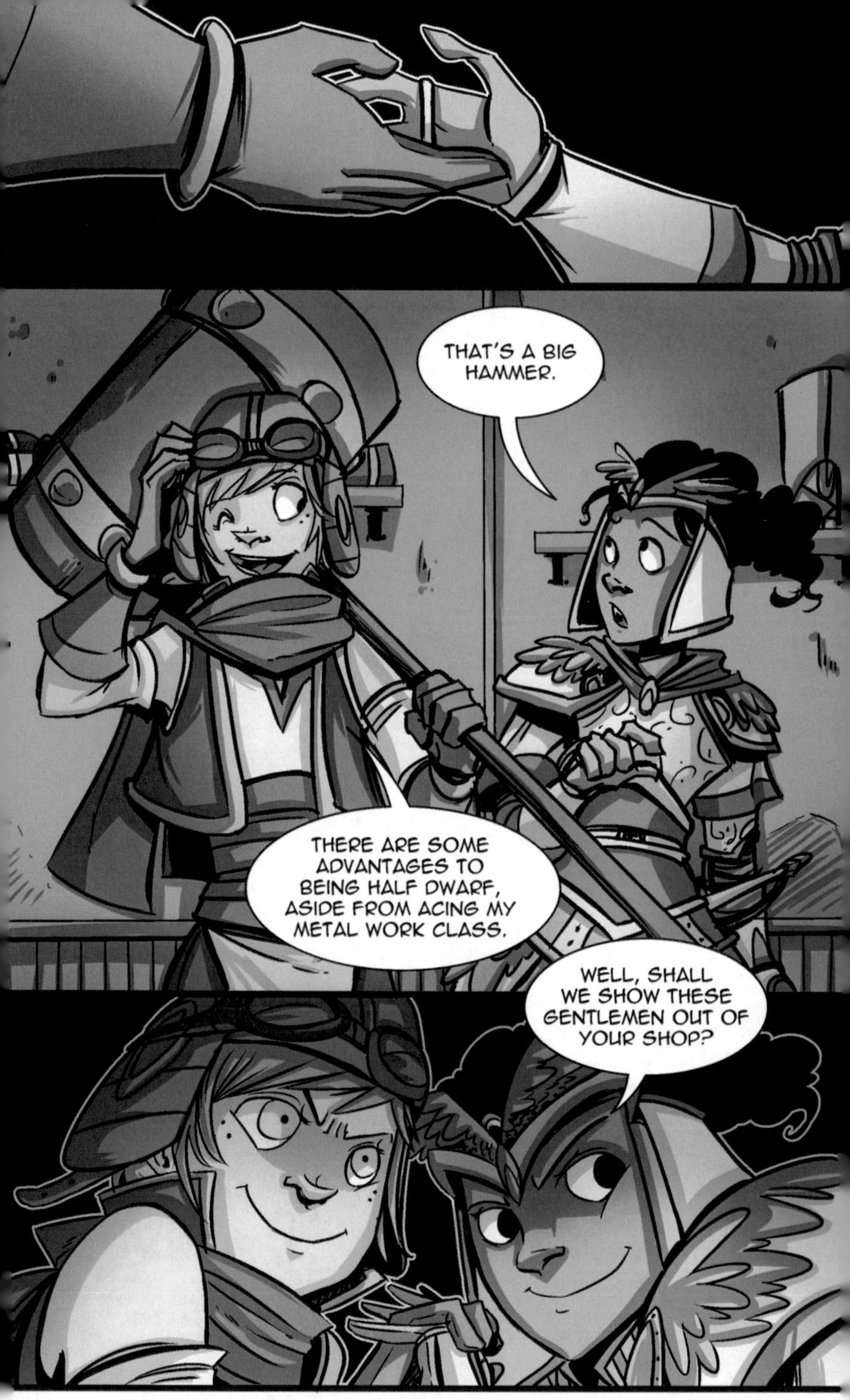
THAT'S A BIG HAMMER.
THERE ARE SOME ADVANTAGES TO BEING HALF DWARF, ASIDE FROM ACING MY METAL WORK CLASS.
WELL, SHALL WE SHOW THESE GENTLEMEN OUT OF YOUR SHOP?

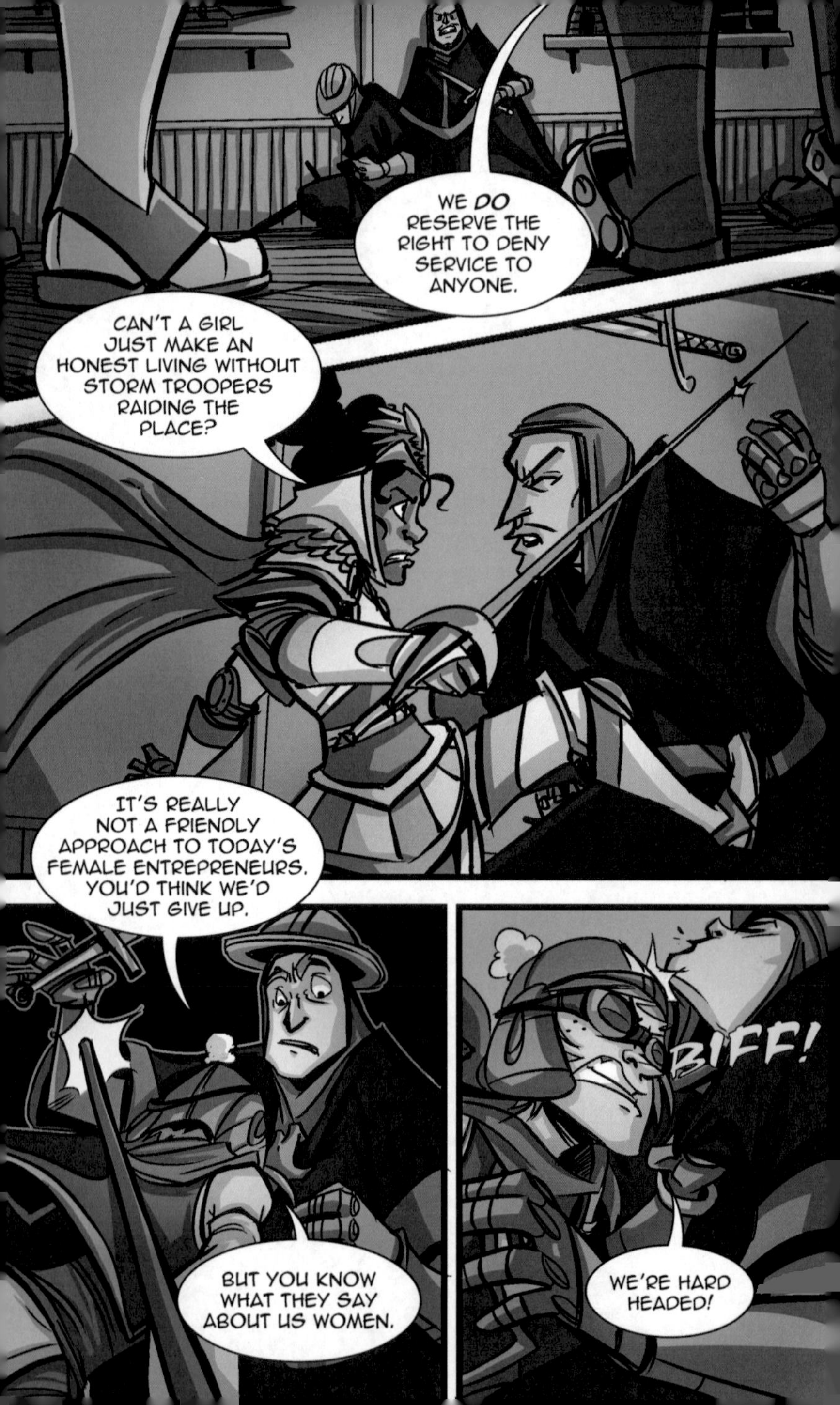
WE *DO* RESERVE THE RIGHT TO DENY SERVICE TO ANYONE.
CAN'T A GIRL JUST MAKE AN HONEST LIVING WITHOUT STORM TROOPERS RAIDING THE PLACE?
IT'S REALLY NOT A FRIENDLY APPROACH TO TODAY'S FEMALE ENTREPRENEURS. YOU'D THINK WE'D JUST GIVE UP.
BUT YOU KNOW WHAT THEY SAY ABOUT US WOMEN.
WE'RE HARD HEADED!
BIFF!

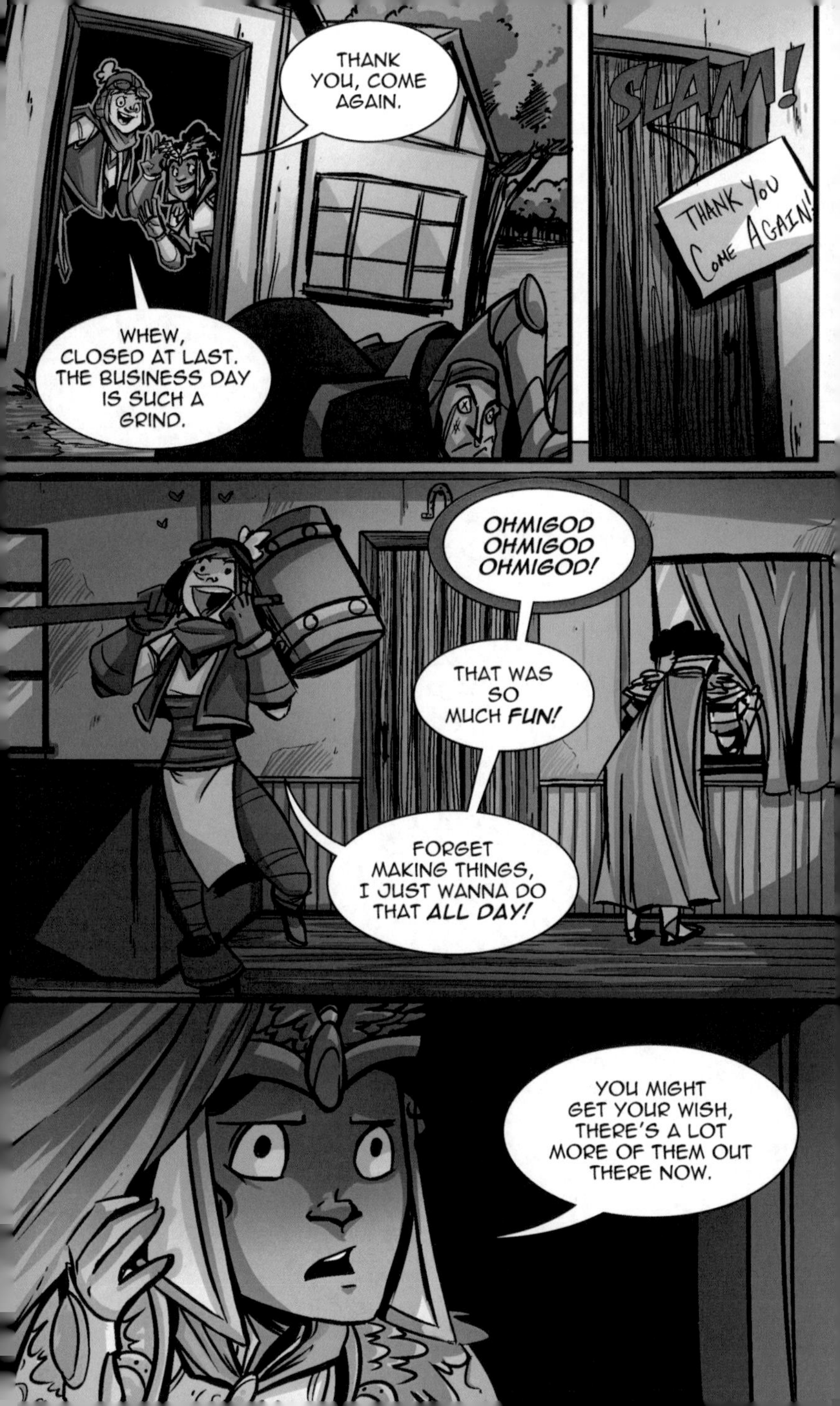
THANK YOU, COME AGAIN.
WHEW, CLOSED AT LAST. THE BUSINESS DAY IS SUCH A GRIND.
SLAM!
THANK YOU COME AGAIN!
OHMIGOD OHMIGOD OHMIGOD!
THAT WAS SO MUCH FUN!
FORGET MAKING THINGS, I JUST WANNA DO THAT ALL DAY!
YOU MIGHT GET YOUR WISH, THERE'S A LOT MORE OF THEM OUT THERE NOW.

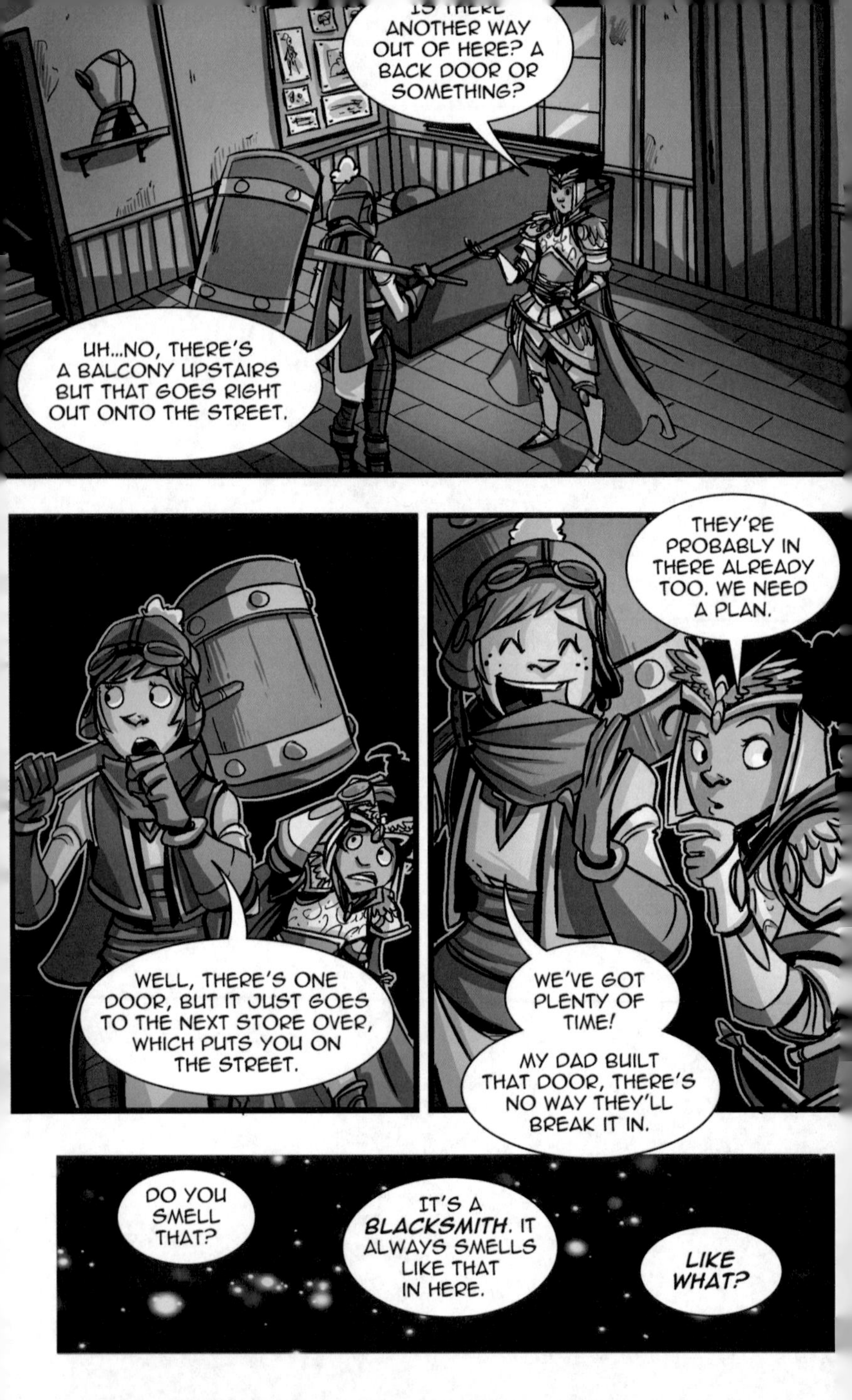
IS THERE ANOTHER WAY OUT OF HERE? A BACK DOOR OR SOMETHING?
UH...NO, THERE'S A BALCONY UPSTAIRS BUT THAT GOES RIGHT OUT ONTO THE STREET.
WELL, THERE'S ONE DOOR, BUT IT JUST GOES TO THE NEXT STORE OVER, WHICH PUTS YOU ON THE STREET.
THEY'RE PROBABLY IN THERE ALREADY TOO. WE NEED A PLAN.
WE'VE GOT PLENTY OF TIME!
MY DAD BUILT THAT DOOR, THERE'S NO WAY THEY'LL BREAK IT IN.
DO YOU SMELL THAT?
IT'S A *BLACKSMITH*. IT ALWAYS SMELLS LIKE THAT IN HERE.
LIKE WHAT?

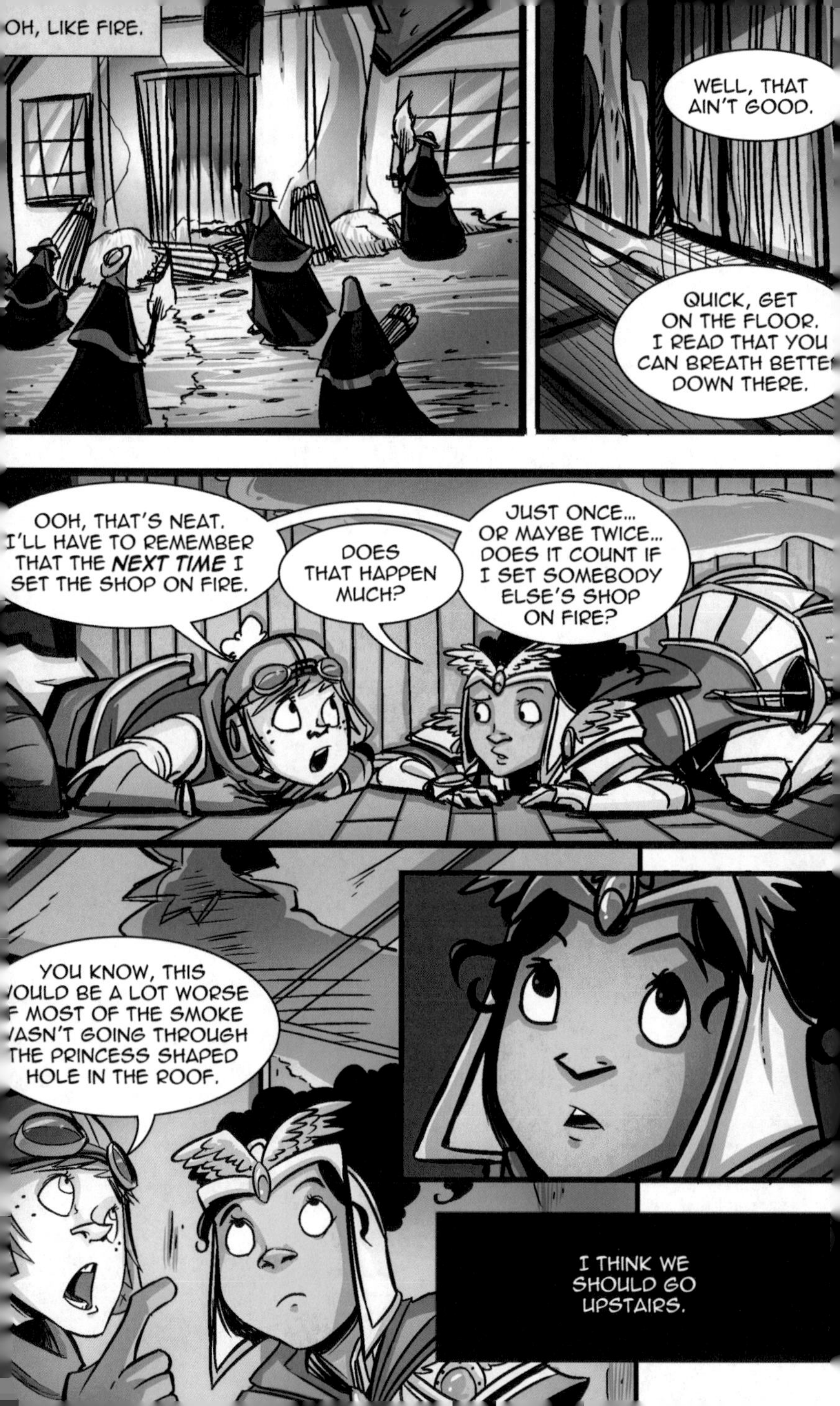

OH, LIKE FIRE.
WELL, THAT AIN'T GOOD.
QUICK, GET ON THE FLOOR. I READ THAT YOU CAN BREATH BETTE
DOWN THERE.
OOH, THAT'S NEAT. I'LL HAVE TO REMEMBER THAT THE NEXT TIME I SET THE SHOP ON FIRE.
DOES THAT HAPPEN MUCH?
JUST ONCE... OR MAYBE TWICE... DOES IT COUNT IF I SET SOMEBODY ELSE'S SHOP ON FIRE?
YOU KNOW, THIS /OULD BE A LOT WORSE F MOST OF THE SMOKE /ASN'T GOING THROUGH THE PRINCESS SHAPED HOLE IN THE ROOF.
I THINK WE SHOULD GO UPSTAIRS.

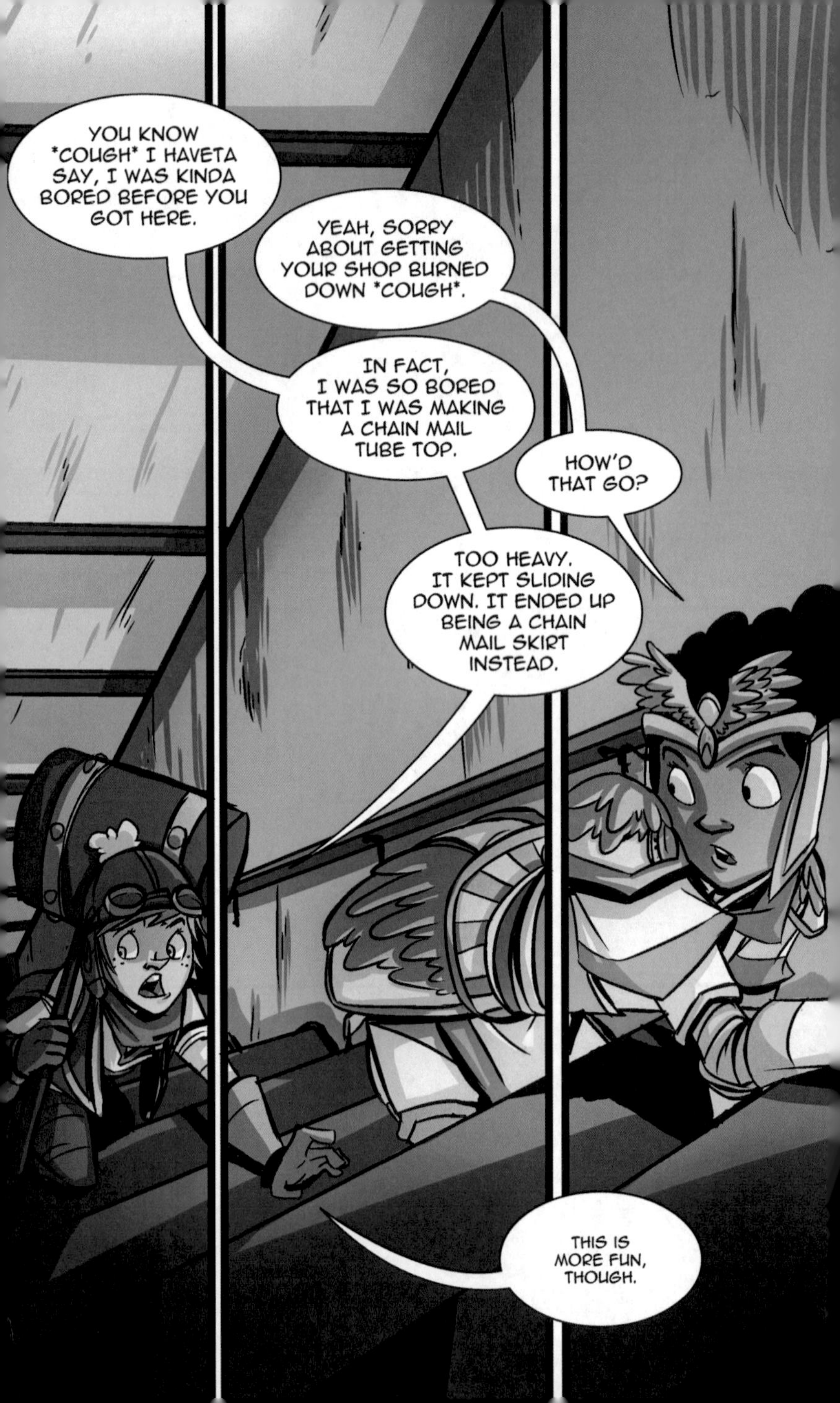
YOU KNOW *COUGH* I HAVETA SAY, I WAS KINDA BORED BEFORE YOU GOT HERE.
YEAH, SORRY ABOUT GETTING YOUR SHOP BURNED DOWN *COUGH*.
IN FACT, I WAS SO BORED THAT I WAS MAKING A CHAIN MAIL TUBE TOP.
HOW'D THAT GO?
TOO HEAVY. IT KEPT SLIDING DOWN. IT ENDED UP BEING A CHAIN MAIL SKIRT INSTEAD.
THIS IS MORE FUN, THOUGH.

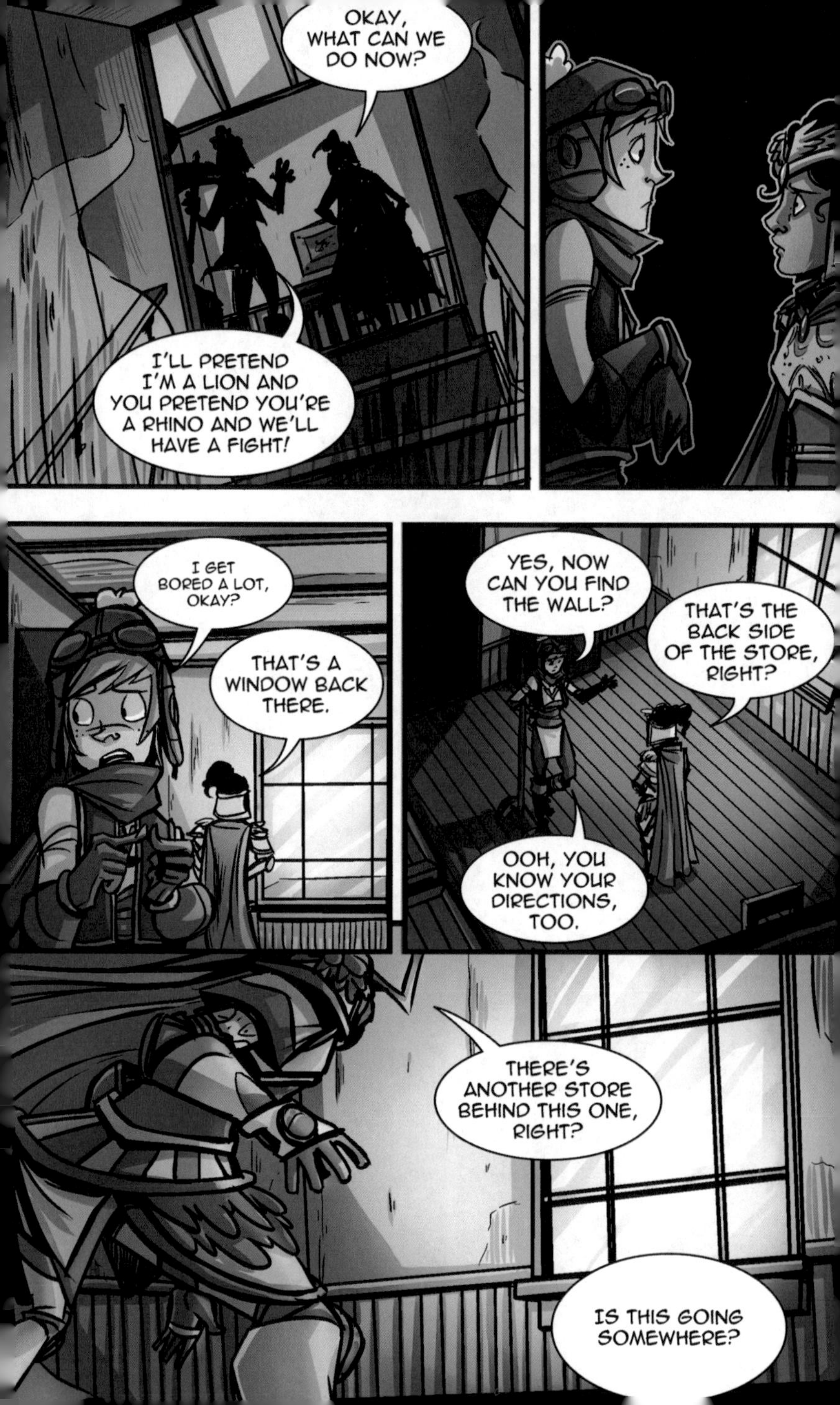
OKAY, WHAT CAN WE DO NOW?
I'LL PRETEND I'M A LION AND YOU PRETEND YOU'RE A RHINO AND WE'LL HAVE A FIGHT!
I GET BORED A LOT, OKAY?
THAT'S A WINDOW BACK THERE.
YES, NOW CAN YOU FIND THE WALL?
THAT'S THE BACK SIDE OF THE STORE, RIGHT?
OOH, YOU KNOW YOUR DIRECTIONS, TOO.
THERE'S ANOTHER STORE BEHIND THIS ONE, RIGHT?
IS THIS GOING SOMEWHERE?

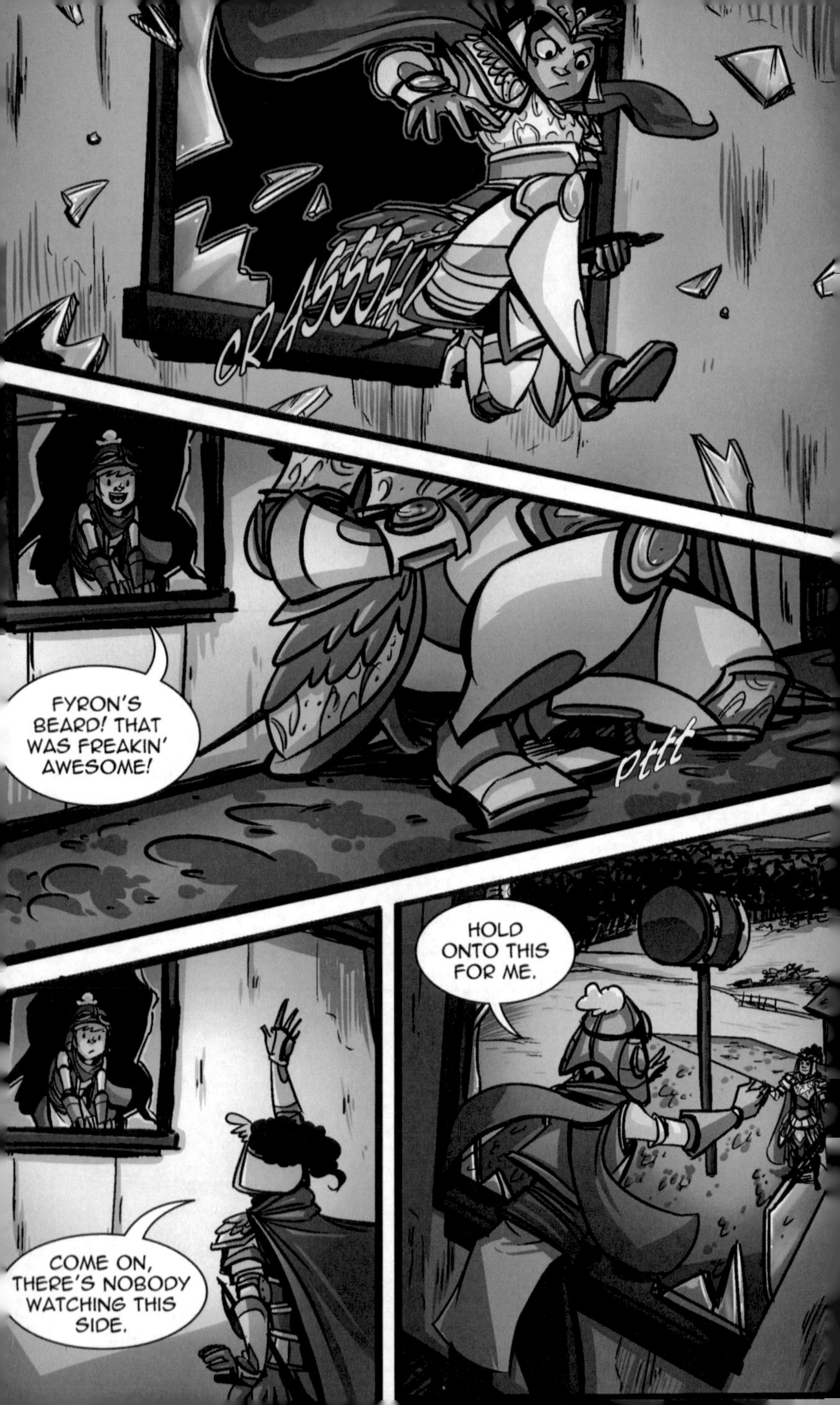
CRASSSH!
FYRON'S BEARD! THAT WAS FREAKIN' AWESOME!
pttt
COME ON, THERE'S NOBODY WATCHING THIS SIDE.
HOLD ONTO THIS FOR ME.

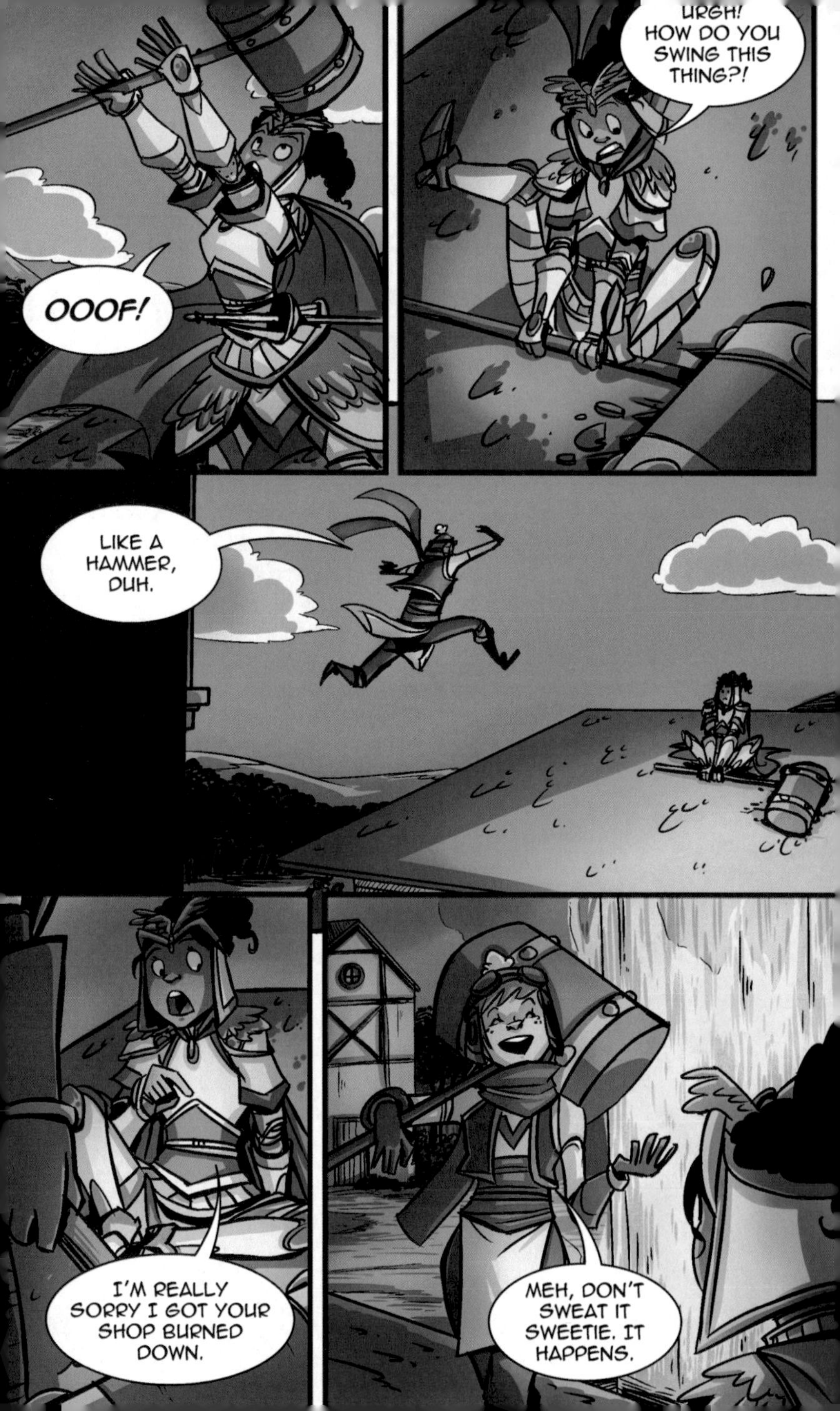
OOOF!
URGH! HOW DO YOU SWING THIS THING?!
LIKE A HAMMER, DUH.
I'M REALLY SORRY I GOT YOUR SHOP BURNED DOWN.
MEH, DON'T SWEAT IT SWEETIE. IT HAPPENS.

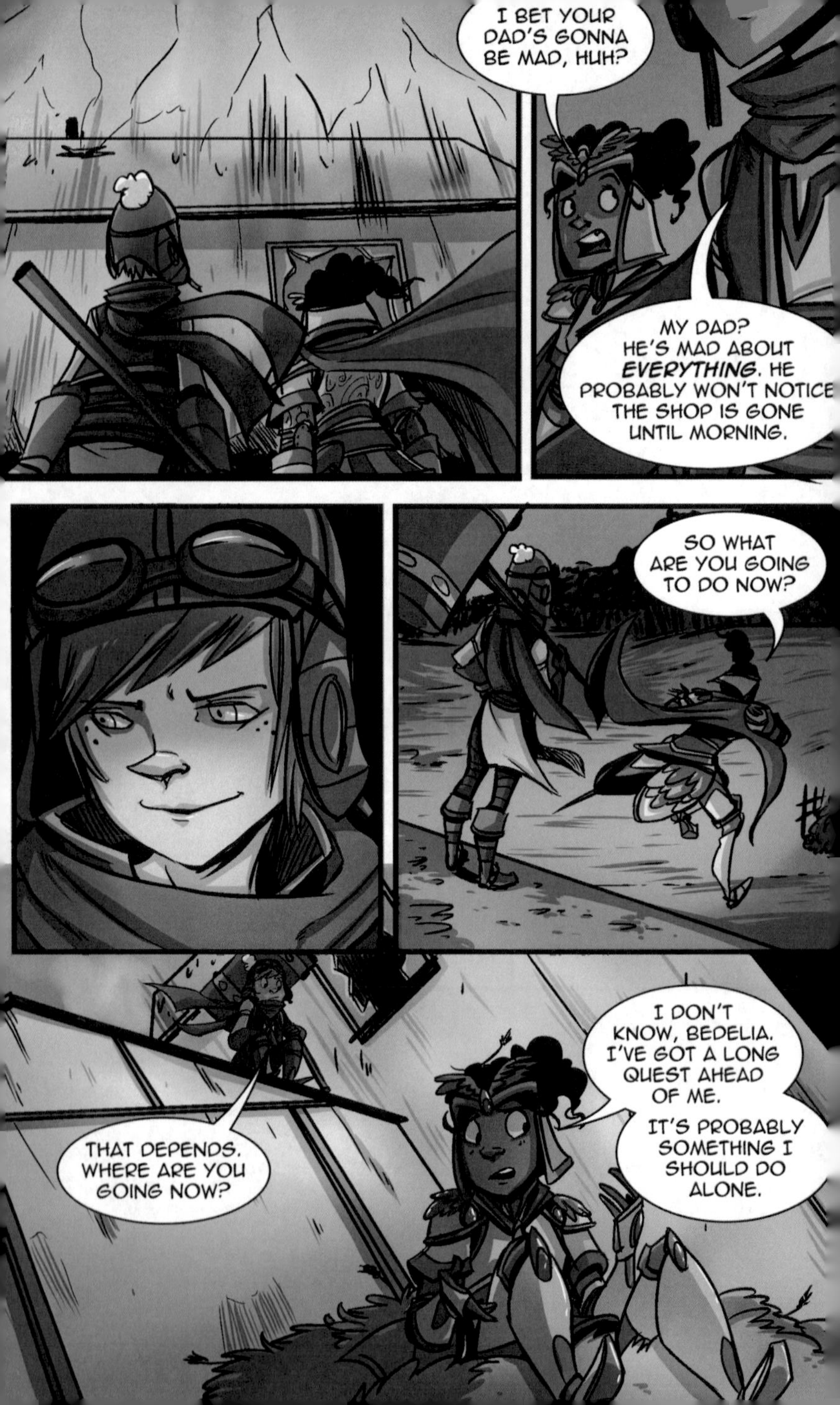
I BET YOUR DAD'S GONNA BE MAD, HUH?
MY DAD? HE'S MAD ABOUT *EVERYTHING*. HE PROBABLY WON'T NOTICE THE SHOP IS GONE UNTIL MORNING.
SO WHAT ARE YOU GOING TO DO NOW?
THAT DEPENDS. WHERE ARE YOU GOING NOW?
I DON'T KNOW, BEDELIA. I'VE GOT A LONG QUEST AHEAD OF ME.
IT'S PROBABLY SOMETHING I SHOULD DO ALONE.

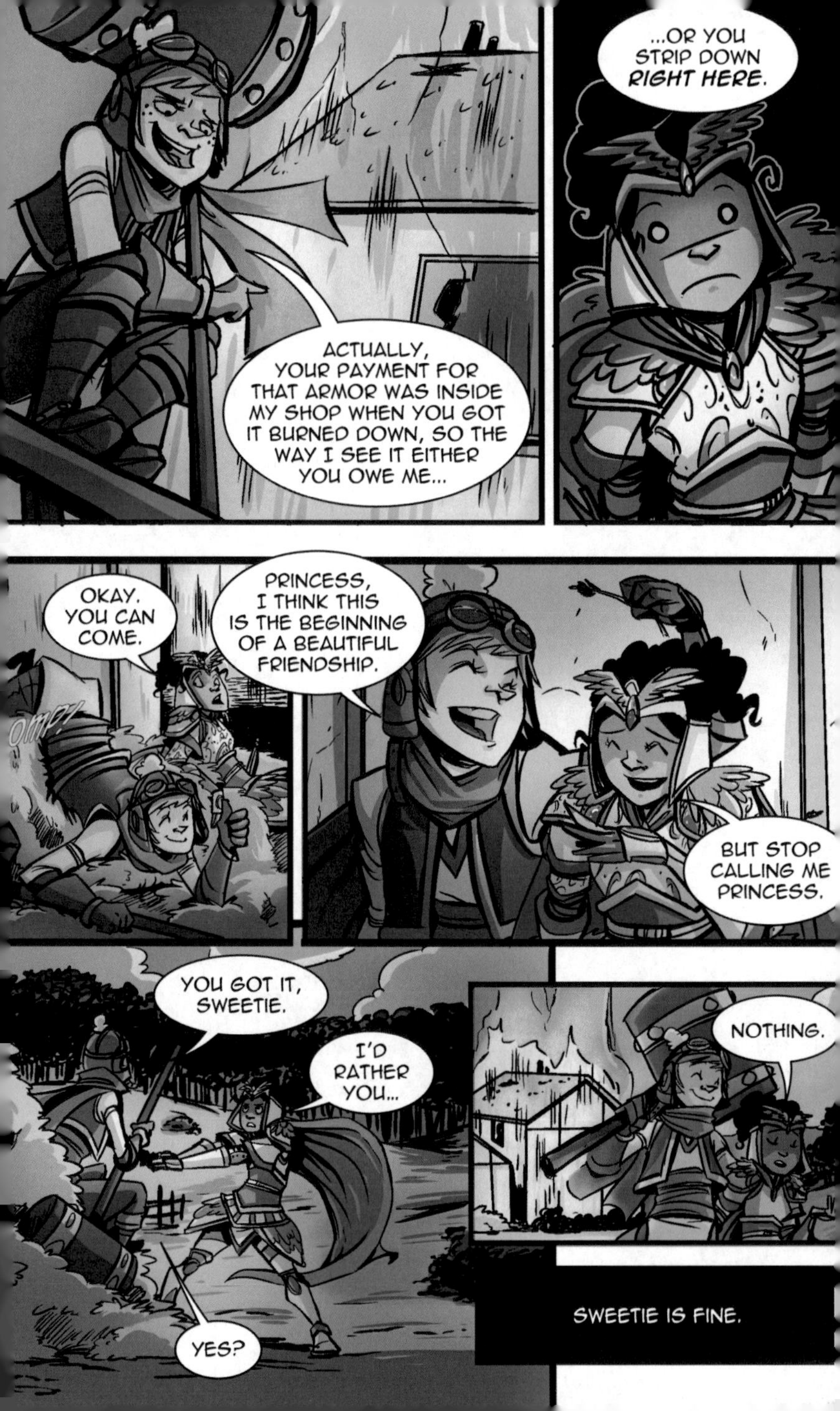
ACTUALLY, YOUR PAYMENT FOR THAT ARMOR WAS INSIDE MY SHOP WHEN YOU GOT IT BURNED DOWN, SO THE WAY I SEE IT EITHER YOU OWE ME...
...OR YOU STRIP DOWN RIGHT HERE.
OMP!
OKAY. YOU CAN COME.
PRINCESS, I THINK THIS IS THE BEGINNING OF A BEAUTIFUL FRIENDSHIP.
BUT STOP CALLING ME PRINCESS.
YOU GOT IT, SWEETIE.
I'D RATHER YOU...
YES?
NOTHING.
SWEETIE IS FINE.

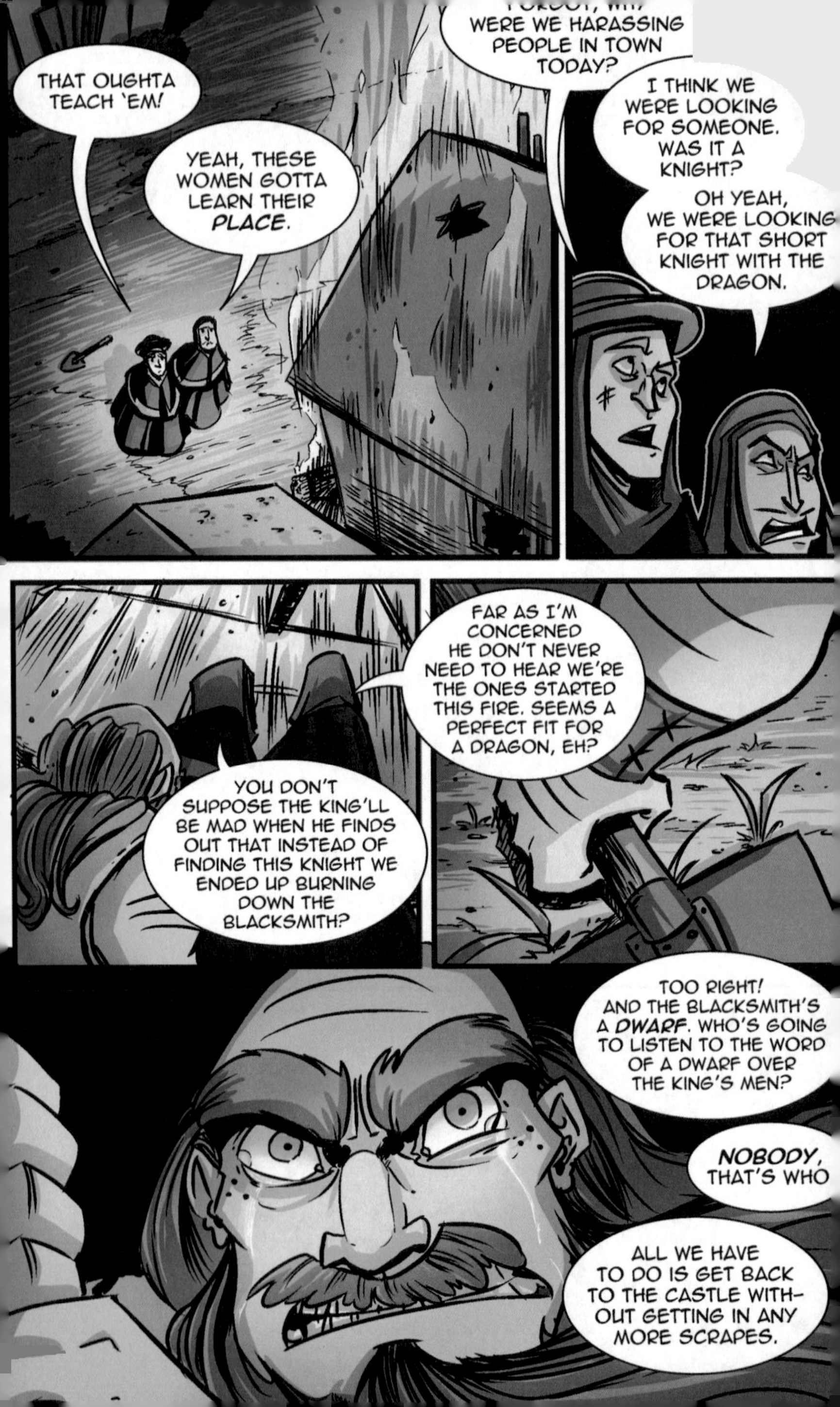
THAT OUGHTA TEACH 'EM!
YEAH, THESE WOMEN GOTTA LEARN THEIR *PLACE*.
WERE WE HARASSING PEOPLE IN TOWN TODAY?
I THINK WE WERE LOOKING FOR SOMEONE. WAS IT A KNIGHT?
OH YEAH, WE WERE LOOKING FOR THAT SHORT KNIGHT WITH THE DRAGON.
YOU DON'T SUPPOSE THE KING'LL BE MAD WHEN HE FINDS OUT THAT INSTEAD OF FINDING THIS KNIGHT WE ENDED UP BURNING DOWN THE BLACKSMITH?
FAR AS I'M CONCERNED HE DON'T NEVER NEED TO HEAR WE'RE THE ONES STARTED THIS FIRE. SEEMS A PERFECT FIT FOR A DRAGON, EH?
TOO RIGHT! AND THE BLACKSMITH'S A *DWARF*. WHO'S GOING TO LISTEN TO THE WORD OF A DWARF OVER THE KING'S MEN?
NOBODY, THAT'S WHO
ALL WE HAVE TO DO IS GET BACK TO THE CASTLE WITH-OUT GETTING IN ANY MORE SCRAPES.

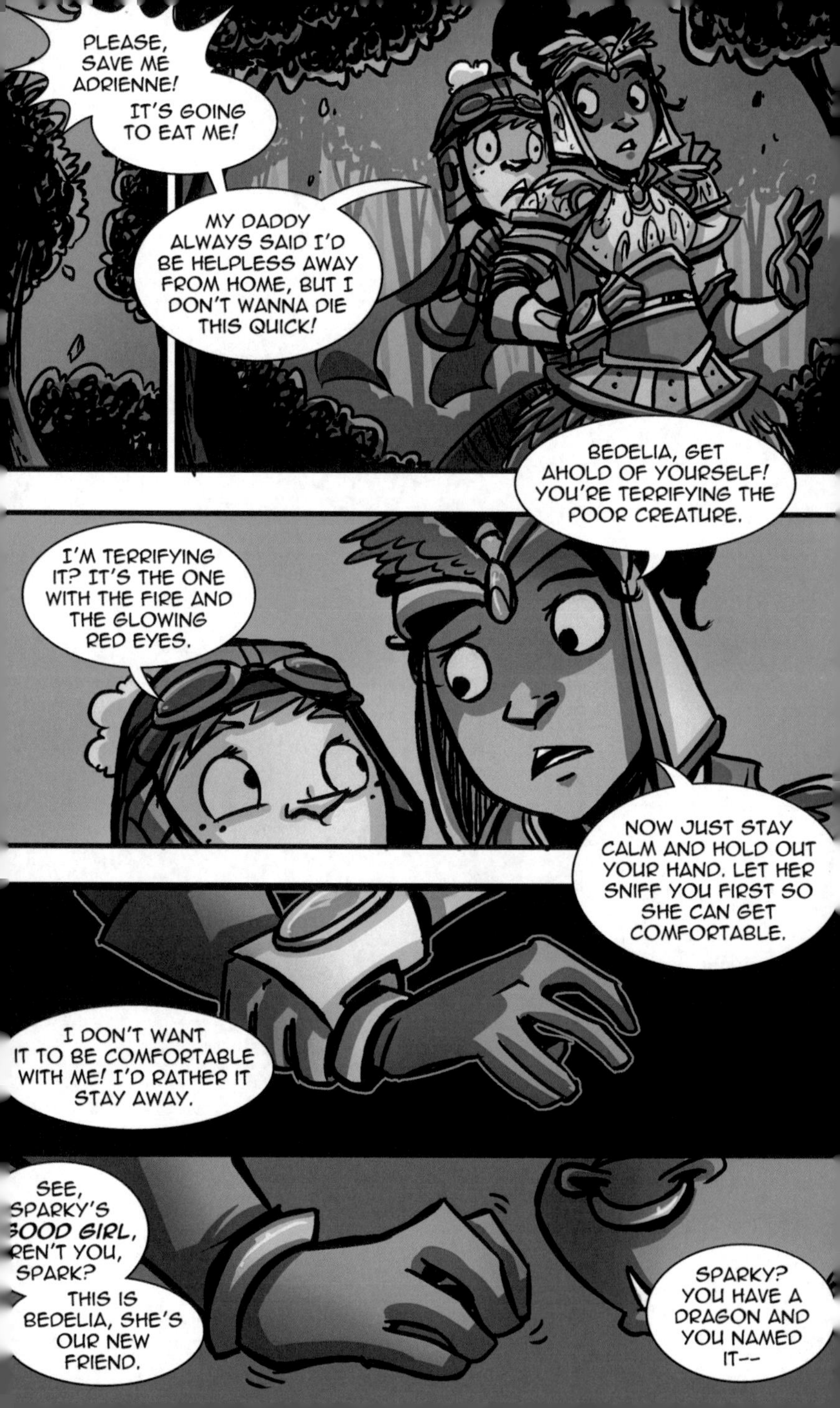
PLEASE, SAVE ME ADRIENNE!
IT'S GOING TO EAT ME!
MY DADDY ALWAYS SAID I'D BE HELPLESS AWAY FROM HOME, BUT I DON'T WANNA DIE THIS QUICK!
BEDELIA, GET AHOLD OF YOURSELF! YOU'RE TERRIFYING THE POOR CREATURE.
I'M TERRIFYING IT? IT'S THE ONE WITH THE FIRE AND THE GLOWING RED EYES.
NOW JUST STAY CALM AND HOLD OUT YOUR HAND. LET HER SNIFF YOU FIRST SO SHE CAN GET COMFORTABLE.
I DON'T WANT IT TO BE COMFORTABLE WITH ME! I'D RATHER IT STAY AWAY.
SEE, SPARKY'S *OOD GIRL*, REN'T YOU, SPARK?
THIS IS BEDELIA, SHE'S OUR NEW FRIEND.
SPARKY? YOU HAVE A DRAGON AND YOU NAMED IT--

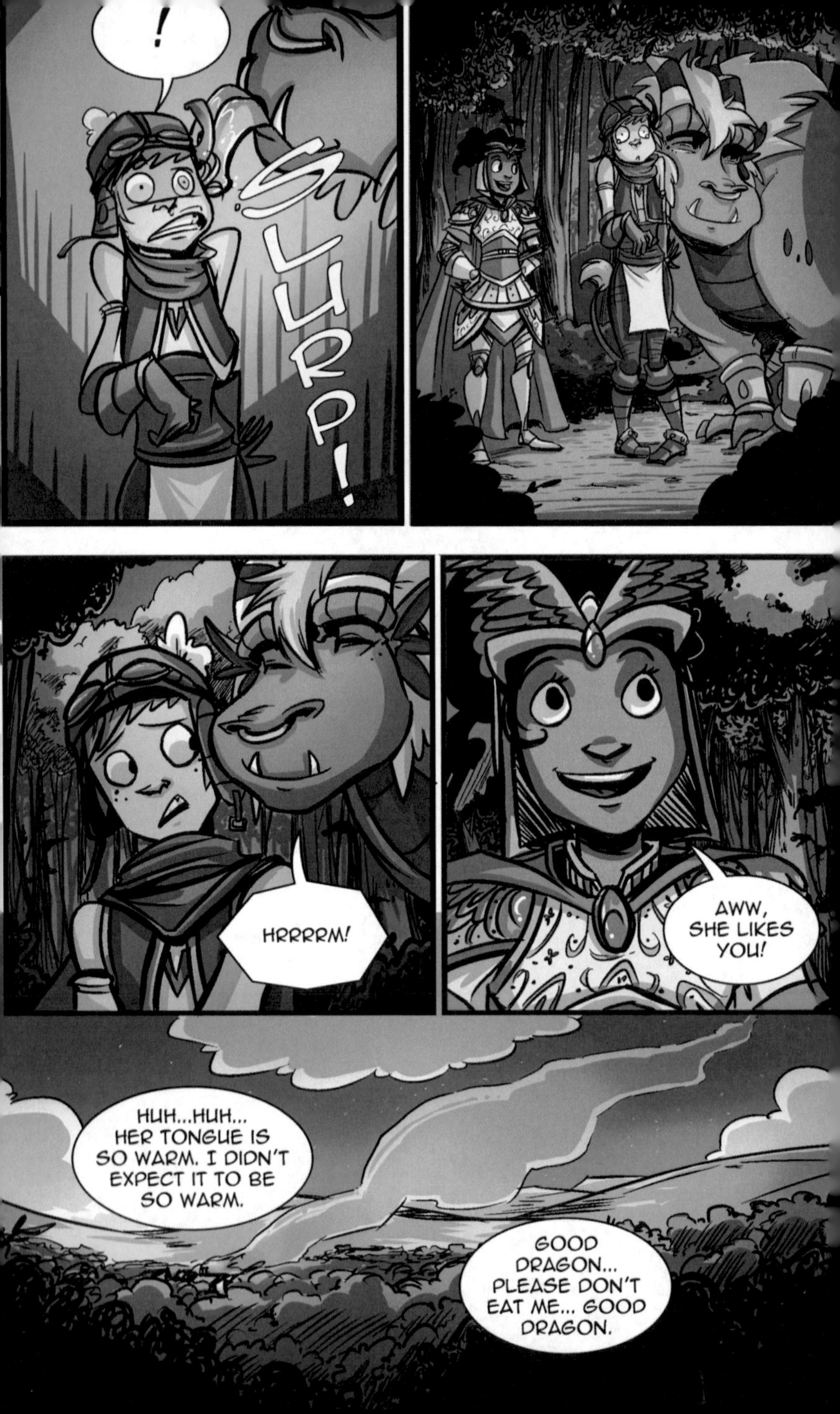
!
SLURP!
HRRRRM!
AWW, SHE LIKES YOU!
HUH...HUH... HER TONGUE IS SO WARM. I DIDN'T EXPECT IT TO BE SO WARM.
GOOD DRAGON... PLEASE DON'T EAT ME... GOOD DRAGON.

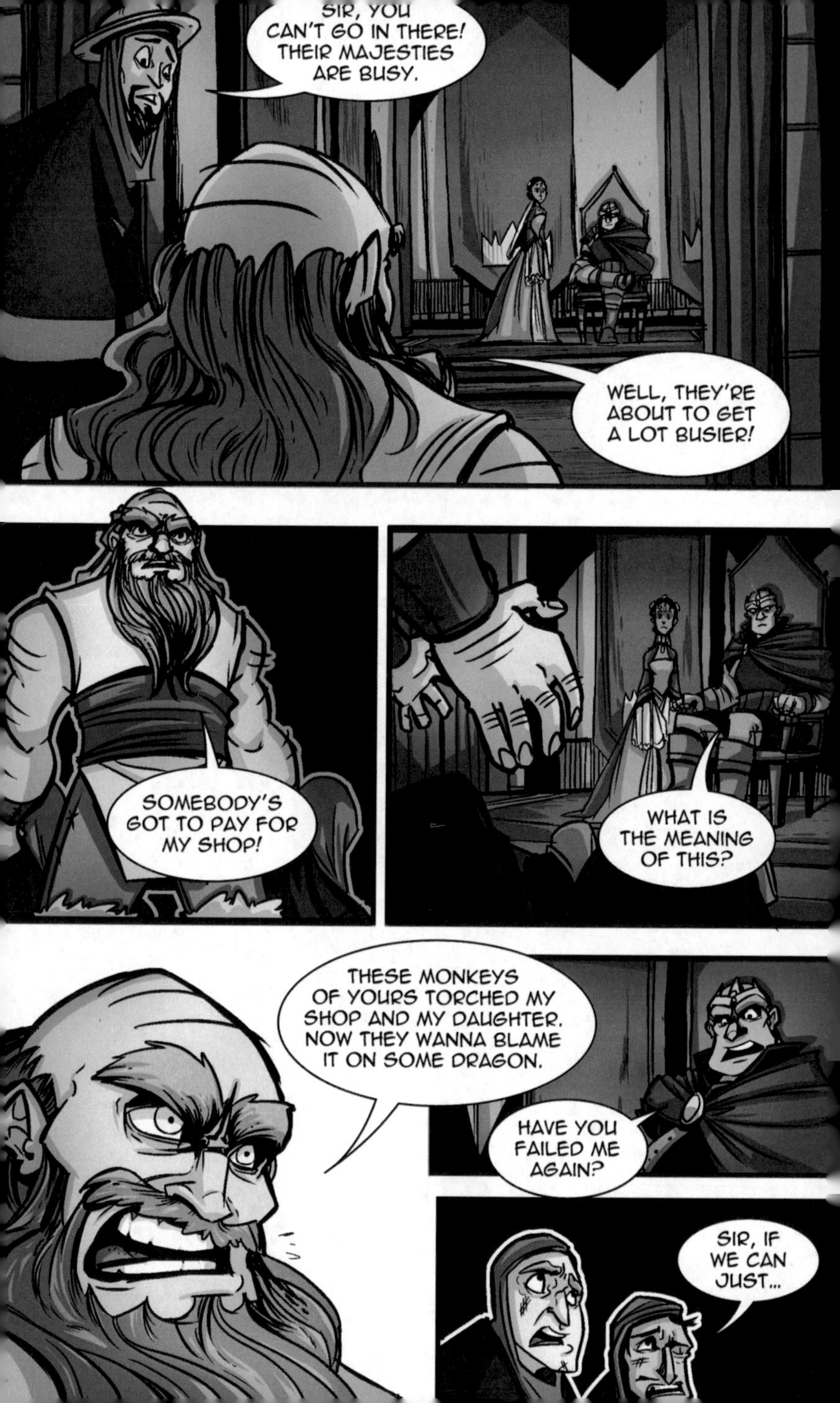
SIR, YOU CAN'T GO IN THERE! THEIR MAJESTIES ARE BUSY.
WELL, THEY'RE ABOUT TO GET A LOT BUSIER!
SOMEBODY'S GOT TO PAY FOR MY SHOP!
WHAT IS THE MEANING OF THIS?
THESE MONKEYS OF YOURS TORCHED MY SHOP AND MY DAUGHTER. NOW THEY WANNA BLAME IT ON SOME DRAGON.
HAVE YOU FAILED ME AGAIN?
SIR, IF WE CAN JUST...

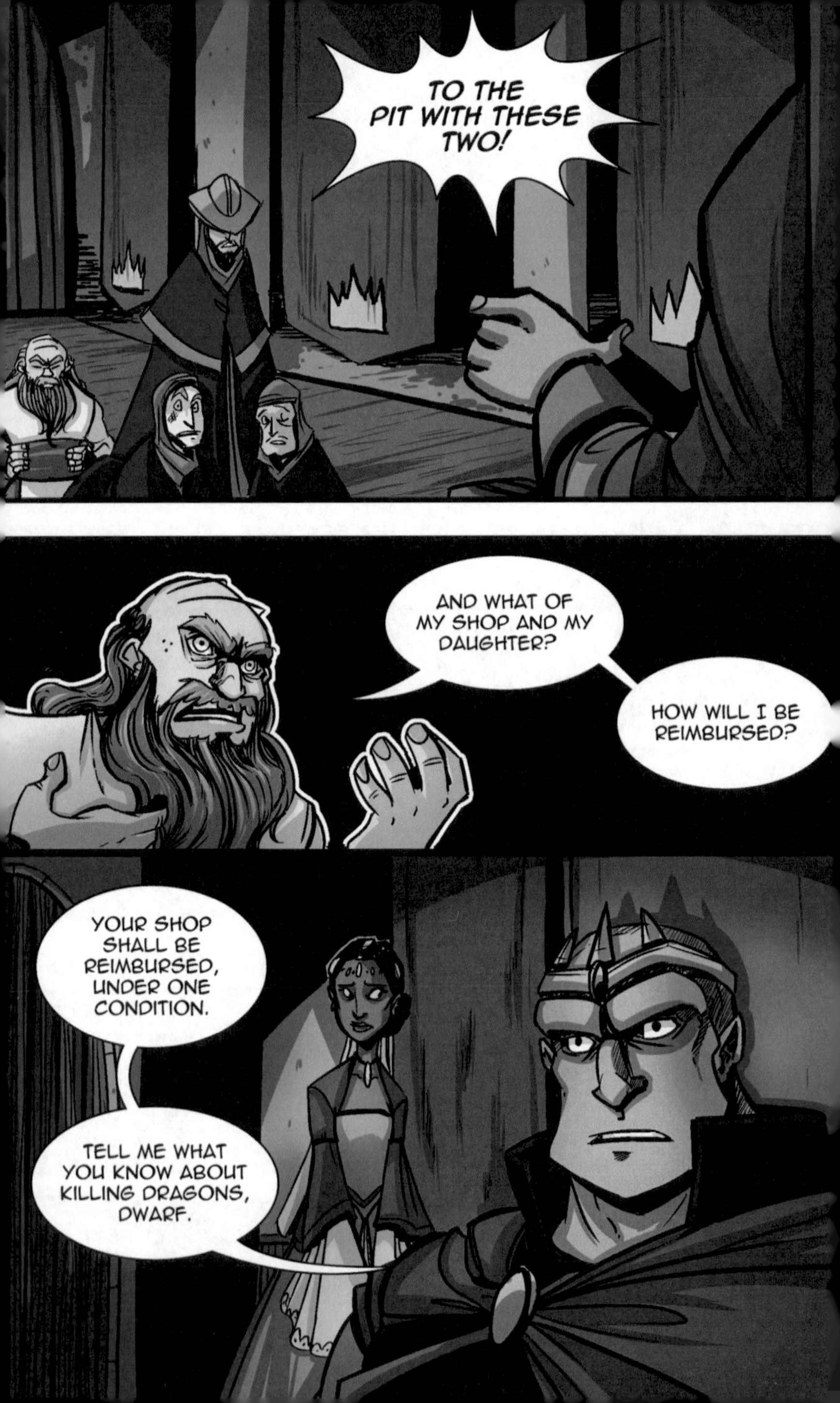
TO THE PIT WITH THESE TWO!
AND WHAT OF MY SHOP AND MY DAUGHTER?
HOW WILL I BE REIMBURSED?
YOUR SHOP SHALL BE REIMBURSED, UNDER ONE CONDITION.
TELL ME WHAT YOU KNOW ABOUT KILLING DRAGONS, DWARF.

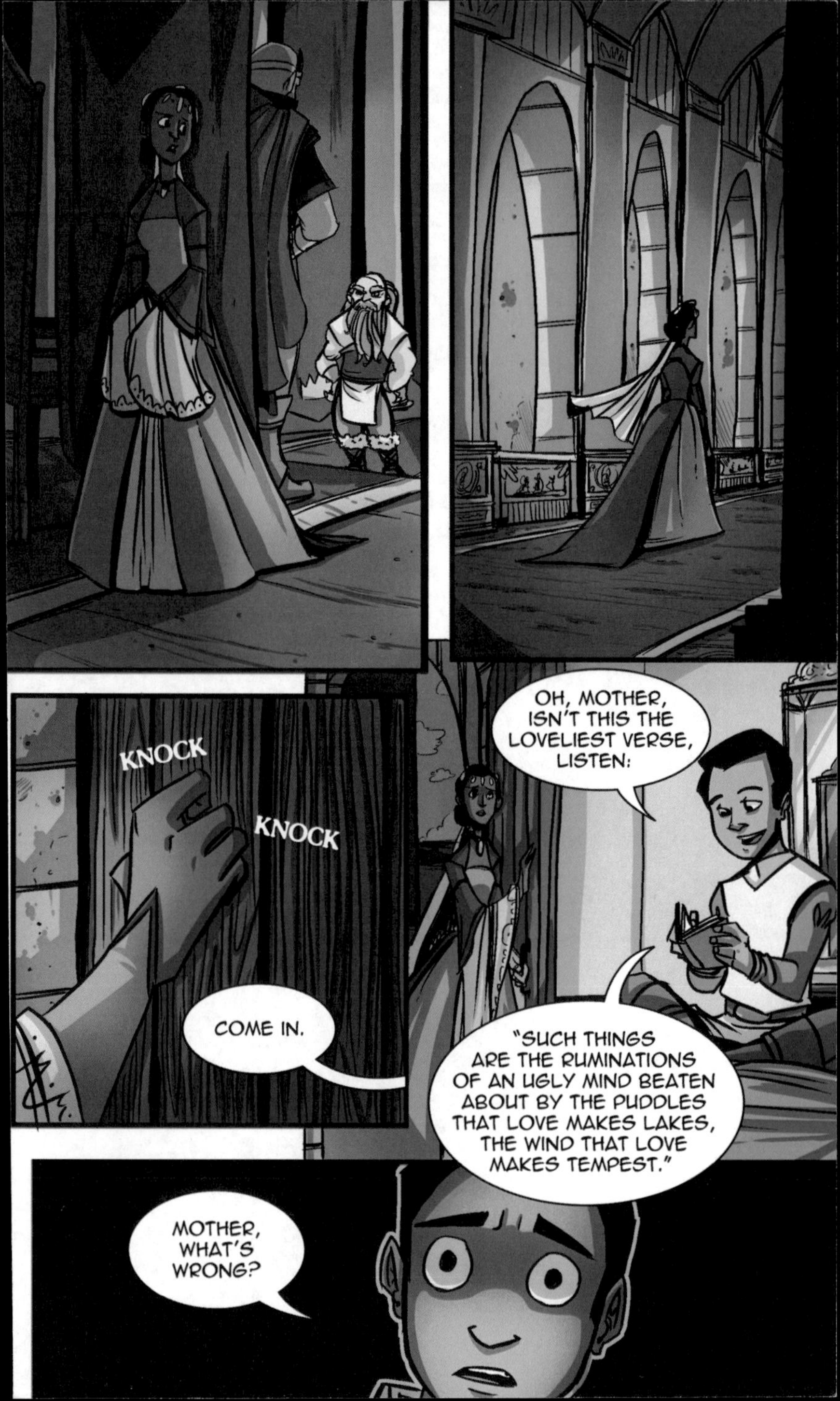
KNOCK
KNOCK
COME IN.
OH, MOTHER, ISN'T THIS THE LOVELIEST VERSE, LISTEN:
"SUCH THINGS ARE THE RUMINATIONS OF AN UGLY MIND BEATEN ABOUT BY THE PUDDLES THAT LOVE MAKES LAKES, THE WIND THAT LOVE MAKES TEMPEST."
MOTHER, WHAT'S WRONG?

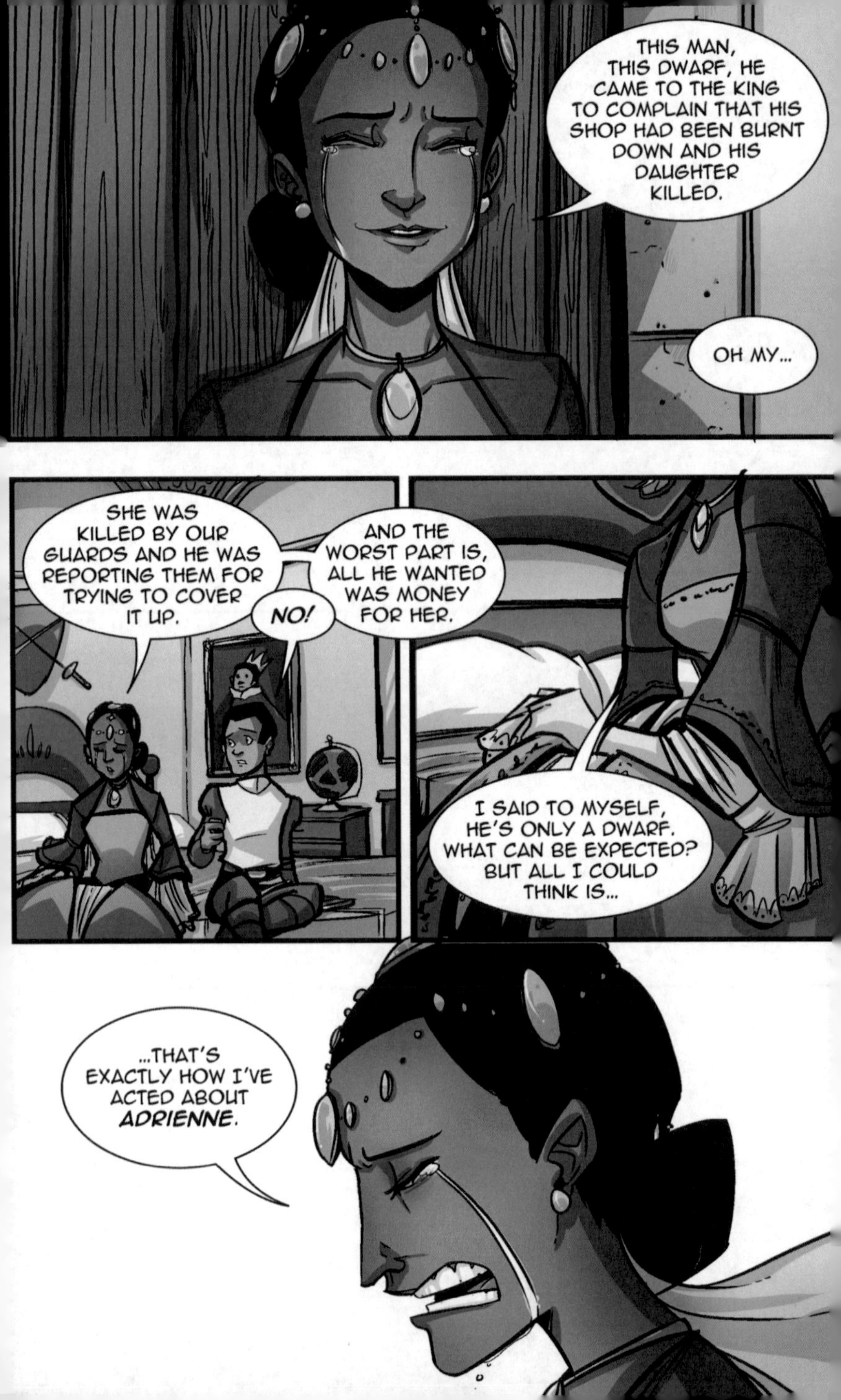
THIS MAN, THIS DWARF, HE CAME TO THE KING TO COMPLAIN THAT HIS SHOP HAD BEEN BURNT DOWN AND HIS DAUGHTER KILLED.
OH MY...
SHE WAS KILLED BY OUR GUARDS AND HE WAS REPORTING THEM FOR TRYING TO COVER IT UP.
NO!
AND THE WORST PART IS, ALL HE WANTED WAS MONEY FOR HER.
I SAID TO MYSELF, HE'S ONLY A DWARF. WHAT CAN BE EXPECTED? BUT ALL I COULD THINK IS...
...THAT'S EXACTLY HOW I'VE ACTED ABOUT *ADRIENNE*.

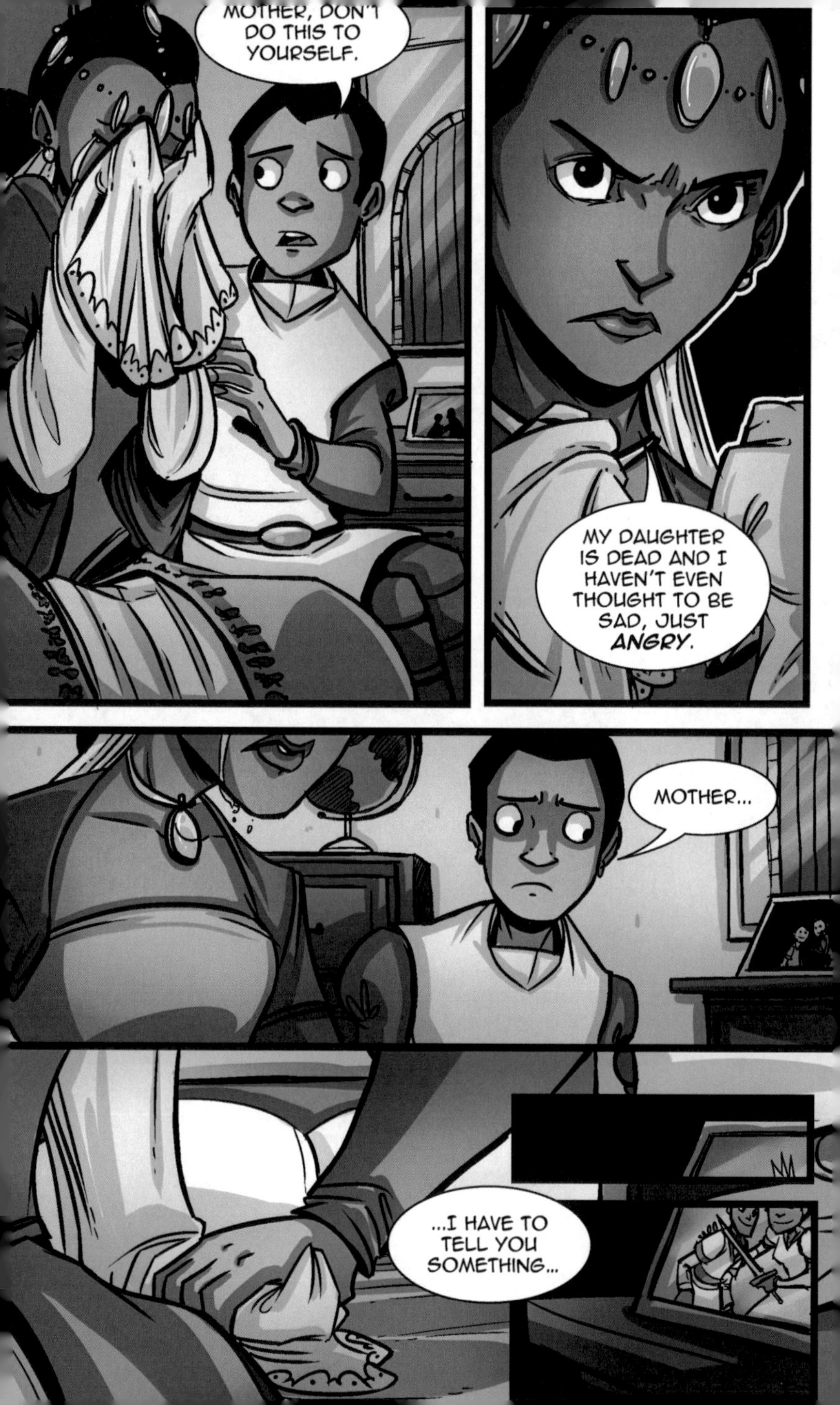
MOTHER, DON'T DO THIS TO YOURSELF.
MY DAUGHTER IS DEAD AND I HAVEN'T EVEN THOUGHT TO BE SAD, JUST ANGRY.
MOTHER...
[redacted]
...I HAVE TO TELL YOU SOMETHING...

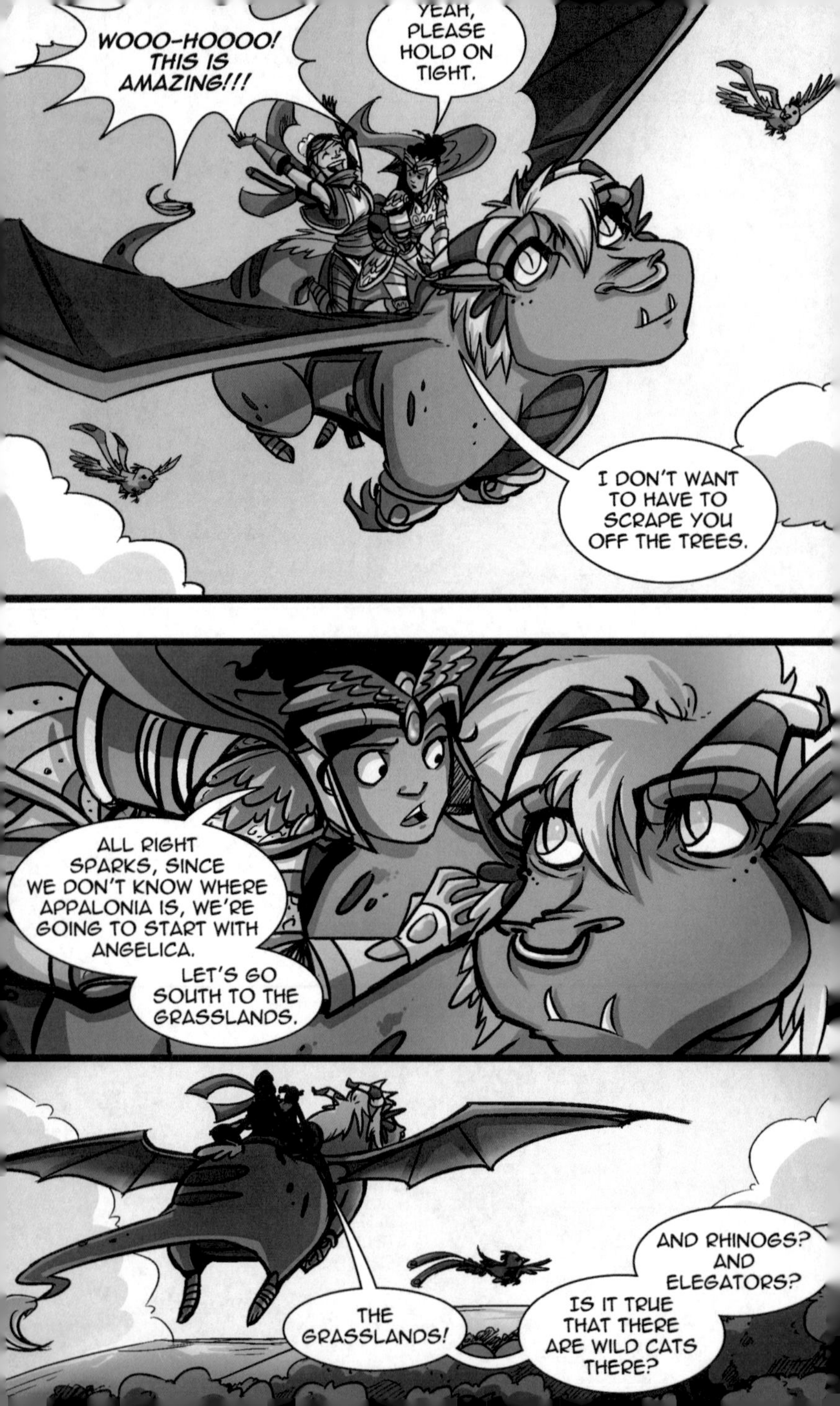
WOOO-HOOOO! THIS IS AMAZING!!!
YEAH, PLEASE HOLD ON TIGHT.
I DON'T WANT TO HAVE TO SCRAPE YOU OFF THE TREES.
ALL RIGHT SPARKS, SINCE WE DON'T KNOW WHERE APPALONIA IS, WE'RE GOING TO START WITH ANGELICA.
LET'S GO SOUTH TO THE GRASSLANDS.
THE GRASSLANDS!
IS IT TRUE THAT THERE ARE WILD CATS THERE?
AND RHINOGS? AND ELEGATORS?

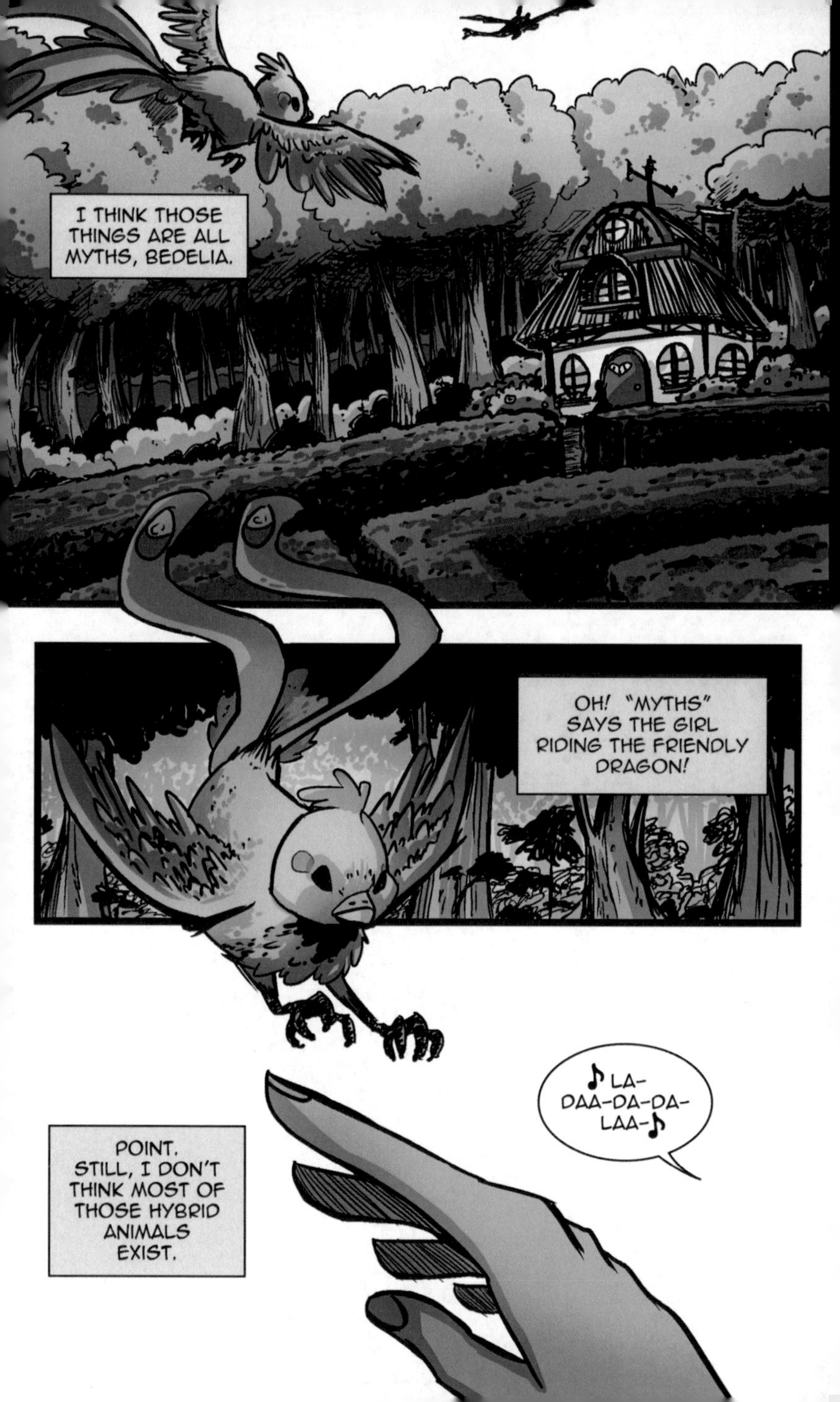
I THINK THOSE THINGS ARE ALL MYTHS, BEDELIA.
OH! "MYTHS" SAYS THE GIRL RIDING THE FRIENDLY DRAGON!
POINT. STILL, I DON'T THINK MOST OF THOSE HYBRID ANIMALS EXIST.
♪ LA-DAA-DA-DA-LAA-♪

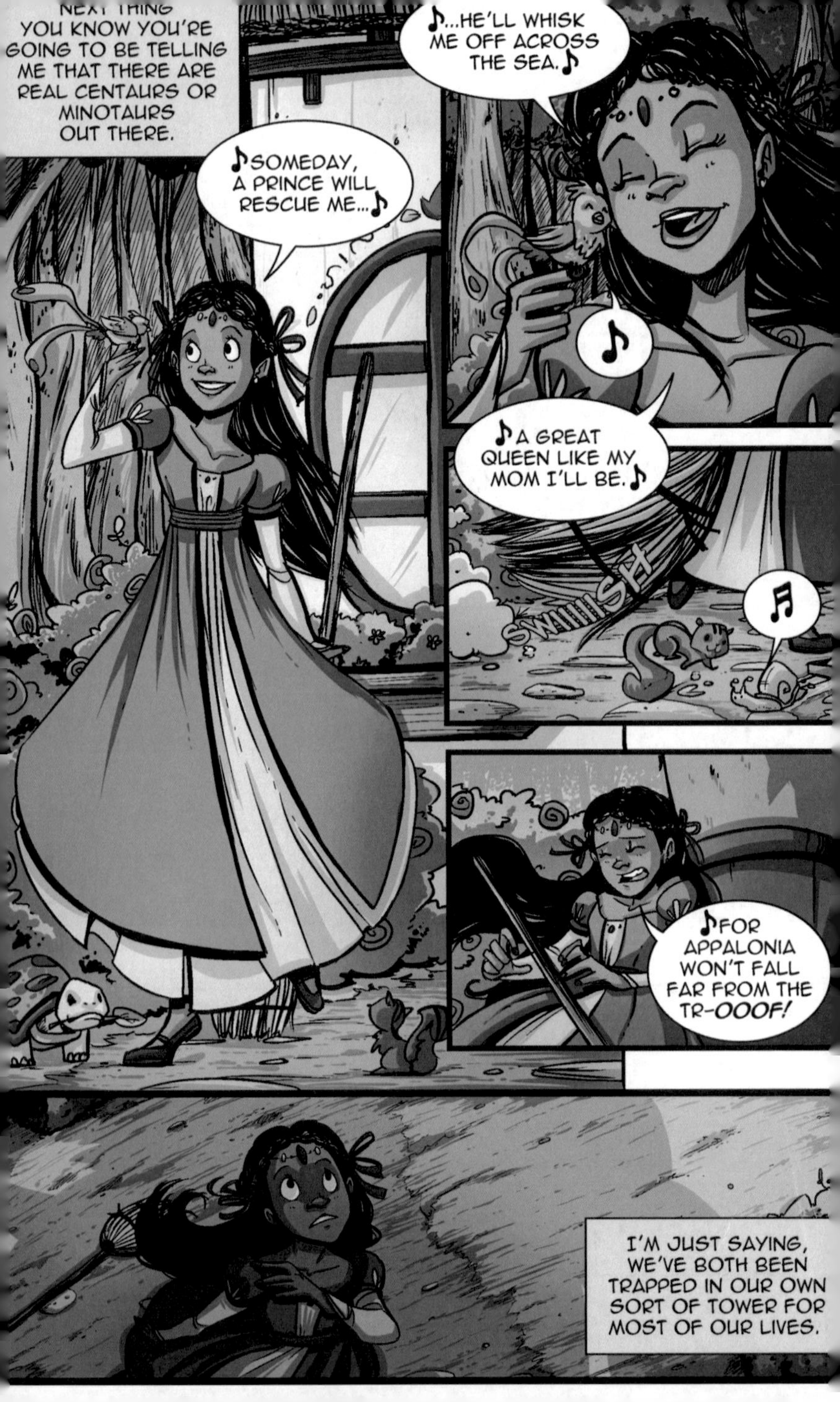
NEXT THING YOU KNOW YOU'RE GOING TO BE TELLING ME THAT THERE ARE REAL CENTAURS OR MINOTAURS OUT THERE.
♪SOMEDAY, A PRINCE WILL RESCUE ME...♪
♪...HE'LL WHISK ME OFF ACROSS THE SEA.♪
♪
♪A GREAT QUEEN LIKE MY MOM I'LL BE.♪
SWIIIISH
♬
♪FOR APPALONIA WON'T FALL FAR FROM THE TR-OOOF!
I'M JUST SAYING, WE'VE BOTH BEEN TRAPPED IN OUR OWN SORT OF TOWER FOR MOST OF OUR LIVES.

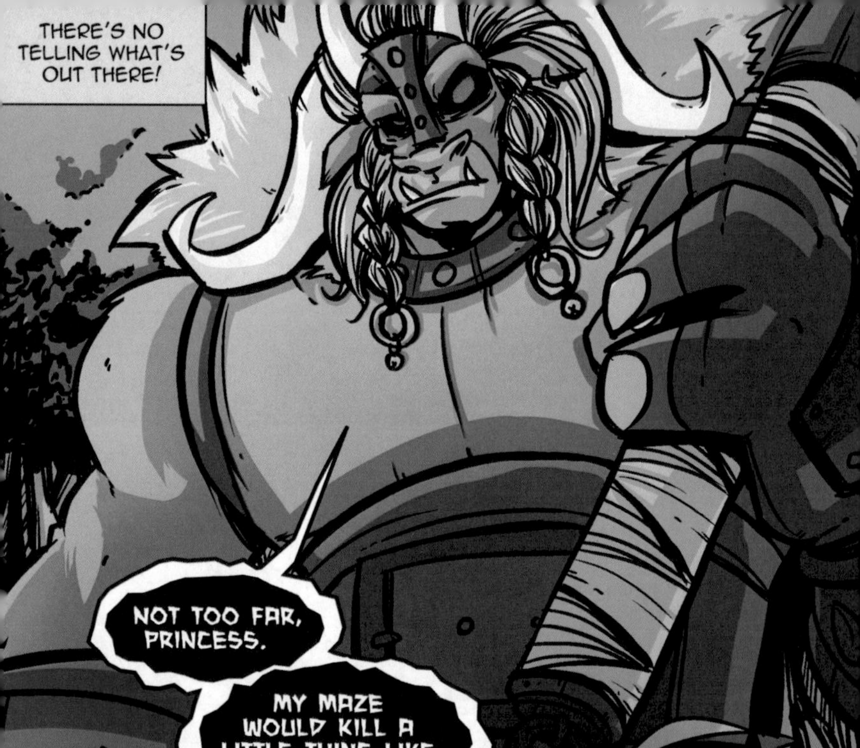
THERE'S NO TELLING WHAT'S OUT THERE!
NOT TOO FAR, PRINCESS.
MY MAZE WOULD KILL A LITTLE THING LIKE YOURSELF.

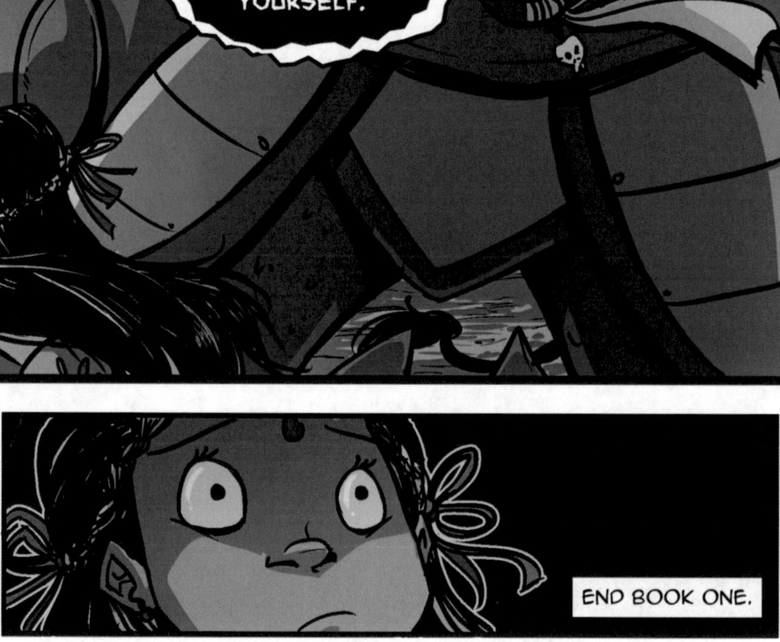
END BOOK ONE.

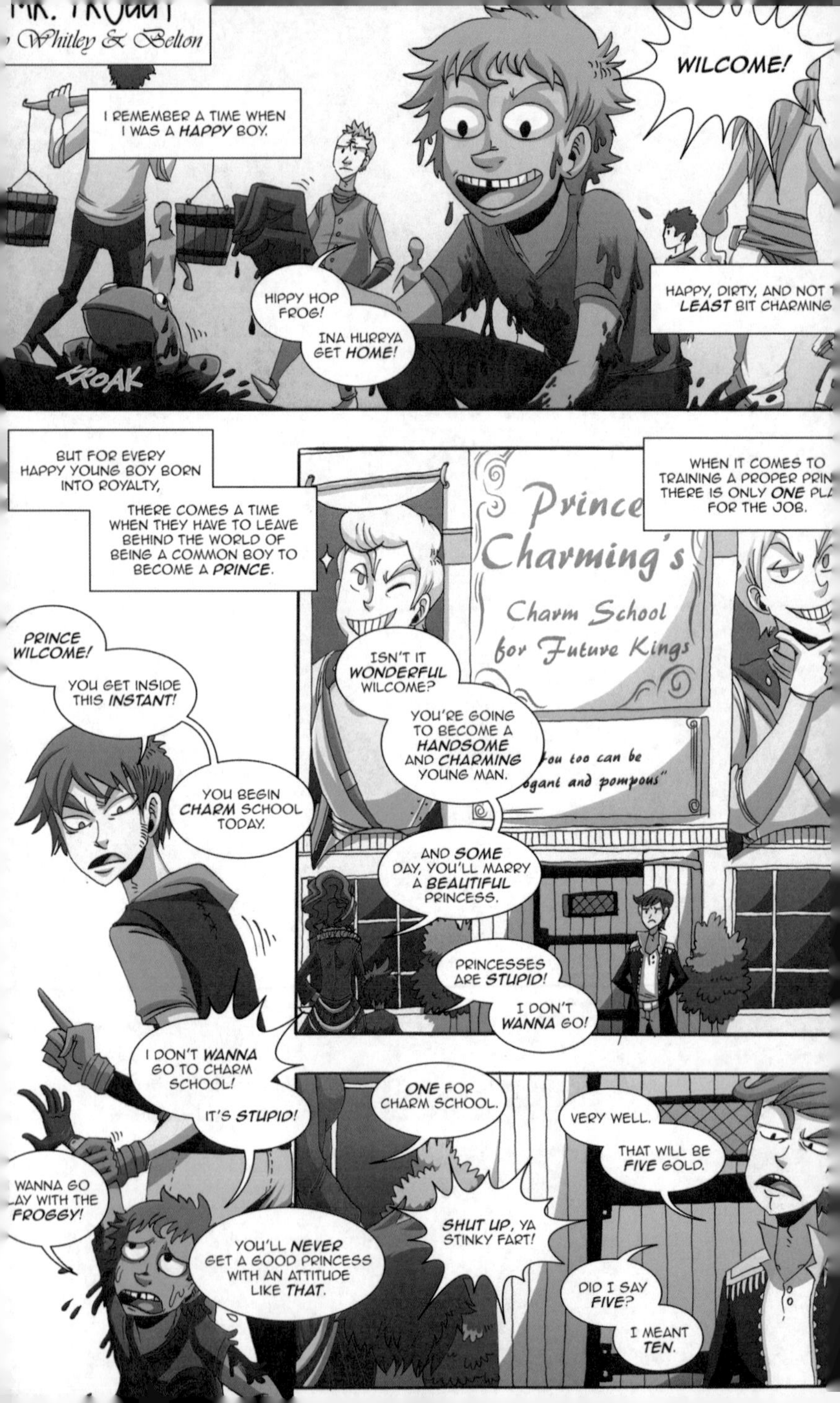
MR. TROAT
Whitley & Belton
I REMEMBER A TIME WHEN I WAS A HAPPY BOY.
WILCOME!
HIPPY HOP FROG!
INA HURRYA GET HOME!
KROAK
HAPPY, DIRTY, AND NOT
LEAST BIT CHARMING
BUT FOR EVERY HAPPY YOUNG BOY BORN INTO ROYALTY,
THERE COMES A TIME WHEN THEY HAVE TO LEAVE BEHIND THE WORLD OF BEING A COMMON BOY TO BECOME A PRINCE.
WHEN IT COMES TO TRAINING A PROPER PRIN
THERE IS ONLY ONE PLA
FOR THE JOB.
Prince Charming's
Charm School for Future Kings
"You too can be
ogant and pompous"
PRINCE WILCOME!
YOU GET INSIDE THIS INSTANT!
YOU BEGIN CHARM SCHOOL TODAY.
ISN'T IT WONDERFUL WILCOME?
YOU'RE GOING TO BECOME A HANDSOME AND CHARMING YOUNG MAN.
AND SOME DAY, YOU'LL MARRY A BEAUTIFUL PRINCESS.
PRINCESSES ARE STUPID!
I DON'T WANNA GO!
I DON'T WANNA GO TO CHARM SCHOOL!
IT'S STUPID!
WANNA GO
AY WITH THE FROGGY!
YOU'LL NEVER GET A GOOD PRINCESS WITH AN ATTITUDE LIKE THAT.
ONE FOR CHARM SCHOOL.
SHUT UP, YA STINKY FART!
VERY WELL.
THAT WILL BE FIVE GOLD.
DID I SAY FIVE?
I MEANT TEN.

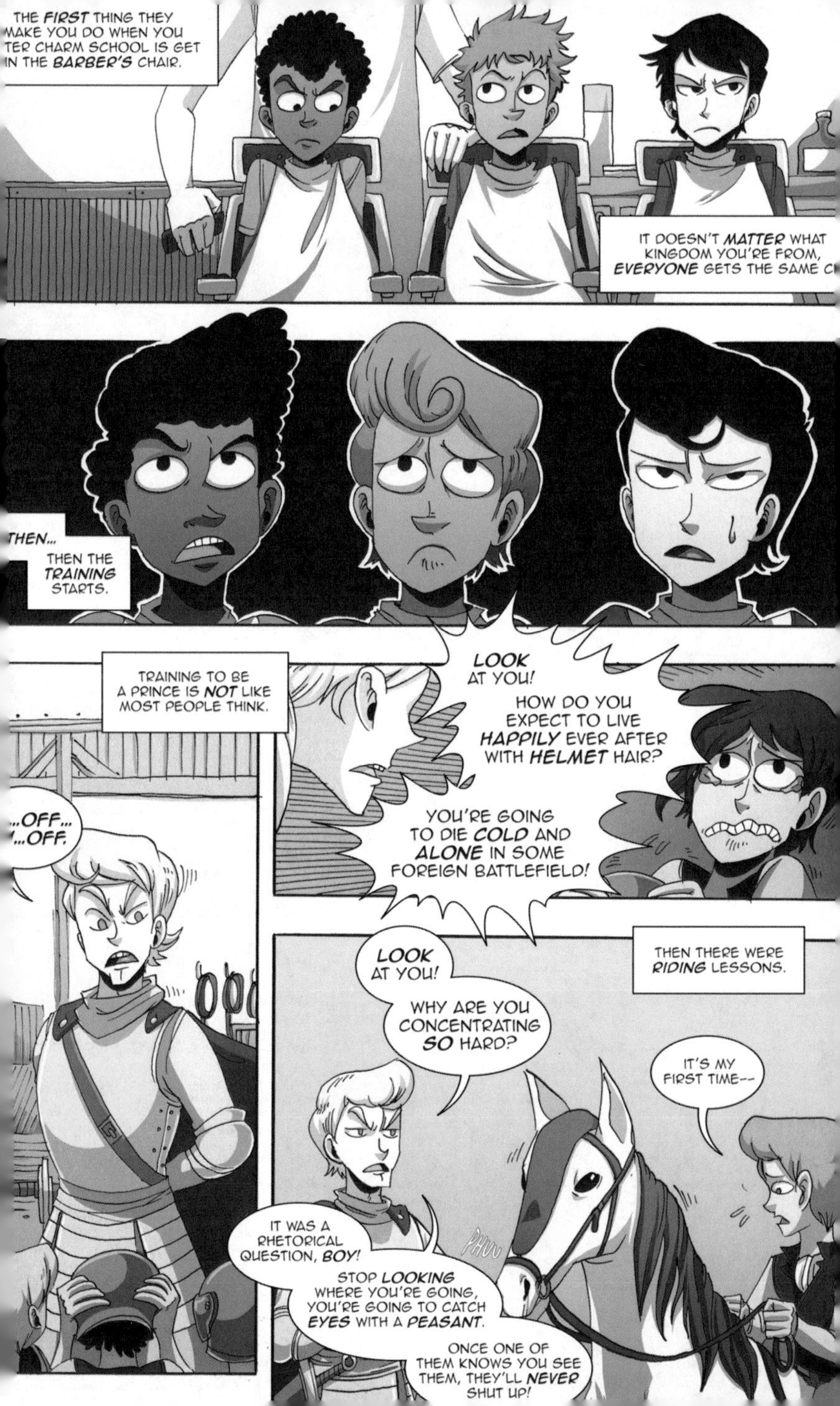
THE FIRST THING THEY MAKE YOU DO WHEN YOU TER CHARM SCHOOL IS GET IN THE BARBER'S CHAIR.
IT DOESN'T MATTER WHAT KINGDOM YOU'RE FROM, EVERYONE GETS THE SAME C
THEN...
THEN THE TRAINING STARTS.
TRAINING TO BE A PRINCE IS NOT LIKE MOST PEOPLE THINK.
...OFF...
...OFF.
LOOK AT YOU!
HOW DO YOU EXPECT TO LIVE HAPPILY EVER AFTER WITH HELMET HAIR?
YOU'RE GOING TO DIE COLD AND ALONE IN SOME FOREIGN BATTLEFIELD!
THEN THERE WERE RIDING LESSONS.
LOOK AT YOU!
WHY ARE YOU CONCENTRATING SO HARD?
IT'S MY FIRST TIME--
IT WAS A RHETORICAL QUESTION, BOY!
STOP LOOKING WHERE YOU'RE GOING, YOU'RE GOING TO CATCH EYES WITH A PEASANT.
ONCE ONE OF THEM KNOWS YOU SEE THEM, THEY'LL NEVER SHUT UP!
PHUU

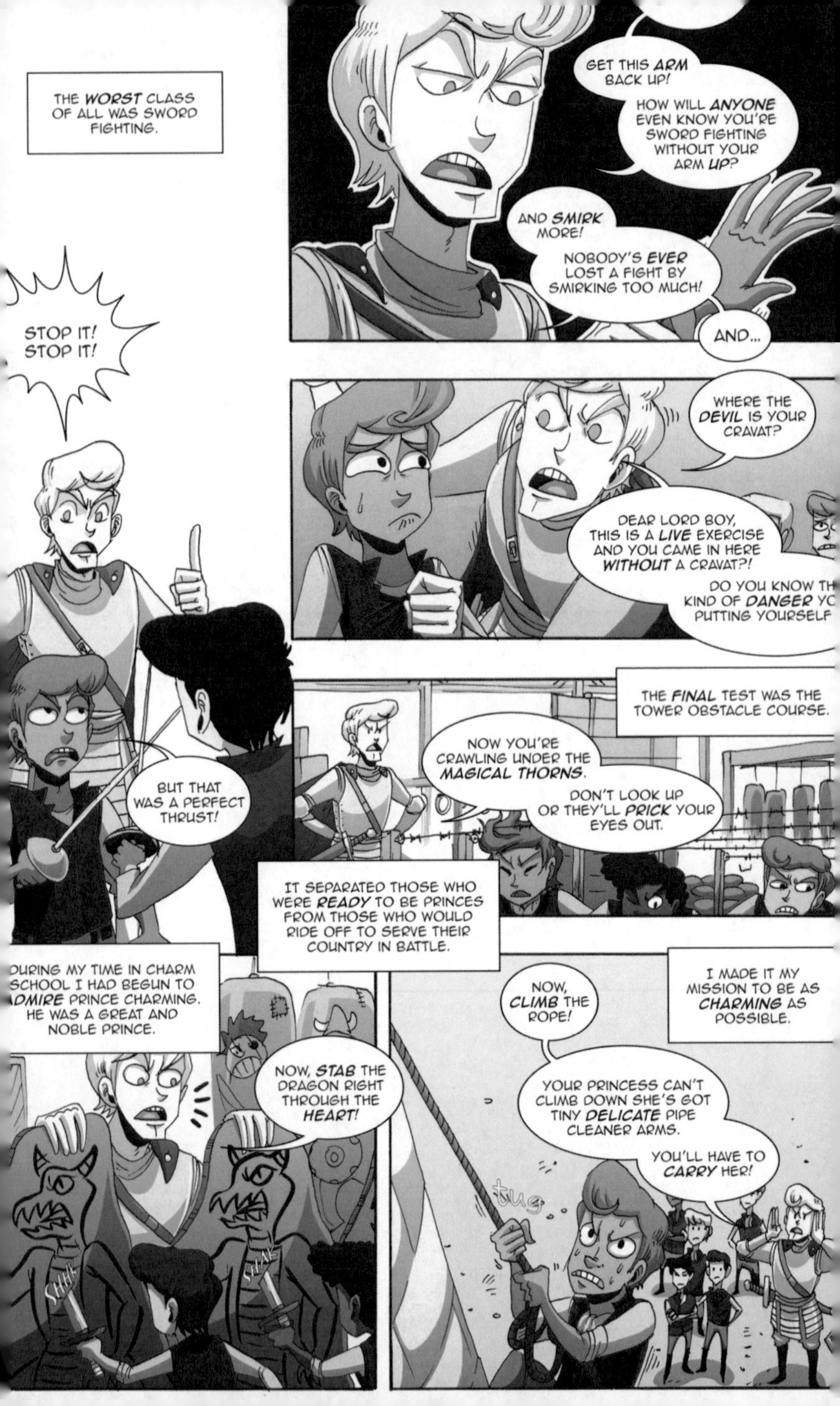
THE *WORST* CLASS OF ALL WAS SWORD FIGHTING.
GET THIS *ARM* BACK UP!
HOW WILL *ANYONE* EVEN KNOW YOU'RE SWORD FIGHTING WITHOUT YOUR ARM *UP*?
AND *SMIRK* MORE!
NOBODY'S *EVER* LOST A FIGHT BY SMIRKING TOO MUCH!
AND...
STOP IT! STOP IT!
BUT THAT WAS A PERFECT THRUST!
WHERE THE *DEVIL* IS YOUR CRAVAT?
DEAR LORD BOY, THIS IS A *LIVE* EXERCISE AND YOU CAME IN HERE *WITHOUT* A CRAVAT?!
DO YOU KNOW TH KIND OF *DANGER* YO PUTTING YOURSELF
THE *FINAL* TEST WAS THE TOWER OBSTACLE COURSE.
NOW YOU'RE CRAWLING UNDER THE *MAGICAL THORNS*.
DON'T LOOK UP OR THEY'LL *PRICK* YOUR EYES OUT.
IT SEPARATED THOSE WHO WERE *READY* TO BE PRINCES FROM THOSE WHO WOULD RIDE OFF TO SERVE THEIR COUNTRY IN BATTLE.
DURING MY TIME IN CHARM SCHOOL I HAD BEGUN TO *ADMIRE* PRINCE CHARMING. HE WAS A GREAT AND NOBLE PRINCE.
NOW, *STAB* THE DRAGON RIGHT THROUGH THE *HEART*!
SHHK
SHAK
I MADE IT MY MISSION TO BE AS *CHARMING* AS POSSIBLE.
NOW, *CLIMB* THE ROPE!
YOUR PRINCESS CAN'T CLIMB DOWN SHE'S GOT TINY *DELICATE* PIPE CLEANER ARMS.
YOU'LL HAVE TO *CARRY* HER!
tug

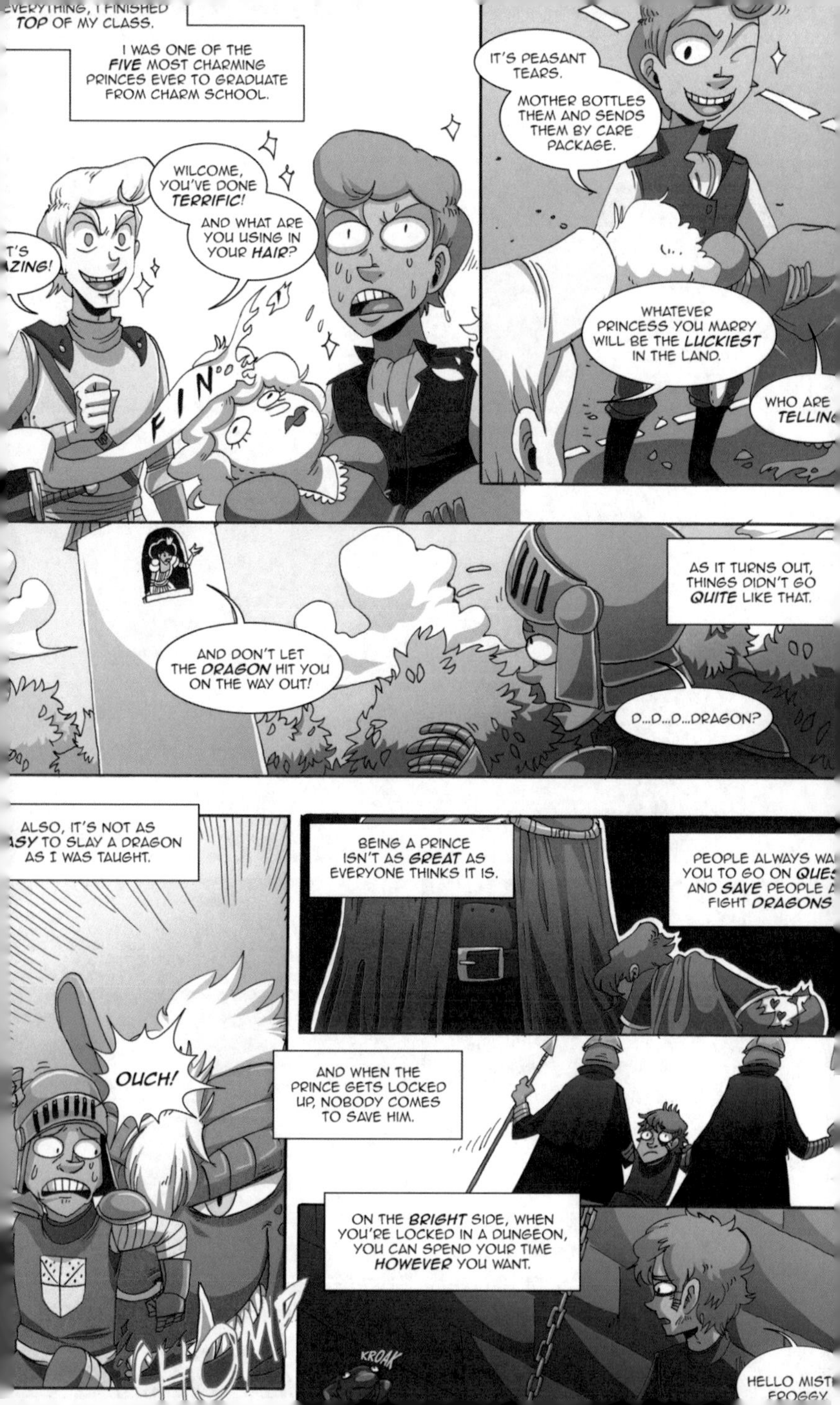

EVERYTHING, I FINISHED TOP OF MY CLASS.
I WAS ONE OF THE FIVE MOST CHARMING PRINCES EVER TO GRADUATE FROM CHARM SCHOOL.
WILCOME, YOU'VE DONE TERRIFIC!
AND WHAT ARE YOU USING IN YOUR HAIR?
FIN
IT'S PEASANT TEARS.
MOTHER BOTTLES THEM AND SENDS THEM BY CARE PACKAGE.
WHATEVER PRINCESS YOU MARRY WILL BE THE LUCKIEST IN THE LAND.
WHO ARE TELLIN
AS IT TURNS OUT, THINGS DIDN'T GO QUITE LIKE THAT.
AND DON'T LET THE DRAGON HIT YOU ON THE WAY OUT!
D...D...D...DRAGON?
ALSO, IT'S NOT AS ASY TO SLAY A DRAGON AS I WAS TAUGHT.
OUCH!
CHOMP
KROAK
BEING A PRINCE ISN'T AS GREAT AS EVERYONE THINKS IT IS.
PEOPLE ALWAYS WA YOU TO GO ON QUES AND SAVE PEOPLE A FIGHT DRAGONS
AND WHEN THE PRINCE GETS LOCKED UP, NOBODY COMES TO SAVE HIM.
ON THE BRIGHT SIDE, WHEN YOU'RE LOCKED IN A DUNGEON, YOU CAN SPEND YOUR TIME HOWEVER YOU WANT.
HELLO MIST FROGGY

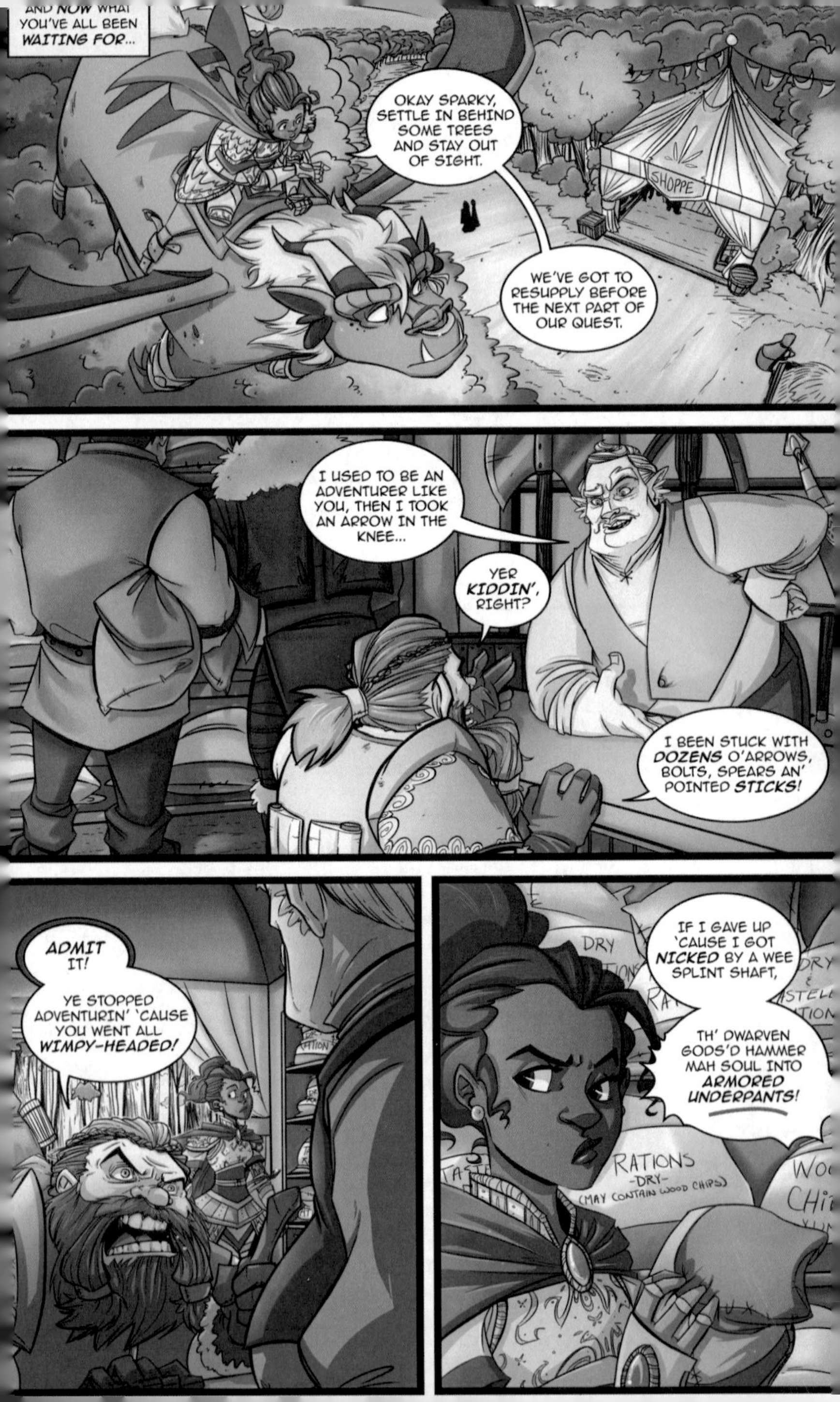
AND NOW WHAT YOU'VE ALL BEEN WAITING FOR...
OKAY SPARKY, SETTLE IN BEHIND SOME TREES AND STAY OUT OF SIGHT.
WE'VE GOT TO RESUPPLY BEFORE THE NEXT PART OF OUR QUEST.
SHOPPE
I USED TO BE AN ADVENTURER LIKE YOU, THEN I TOOK AN ARROW IN THE KNEE...
YER KIDDIN', RIGHT?
I BEEN STUCK WITH DOZENS O'ARROWS, BOLTS, SPEARS AN' POINTED STICKS!
ADMIT IT!
YE STOPPED ADVENTURIN' 'CAUSE YOU WENT ALL WIMPY-HEADED!
IF I GAVE UP 'CAUSE I GOT NICKED BY A WEE SPLINT SHAFT,
TH' DWARVEN GODS'D HAMMER MAH SOUL INTO ARMORED UNDERPANTS!
RATIONS -DRY- (MAY CONTAIN WOOD CHIPS)

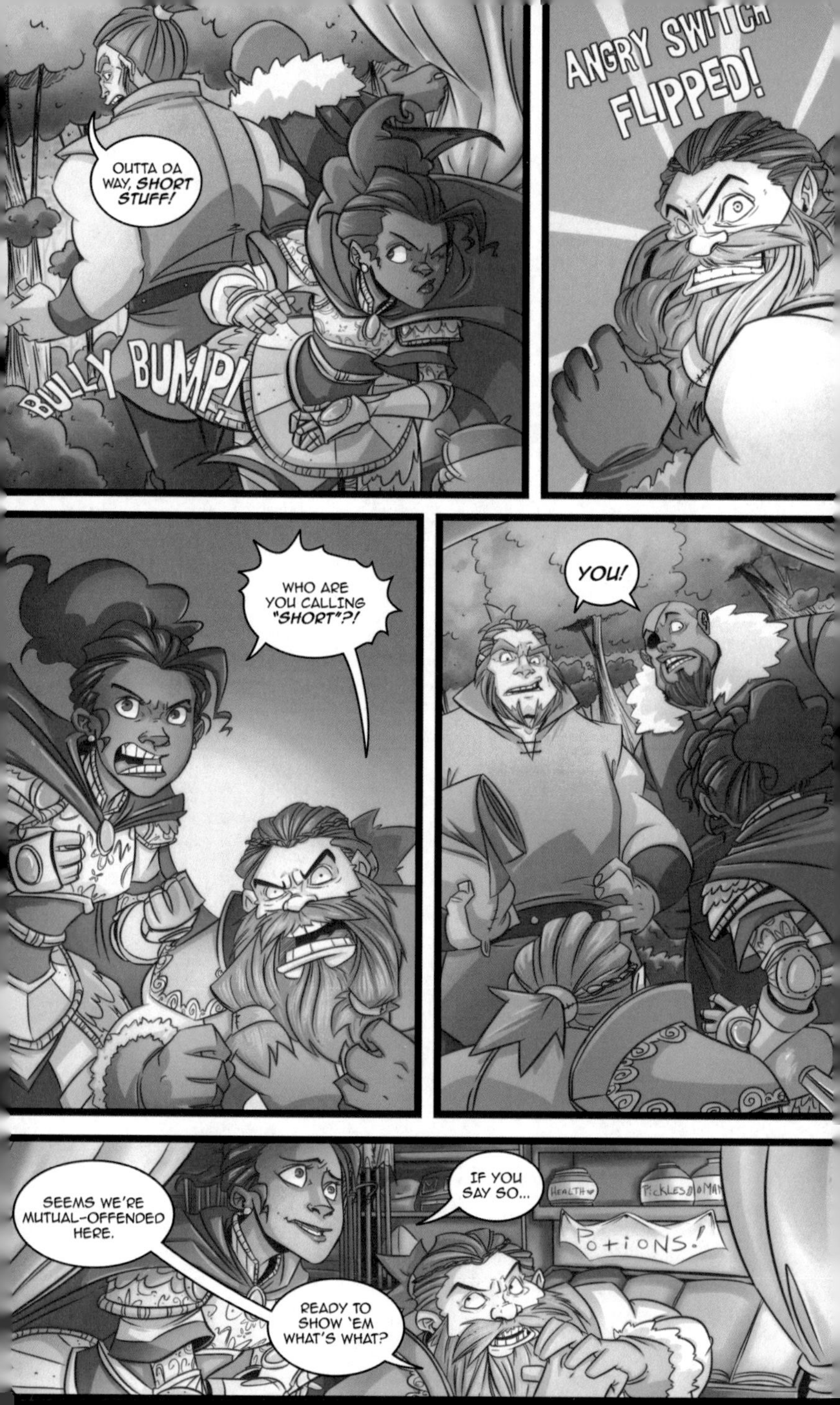
OUTTA DA WAY, SHORT STUFF!
BULLY BUMP!
ANGRY SWITCH FLIPPED!
WHO ARE YOU CALLING "SHORT"?!
YOU!
SEEMS WE'RE MUTUAL-OFFENDED HERE.
IF YOU SAY SO...
HEALTH
PICKLES
POTIONS!
READY TO SHOW 'EM WHAT'S WHAT?

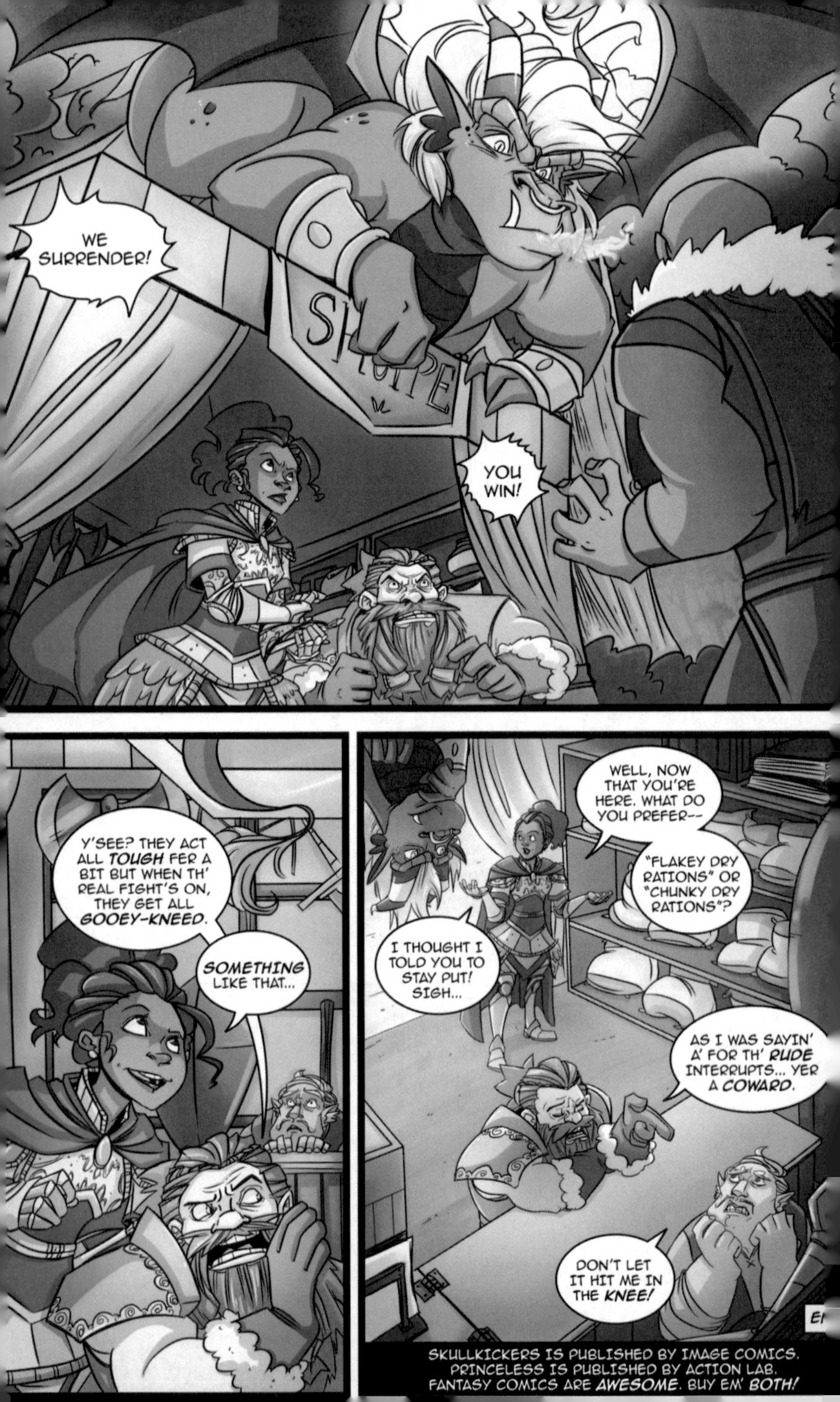
WE SURRENDER!
SHOPPE
YOU WIN!
Y'SEE? THEY ACT ALL TOUGH FER A BIT BUT WHEN TH' REAL FIGHT'S ON, THEY GET ALL GOOEY-KNEED.
SOMETHING LIKE THAT...
WELL, NOW THAT YOU'RE HERE. WHAT DO YOU PREFER--
"FLAKEY DRY RATIONS" OR "CHUNKY DRY RATIONS"?
I THOUGHT I TOLD YOU TO STAY PUT! SIGH...
AS I WAS SAYIN' A' FOR TH' RUDE INTERRUPTS... YER A COWARD.
DON'T LET IT HIT ME IN THE KNEE!
SKULLKICKERS IS PUBLISHED BY IMAGE COMICS.
PRINCELESS IS PUBLISHED BY ACTION LAB.
FANTASY COMICS ARE AWESOME. BUY EM' BOTH!

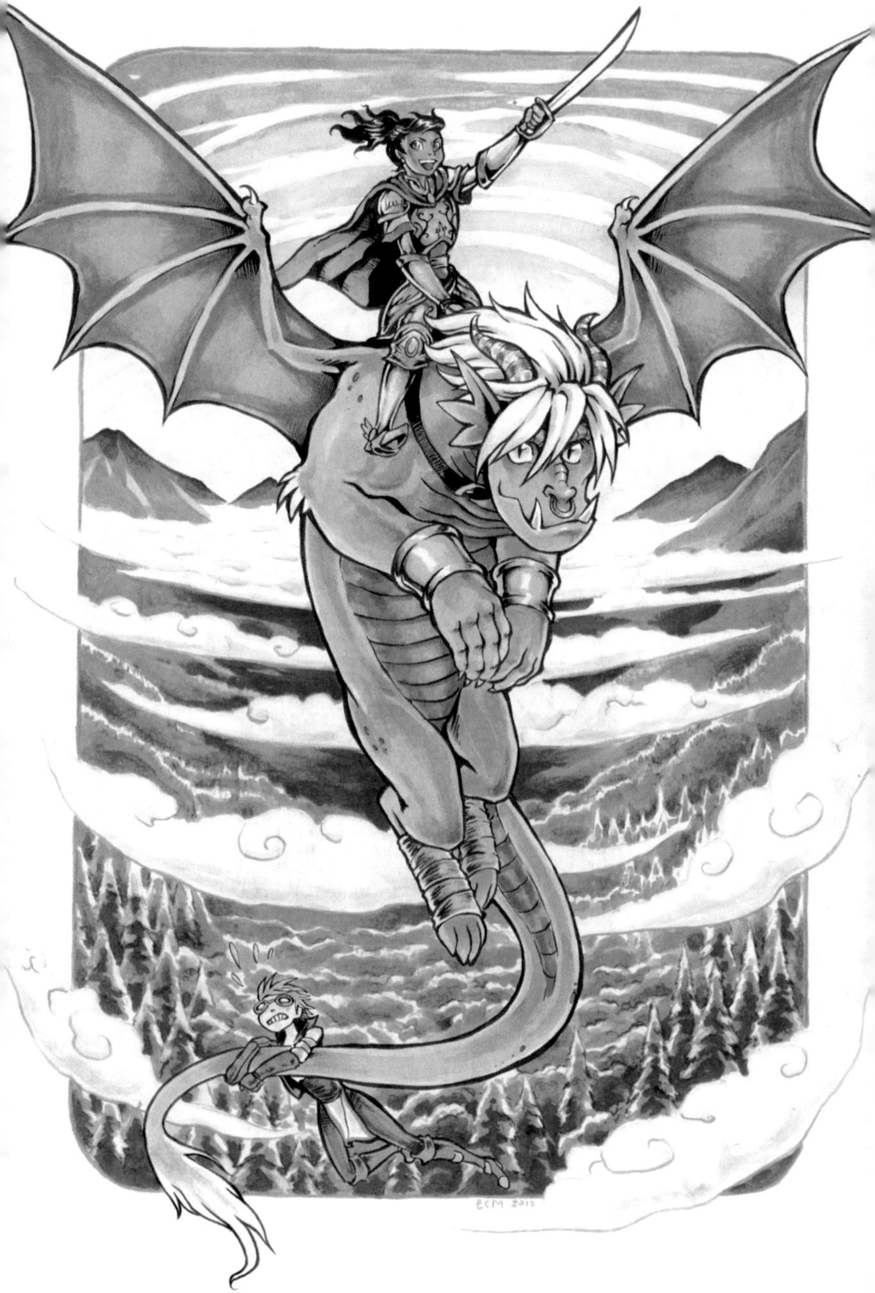
ECM 2012

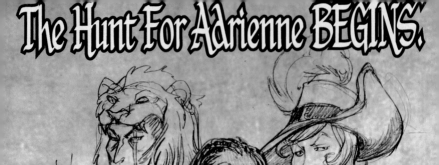

The Hunt For Adrienne BEGINS.

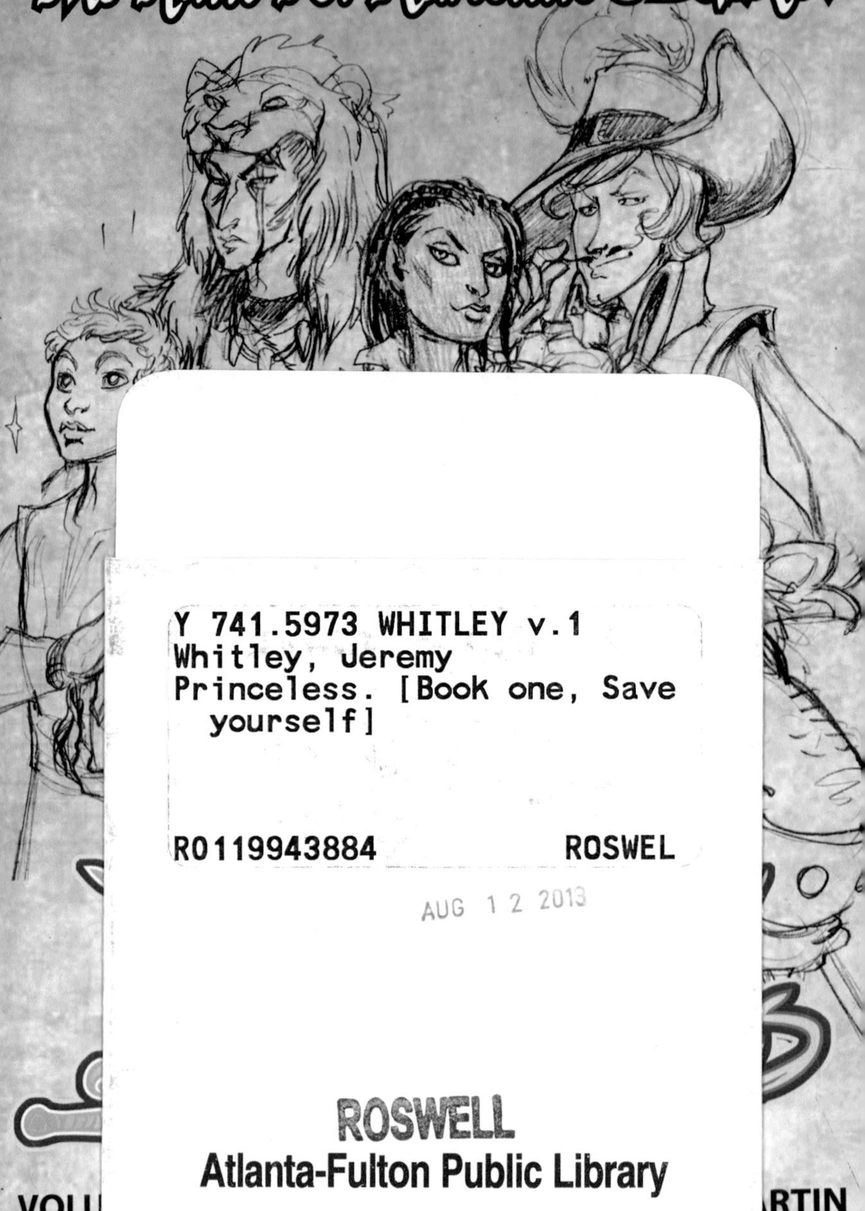

VOLU ... ARTIN

FALL 2012